Group 1

Jane   234-0557
John   234-1862
Mary Pat 865-2148

Small Business Management: Essentials of Entrepreneurship

Small Business Management: Essentials of Entrepreneurship

Lawrence A. Klatt

Florida Atlantic University

Wadsworth Publishing Company, Inc.
Belmont, California

Designer: Russ Leong

© 1973 by Wadsworth Publishing Company, Inc., Belmont, California 94002. All rights reserved. No part of this book may be reproduced, stored in a retrieval system, or transcribed, in any form or by any means, electronic, mechanical, photocopying, recording or otherwise, without the prior written permission of the publisher.

ISBN 0-534-00324-9
L. C. Cat. Card No. 73-83924
Printed in the United States of America

2 3 4 5 6 7 8 9 10—77 76 75

Preface

If the owner–manager of a small firm is to survive, prosper, and grow in today's highly competitive market, he must have more to offer than a "better mousetrap" or a "knack for getting along with people." Due to the high rate of fatalities among new small businesses, managers are becoming more aware of the need for managerial knowledge that will help them improve their effectiveness.

This book is an attempt to summarize the essential concepts and techniques related to the managerial problems of a small firm. Written in nontechnical language from the utilitarian viewpoint of a present or potential businessman, the book focuses on those areas necessary for successful entrepreneurship. The author provides a framework for those aspects of management that are basic to small business operations while at the same time recognizing the need for individual application to problems unique to certain types of businesses.

Accordingly, this short volume does not cover in detail the literature discussing special areas of small business development and operation. If the reader has a need for in-depth treatment of a particular subject, he will want to consult the standard readings or textbooks suggested at the end of each chapter. Charts and tables are used frequently to condense information that would otherwise require many pages to present.

In order to point up the real-life implications of the concepts of entrepreneurship presented in the text, each chapter is followed by a brief managerial situation, or incident, developed around a related management concept, problem, or practice. These incidents, which follow one small business from its inception through its growth and operational changes, should suggest to the reader some of the decision-making tasks confronting the entrepreneur. In addition, three comprehensive cases are included in an appendix to give the reader a feel for the problems and practices involved in starting and managing a business.

As a manual on small business management, this book will prove useful to a wide variety of readers. It should provide a useful summary of ideas for the small businessman interested in increasing his knowledge of managing a small business. It will also be appropriate for the student in a college or adult extension course who would like to become a successful entrepreneur.

The author gratefully acknowledges the contributions of those who have reviewed the manuscript, including Murray P. Leavitt of DeAnza College, John D. Minch of Cabrillo College, and Donald R. Webb of the University of Missouri. A special word of appreciation goes to Adrienne Harris for an outstanding job of editing the manuscript.

A special, belated acknowledgment should be made to Richard N. Farmer of Indiana University, who wrote the situations that follow each chapter in the text and who accidently failed to receive credit in the first printing of the book.

Contents

Part One: Foundations of Entrepreneurship

1: Small Business and the Economy 3

What Is a Small Business? 3   Scope and Trends of Small Business 5   Factors in Small Business Failure 6   Avoiding Small Business Failure 9   Future Outlook for Small Business 10

Incident 1: I'm Not All Right, Jack 12

2: The Entrepreneur 15

Rewards and Costs of Entrepreneurship 16   Working for Others 17   The Entrepreneur Type 18   Introspection and Self-Selection 20

Incident 2: The Future Winner 25

Part Two: Management: The Key to Successful Entrepreneurship

3: Setting Goals 31

The Planning Function 31   Steps in Planning 32   Time Period 33   Objectives 34   Policies 35   Long-Range Planning 36   Short-Range Planning 36   Planning and Objectives 37   Some Final Comments on Establishing Goals 41

Incident 3: The Plan Emerges 42

Contents

4: Implementing Goals 47

Decision Making and Planning 55   Creativity in Planning and Decision Making 57   Creative Techniques 59

Incident 4: Writing It Down 62

5: Reaching Goals 65

Organizing 65   Organizational Structure 66   Organization in Practice: A Case Study 67   Principles of Organization 69   Committees 71   Informal Organization 72   Actuating 73   Controlling 78

Incident 5: Getting Organized 81

Part Three: Starting the Business

6: Two Paths to Entrepreneurship 89

Buying a Small Business 89   Starting a New Business 96

Incident 6: What's It Worth? 100

7: Choosing a Location and Form of Organization 105

Location 105   Form of Organization 115

Incident 7: You Can't Get There from Here—Or Can You? 121

8: Getting Capital and Credit 125

Determining Capital Requirements 126   Sources of Initial Funds 128   Establishing Credit Relationships 134

Incident 8: Money Problems 137

Contents ix

9: How about a Franchise? 141

What Is a Franchise? 142   Advantages of Franchising 142   Disadvantages of Franchising 143   Finding Franchise Opportunities 143   Factors to Consider about the Franchise 145   Checklist for Evaluating a Franchise 147   Some Final Thoughts on Franchising 149

Incident 9: Franchise Potential 150

Part Four: Operating the Business

10: Marketing Practices 155

Emergence of Marketing Activity 155   The Marketing Concept: A Better Way To Do Business 157   Marketing Decision Making 158   Elements of Marketing Strategy 160   Credit: The Other Dimension of Marketing 175   Future Outlook 176   Appendix: Effective Advertising 176

Incident 10: Marketing Problems 187

11: Financial Management 193

Basic Accounting Definitions 194   Fundamental Accounting Equation 195   Financial Statements 196   Financial Planning 200   Cost of Capital 204   Current-Asset Management 207   Fixed-Asset Management 211   Managing Tax Obligations 212

Incident 11: Financial Problems Revisited 214

12: Managing the Human Resource 219

Hiring New Employees 220   Recruitment 220   Selection 222   Training and Developing Employees 226   Compensating Employees 228

Human Relations 232   Union Relations 233
Appendix: The Union Contract 236

Incident 12: Finding the Right Man 237

13: The Production Process 241

Product Design 242   Production Planning and
Control 242   Plant Layout 243   Plant
Maintenance 245   Work Improvement 246
Production Standards 248   Inventory Control 249
Quality Control 251   Quantitative Analysis 255
Appendix: Quantitative Analysis Techniques 256

Incident 13: Getting the Work Organized 264

Part Five: Resources for Managerial Decision Making

14: Where to Go for Advice and Assistance 269

The Professionals 269   Small Business
Administration 273   Trade Associations 275
Educational and Business Groups 275   Other
Governmental Agencies 276   The Small
Businessman Himself 276   Appendix: SBA
Publications 278

Incident 14: The Manager 279

Part Six: Comprehensive Cases

Case Study 1: The J & P Superette 285

Case Study 2: Air Comfort, Incorporated 295

Case Study 3: Southern Mobile Homes, Inc. 301

Index 309

Part One Foundations of Entrepreneurship

Small Business and the Economy

Chapter 1

The small, independently owned business has always had a vital role to play in the American economy, and it continues to represent an avenue of opportunity for millions of enterprising individuals. Three decades ago there were already more than 3 million small businesses in this country; by 1961 the number had grown to 4.5 million. Today it is estimated that approximately 5.4 million small businesses are in existence, with a forecast of 5.7 million by 1975.[1]

These statistics do not entirely convey the importance of the small business to the American public, however. The small business represents one of the few areas open to the enterprising individual who seeks to escape the bureaucracy of large organizations. It is one of the few opportunities for owners and employees and owners and customers to meet face to face. Indeed, small business is an integral part of the American Dream, as one group of researchers noted: "The entrepreneurial dream is still today the haven for the common man. . . . Many Americans, at least once in their lives, dream the dream of owning a business that they have created."[2]

What Is a Small Business?

Most people would agree that the neighborhood pizza parlor is a small business, while an automobile manufacturer is a big business. Between

---

[1] Harold K. Charlesworth, "The Uncertain Future of Small Business: Can This Picture Be Changed?" *M.S.U. Business Topics* 18, No. 2 (Spring 1970), p. 14.

[2] Orvis Collins et al., "The Enterprising Man and the Business Executive," *M.S.U. Business Topics* (Winter 1964), p. 19.

these two extremes, we would probably find little agreement about what is "big" or "small," for size is a relative concept. What is "small" in one industry in terms of employees or sales may be "big" in another industry. For example, American Motors, with total sales of over $1 billion, would be a "giant" in many industries, yet its share of the domestic automobile market is only about 3 percent, making it very small compared to General Motors, Chrysler, or Ford.

Where then do we draw the line between big and small, or, in other words, how big is small? In practice, many different standards have been applied at various times to fit particular legislation or studies. For example, the Small Business Act of 1953 defines a small business firm as "one which is independently owned and operated and not dominant in its field of operation." However, in order to implement this rather broad definition, the Small Business Administration (SBA) has developed detailed definitions for each industry, with many exceptions to each definition.[3]

Perhaps the most workable definition of a small business firm is the one put forth by the Committee for Economic Development. They suggest that a small business is characterized by at least two of the following features:

1. *Management is independent.* Usually the managers are also owners.
2. *Capital* is supplied and ownership is held by an individual or a small group.
3. *Area of operations is localized.* While workers and owners are in one home community, markets need not be local.
4. *The size of the firm is small relative to the industry.* The size of the top bracket varies greatly so that what might seem large in one field would definitely be smaller in another.[4]

For the most part, our discussion of management concepts and practices will be intended for firms that fit the above C.E.D. characteristics — independent management, owner capital from an individual or small group, small size relative to other companies in the industry, and localized operation. At the same time, to be more useful to our readers, we shall omit from our discussion the extremely small businesses, such as those built around a professional service. For example, a practicing physician with an office, nurse, and receptionist probably has more to gain by concentrating his effort on developing expertise in his profession and delegating his business activities to an outside specialist or an employee hired for that purpose. However, if this physician later opens

---

[3] See Addison W. Parris, *The Small Business Administration* (New York: Praeger, 1967), Ch. 2.
[4] From *Meeting the Special Problems of Small Business* (New York: Committee for Economic Development, 1947), p. 14.

a small clinic and finds himself "managing" as well as "healing," he would hopefully find this book interesting and helpful.

Scope and Trends of Small Business

Although most business firms are small, they are distributed disproportionately throughout the various industries. In certain sectors of the economy, including wholesale trade, retail trade, service industries, and contract construction, small business predominates. In industries like manufacturing, in which economies of scale and large initial investment are necessary, large business firms prevail. However, even in a large-scale industry like automobile manufacturing, small firms have an important role. While three giant corporations may dominate the industry, thousands of small firms, such as dealerships, auto parts stores, and tool and die shops, are needed for the big corporations to function.

According to one expert, small firms predominate in industries or segments of industries that exhibit certain general attributes:

1. Technological requirements are minimal.
2. Managerial experience requirements perceived as unimportant.
3. Capital requirements are low.
4. Localized nature of the market.[5]

These economic and managerial conditions conducive to small firms also create substantial problems. For example, it has been estimated that more than 90 percent of the small businesses established are organized because of easy entry. Furthermore, it is reasonable to assume that virtually every one of the 450,000 to 500,000 new businesses launched in a typical year is started by an entrepreneur with high expectations. But the same conditions that permit ease of entry also make overcrowding inevitable in most industries, and only those entrepreneurs with the necessary management skills can survive.

In what direction are new enterprises heading? Over half of the new small businesses are retail operations of some type, including restaurants. New franchise outlets account for 5 to 10 percent of the new business operations. Service and recreation fields are growing at the fastest rate. For example, campgrounds, motels, instant printing centers, placement centers, and indoor tennis courts are being set up by the hundreds. According to an article in the *Wall*

---

[5] J. Fred Weston, *The Financing of Small Business* (New York: Macmillan, 1967), p. 46.

Street Journal, due to the growth of permanent-press clothing, coin-operated dry-cleaning shops are opening at the rate of 2,000 each year. A trip to almost any shopping center will also confirm that consumer affluence has precipitated an apparently endless variety of specialty retail outlets.

Unfortunately, according to past mortality rates, about half of these new small businesses will survive no longer than 18 months. Which will succeed and which will fail?

Factors in Small Business Failure

All businesses, regardless of size, have an element of risk. Small businesses, however, have a much greater risk than do large businesses. For example, from 1959 to 1969, nine out of ten business firms that failed had liabilities of less than $100,000, with six out of nine failing firms having liabilities of less than $25,000.

As illustrated in Figure 1-1, the rate of business failures is closely correlated to general business conditions in the country. For example, as sales and profits decreased during the economic downturn of 1970, the number of businesses that went bankrupt—or otherwise failed with loss to creditors—rose 17 percent, from 9,154 in 1969 to 10,748. According to Dun & Bradstreet, the failure

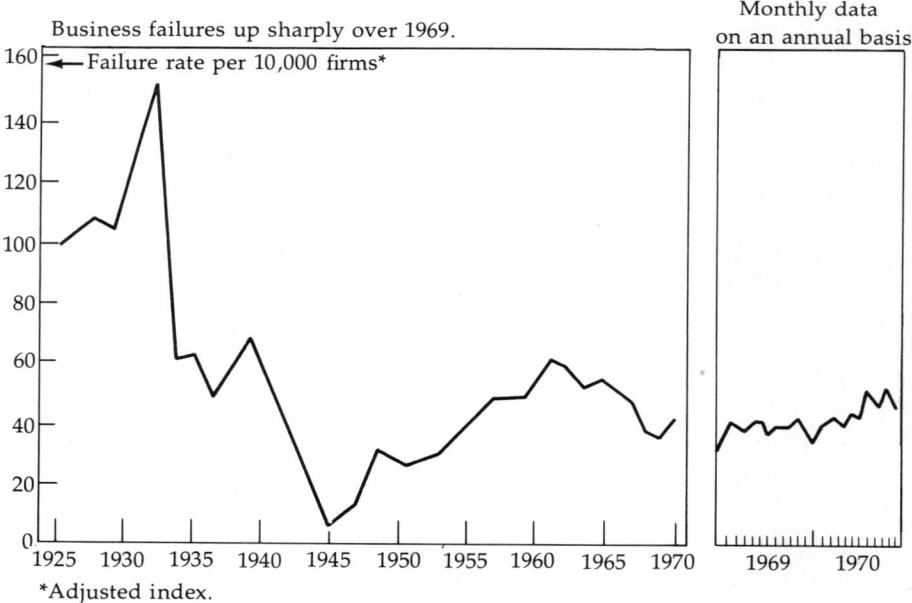

Figure 1-1. Rate of Business Failures (Source: Dun & Bradstreet, Inc.).

rate per 10,000 firms was higher in every month of 1970 than it had been for the same month in 1969.

The number of new businesses is also influenced strongly by general business conditions (see Figure 1-2). For example, the 1970 rate of growth was roughly 30 percent below the average rate experienced in recent years. The turnover among firms is phenomenal; in recent years, *over* 400,000 firms have been started annually, with 350,000 to 400,000 annually discontinued. Dun & Bradstreet report that more than 5,000 listings in their reference book are changed each day, as new names are listed, discontinued businesses deleted, and credit ratings revised.

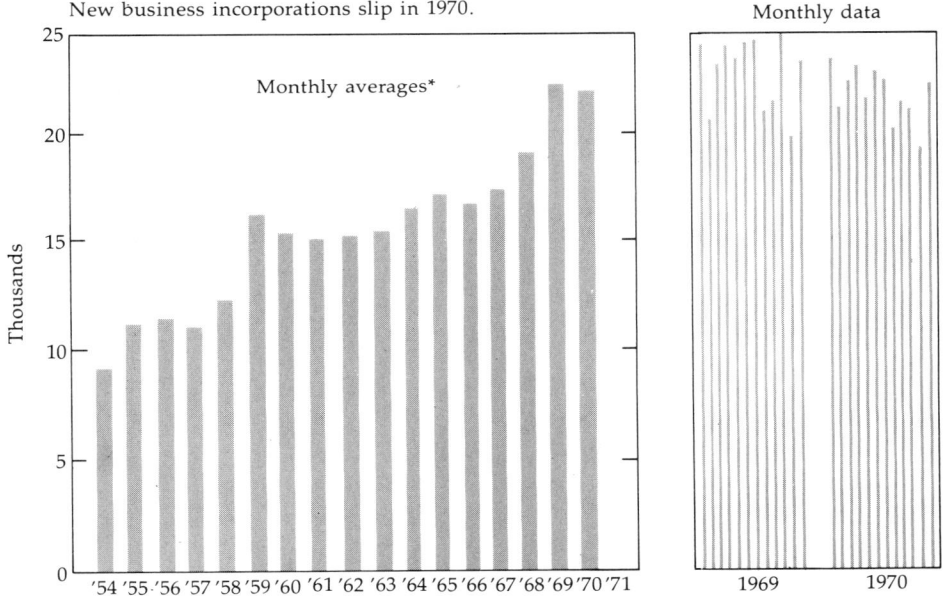

Figure 1-2. New Business Incorporations (Source: Dun & Bradstreet, Inc.).

Of course, the risk of failing in a new small business varies significantly by industry and by lines of business within an industry. For example, retailing, in which small business predominates, consistently shows a high rate of failure. At the same time, there is great variability among the lines of business within retailing (see Table 1-1).

Table 1–1. Retail Failure Rates.

Line of Business	Failure Rate per 10,000 Operating Concerns
Women's ready-to-wear	77
Furniture and furnishings	74
Cameras and photographic supplies	67
Books and stationery	57
Gifts	40
Shoes	23
Hardware	16
Women's accessories	14

Source: *The Failure Record Through 1970* (New York: Dun & Bradstreet, Inc., 1971), p. 5.

As a rule, small firms that fail do so in their first 5-year period (see Table 1–2). In a study conducted in Providence, Rhode Island, in the early 1960s, it was found that only 41 of 81 small service and retail firms survived more than two years.[6] Thus, we can conclude that if a small firm can provide for its survival during its first few years, it has a good chance of surviving.

Table 1–2. Age of Business Failures, 1965–1970.

Year	% in Business 5 Years or Less	% in Business 6 to 10 Years	% in Business Over 10 Years
1965	56.9	21.4	21.7
1966	57.4	21.5	21.1
1967	55.3	22.5	22.2
1968	53.9	23.3	22.8
1969	53.2	24.4	22.4
1970	54.9	22.7	22.4

Source: *The Failure Record Through 1970* (New York: Dun & Bradstreet, Inc., 1971), p. 10.

---

[6] Kurt Mayer and Sidney Goldstein, *The First Two Years: Problems of Small Firm Growth and Survival* (Washington, D. C.: Small Business Administration, 1961), pp. 56–57.

Avoiding Small Business Failure

Aside from economic conditions and the fact that certain lines of business are riskier than others, there are other basic causes that account for the high mortality rate of small businesses. Dun & Bradstreet, in their annual studies of business failure, consistently point out that aside from the relatively few failures caused by fraud, poor health, disaster, and marital difficulties, the most important single reason for business failure is *lack of managerial skills* (see Table 1–3).

Table 1–3. Causes of U.S. Business Failures.

Cause		Percent
Neglect		2.3
Fraud		0.9
Poor management		
Lack of experience in the line	10.2	
Lack of managerial experience	13.5	
Unbalanced experience	18.6	
Incompetence	47.8	90.1
Diaster		1.2
Reason unknown		5.5

Source: *The Failure Record Through 1970* (New York: Dun & Bradstreet, Inc., 1971), pp. 11–12.

However, if you ask any owner of a failing small business for his explanation, you rarely will get an admission of poor management. The owner is typically defensive and blames his problems on such factors as poor location, inadequate sales, excessive competition, lack of working capital, and difficulties with receivables and inventories. As one group of experts has noted, "What may be described by the person who fails as 'excessive competition' might instead be ineffectual sales effort . . . 'bad debts' may in reality have been careless extension of credit . . ."[7]

Studies of small business failure all seem to arrive at the same general conclusion: small business managers suffer from (1) lack of training and experience as a manager, and (2) lack of personal qualifications to run a business.

---

[7] Pearce C. Kelley et al., *How to Organize and Operate a Small Business*, 4th ed. (Englewood Cliffs, N.J.: Prentice-Hall, 1968), p. 20.

These two general limitations can cause the entrepreneur the following more specific problems:

1. Starting the venture with inadequate capital.
2. Choosing a poor location and/or an improper legal form of organization.
3. Putting too much capital into fixed assets.
4. Failing to plan and formulate goals.
5. Keeping inadequate financial records.
6. Failing to follow modern management practices.
7. Taking too much out of the business (that is, "living high on the hog").

A report of the Small Business Opportunities Corporation to the Economic Development Administration perceptively summarizes the shortcomings of failing small businesses in depressed areas:

Many of the existing small businessmen are operating marginally and out of ignorance rather than through understanding of the proper techniques for running a business. Little thought was given to such features as choosing a location, layout, controls (inventory and cash notably), merchandising, maintaining suitable records, cash reserves for contingency purposes, etc. Planning in any real sense is conspicuously absent, and forecasting is simply one of the unknowns. Success is associated with hard work and long hours, so that "mule power" is substituted for good business sense, and the financial returns are proportionate to the former in far too many instances to justify the business. Frustration, despondency, and defeatism "spill over" to affect the entire family, which "pitches in" in the effort to maintain an already inadequate income and virtually hopeless situation.[8]

Future Outlook for Small Business

Most everyone engaged in some aspect of small business uses his or her own "crystal ball" to forecast the outlook for small business. The alarming rate of failures and the trend toward bigness and mergers has caused many experts to predict a dismal future. Others are more optimistic in their predictions. For example, Del Goetz, formerly with the Small Business Advisory Service of the

---

[8] *Final Report July 1, 1967–December 31, 1967* (Philadelphia: Small Business Opportunities Corporation, 1968), pp. 27–28.

Bank of America, points out that the government has been encouraging new business formations, especially by blacks. She further believes that better education, technological advances, and the trend toward specialization will provide young people, whose changing values are causing them to turn away from corporations, with opportunities for individual effort in small businesses.

Edward C. Bursk, editor of the *Harvard Business Review*, also feels that certain changing conditions in the economy can give the alert small businessman a competitive advantage. He points out that:

> In spite of predictions to the contrary, such modern influences as automation, statistical decision making, and the cost-price squeeze can bring new opportunities to small businessmen who are prepared to capitalize on them.[9]

Bursk feels that because these three developments force the large business into a pattern of standardization, the small business, with its greater flexibility and adaptability, is therefore in a good position to pick up opportunities that the larger business must bypass.

It is important that the small businessman remember that his success will not come about by attempting to meet big business head-on. It follows from this statement that the small businessman, assuming he has the necessary qualifications, will achieve success by exploiting the attributes of smallness and finding his "niche" in the economy rather than by meeting big business head-on. The attributes of smallness that he can build on are flexibility, ability to adapt quickly to new or changing conditions, and personalized service. These factors, combined with the increasing demand for specialized services and custom products made possible by higher incomes and increased leisure time, suggest that small business will continue to play an important role in the economy of the future.

Of course, whether any particular small business succeeds or fails will depend to a large extent on the owner's personal abilities, his openness to change, and the nature of the assistance available to him. The modest intent of this book is to provide potential or existing entrepreneurs with such practical assistance.

---

[9]Edward C. Bursk, "Pointers on Meeting Competition," *Management Aids for Small Manufacturers*, No. 10 (Washington, D. C.: Small Business Administration, 1964), p. 17.

Incident 1: I'm Not All Right, Jack

"Sam, I've had it!" Pete Smith said, as they sipped their coffee in Pete's kitchen. "Look at us—working our pants off, no money in the bank, and that idiot Martin yelling at us all the time. There's got to be a better way to live!"

"So body and fender work isn't a big deal," Sam replied. "What do you suggest—robbing banks?"

"Sometimes I think that's what Martin does, Sam. We're much better craftsmen than he is, and look at the way he runs the business. Have you seen his invoices? A job that we earn fifty bucks on, he charges one-fifty, or even two hundred. But he owns the place, and we're just working stiffs." Pete moodily sipped his coffee.

"Yeah, if *we* owned the place . . ."

"Sam, why don't we own the place? I mean, why don't we set up our own shop?"

Sam sighed. "Sure, sure. All we'd have to do is find some money, rent a shop, get some tools, find some customers, and try to do all that office stuff while we hammered out fenders. You might as well relax, kid. We're going to be wage slaves all our lives."

"Sam, we've got most of our own tools. And, remember, Jacobs is going out of business. We could get the power equipment from him cheap. We could do it, Sam."

"I'm still supporting my brother-in-law on a deal like that. Remember? He tried to run that pizza parlor. Ended up owing maybe thirty thousand. No, Pete, business is for the big guys, not people like us." He sighed again. "How old are you, Pete?"

"Twenty-five."

"And Martha's maybe twenty-three?"

"Right. And I'm sure she'd go along with my idea. She's always supported me when I needed it."

"Your wife's too nice to have you work eighty hours a week, Pete. You told me last week that she wants to quit her job. If you go into business for yourself, she'll end up making all the money, and you'll end up spending it."

"Look, Sam, what's so hard about running a business? I bet that we could rent a shop, get the tools, and do the job right for maybe eight or nine thousand bucks. Maybe even less, if we worked it right."

"Martin may be a creep, but his checks don't bounce," Sam said.

"Sam, I don't want to spend the next forty years working for someone else. I think that I'll do some thinking about my own company. Let's see—Smith and Company . . . How about Super Body Repair? Hey, I've got it! Smith the Smith, Inc. Remember, blacksmiths used to be called smiths, and that's really what we are, isn't it?"

Sam laughed and got up. "I have to go, Pete. You're too much. I wish that I was young again—when you get to be forty-two, you lose your drive. But listen. If you're really serious, you've got to plan. You know—when we take a look at those crushed fenders, we have to figure out just how all that metal is going to be stretched and bent back. If you plan right, the job goes fine. But if you start hacking and pounding away, then the car ends up a mess. Maybe a business is like that too—you've got to plan ahead. Now you sit down and make up a plan. Then maybe if the plan is good, I'll listen to your wild ideas."

Pete began to look around for some paper. "OK, Sam, you're right. I'll plan the whole thing out for you. You'll see—we can make this thing go!"

1. Pete Smith has four years' experience as a body and fender man. He learned his trade at a vocational school, where he studied for two years after high school. What assets does Pete have that might make him a successful businessman?
2. What will Pete have to learn fast if his new company is to succeed? Why?
3. Is the body and fender repair business a good one for the small businessman? Why or why not? Is Pete likely to get wiped out by big companies?
4. Help Pete out by writing down a basic plan for him. Include the important things he should start thinking about now if he really expects to succeed.

Discussion Questions

1. How significant is small business in today's American economy?
2. Do you see any reason for the many definitions of small business?
3. What are the significant characteristics of a small business as proposed by the Committee for Economic Development?
4. In which sectors of the economy is small business most important? To what do you attribute its strength in these areas?
5. What growth areas do you foresee for tomorrow's small businesses?
6. List and briefly discuss several factors in small business failure.
7. What are two general reasons why owners or managers of small businesses frequently fail? What specific problems result from these more general limitations?
8. What do you see as the outlook for small business 10 years from now? Twenty years from now? Why?
9. Do you feel that small business can meet big business head on? Why or why not?

Suggested Readings

Bostram, Karl, "Why We Need Research for Independent Business," *Journal of Small Business Management* II (January 1964), 14–18.

Bursh, Edward C., "Pointers on Meeting Competition," *Management Aids for Small Manufacturers*, No. 10. Washington, D.C.: Small Business Administration, 1964.

Charlesworth, Harold K., "The Uncertain Future of Small Business: Can This Picture Be Changed?" *Business Topics* 18, No. 2 (Spring 1970), 13–15.

Foley, Eugene C., "Unskilled Managers—The Major Barrier to Small Business Success," *Journal of Small Business Management* III (July 1965), 13–15.

Hollander, Edward D., et al., *The Future of Small Business*, prepared by Robert R. Nathan Associates, Inc. New York: Praeger, 1967.

Kamerchen, David R., "The Persistance of Small Firms: A Pyrrhic Victory," *Marquette Business Review* VIII (Winter 1964), 150–156.

Kelley, Pearce C., Lawyer, Kenneth, and Baumback, Clifford M., *How to Organize and Operate a Small Business*, 4th ed. Englewood Cliffs, N. J.: Prentice-Hall, 1968. Ch. 1 & 2.

Klatt, Lawrence A., ed., *Managing the Dynamic Small Firm: Readings*. Belmont, Calif.: Wadsworth, 1971. See "Problems of the Small Business," pp. 25–49, and "The Future," pp. 329–354.

Mayer, Kurt, and Goldstein, Sidney, *The First Two Years: Problems of Small Firm Growth and Survival*. Washington, D. C.: Small Business Administration, 1961.

Proxmire, William, *Can Small Business Survive?* Chicago: Henry Regnery, 1964.

Ringstrom, N. H., *Case Studies in Business Success and Failure*. Small Business Management Research Report prepared by Oklahoma State University under a grant from the Small Business Administration, Washington, D. C., 1962.

Small Business Advisory Service, "Small Business Success," *Small Business Reports*, VII. San Francisco: Bank of America, 1966.

Weston, J. Fred, "The Position of Small Business in the American Economy." In *The Financing of Small Business*, edited by Irving Pfeffer. New York: Macmillan, 1967.

Wisnewsky, Edward, "Small Business: Political Front or Ideological Problem?" *Marquette Business Review* IV (June 1960), 1–17.

Woodruff, A. M., "Traps to Avoid in Small Business Management," *Management Aids Annual No. 6*. Washington, D. C.: Small Business Administration, 1960. Pp. 9–15.

The Entrepreneur

Chapter 2

The American Dream of being one's own boss and the cultural emphasis on independence are behind many people's desire for business ownership. The idea that any ambitious American with industry, average intelligence, and thrift can save enough money to start a small business and, if he has real drive and ability, can develop it into a successful business still exists for a large portion of the working population.

The findings of at least one study are that the majority of workers in every occupational category have had the goal of going into business for themselves. Furthermore, many of the respondents actually attempted to fulfill this aspiration at some time during their career.[1]

Why do so many people wish to go into business for themselves? Of course, the motivation for economic behavior is exceedingly complex. Such basic human needs as the needs for security, recognition, affection, and self-expression provide the impetus for much of our behavior. The relative importance of these needs, however, varies from person to person and is influenced by such factors as sex, age, occupational experience, and family history, to name a few. To ask an individual why he went into business for himself is likely to result in stereotypical answers such as "to be my own boss" or "to make money." Evidence suggests that such replies are rationalizations rather than statements of basic motivations. For example, a survey of small firm growth and survival found that "the owners in many cases did not consciously

---

[1] For example, see Seymour M. Lipset and Reinhard Bendix, "Social Mobility and Occupational Career Patterns," *American Journal of Sociology* (March 1954), pp. 494–504.

know why they went into business; often they had no clear goals in mind, having little if any appreciation of the business world in general."[2]

Rewards and Costs of Entrepreneurship

Advantages of Self-Employment

Whatever the motivation for starting one's own business, it cannot be denied that self-employment offers distinct advantages. An owner–operator of a business derives a sense of pride and satisfaction in building a valuable investment for the future. Given the opportunity to try his own ideas, he can cultivate a sense of independence. In many cases, a new business may mean an opportunity for a higher income. Moreover, once the business is on a paying basis, it can yield financial and occupational security.

Certainly there are other factors that can motivate a person to start a new business: the opportunity for service, a desire for power, or the need to prove his ability. Further, many entrepreneurs start businesses simply because they are unable to obtain salaried employment, either because of age, physical handicaps, or business depressions. For example, due to recent cutbacks in the aerospace industry many highly paid engineers and technicians have had to find new careers as self-employed consultants or owner–operators of franchise outlets—everything from pizza parlors to motels.

Disadvantages of Self-Employment

Any small businessman will be quick to point out the numerous disadvantages that go along with ownership of a business. Of course, the most important danger is the loss of personal capital. With the opportunity for large profits come serious risks, and many of these risks—such as depressed economic conditions, price fluctuations, and to some extent, labor turmoil—are not entirely within the businessman's control.

While a small businessman may be his own boss, he will also find that there are many other people he must please if he wishes to succeed. Regardless of the nature of the business, he must satisfy his customers. In addition, his creditors and competitors will dictate to him. For example, creditors will be tempted to protect their interests by "advising" on how the business should be operated. Larger lenders will require periodic reports, liens on assets, and explana-

---

[2] Kurt B. Mayer and Sidney Goldstein, *The First Two Years, Problems of Small Firm Growth and Survival* (Washington, D. C.: Small Business Administration, 1961), p. 28.

tions for certain actions. Similarly, competitors will seem to be constantly forcing the entrepreneur to change his strategy as they lower prices, increase their promotion efforts, or introduce new products or services. Building inspectors, health authorities, insurance people, and representatives from various government agencies will also see that he meets certain standards, keeps records, and follows regulations. Even in an established firm, the business income is likely to be less regular than that of a salaried employee. Furthermore, an owner–manager has to be both a doer and a planner; in the final analysis, he must accept sole responsibility for all decisions.[3]

Thus, these disadvantages can become a burden that is distasteful to many individuals and that may require certain essential "entrepreneurial" qualities not found in the "ordinary" person.

Working for Others

This chapter is not meant to be a sales pitch for going into business for oneself; nor is it intended to idealize the entrepreneur. Rather my modest goal is to present some factors that should be considered by the individual contemplating self-employment. To be more objective, therefore, it is paramount that some space be devoted to the advantages and disadvantages of being an employee of another's business.

Advantages of Salaried Employment

1. There is little financial responsibility and very little business risk. The business can do poorly or even "go under" and the employee does not lose his personal savings.
2. Working for a large, well-known firm can be a source of pride to the employee. Similarly, the employee who has a strong need to belong can find a large company with many employees an ideal place to socialize and fulfill these needs.
3. A salaried employee usually works regular hours and need not worry after working hours are over. The employee typically works shorter hours and receives overtime pay if required to work beyond regular hours.
4. Other advantages to salaried employment include regular vacations, more fringe benefits, less responsibility, larger initial income, more stability,

---

[3] For an excellent discussion of the advantages and disadvantages of going into your own business, see "Wendell O. Metcalf, *Starting and Managing a Small Business of Your Own* (Washington, D. C.: Small Business Administration, 1962).

predictability of the future and of one's life style, and generally more limited demands on knowledge and ability.

Disadvantages of Salaried Employment

Being a salaried employee offers several advantages. At the same time it involves several disadvantages, such as:

1. Job security and employment opportunities may fluctuate with changing economic conditions. For example, during the recession of 1970–71, large numbers of highly qualified engineers, scientists, and managerial personnel were laid off or dismissed. In some cases, they have been replaced by younger men at lower salaries.
2. There is no ceiling to the entrepreneur's salary, but most employees come close to their salary maximum by the middle of their careers. Or to put it another way, statistics show that the lifetime earnings of employees are smaller than the earnings of entrepreneurs.
3. An employee is subject to discharge for cause or to transfer from one geographical area to another. Similarly, he is subject to retiring at some age whether he wants to or not.
4. Most big businesses seek out "organization men" who will fit neatly into some niche in the organization structure. Not only does this stifle the employee's opportunity to try out his various abilities and knowledge, but being a "company man" runs contrary to the personality of most true entrepreneurs.

The Entrepreneur Type

According to an investigation conducted by Orvis F. Collins and David G. Moore,[4] the entrepreneur is a type of person who differs qualitatively from the salaried manager in a large business organization. In attempting to find out why some men strike out on their own while others join the established organizations, the researchers found certain significant differences in background and attitudes between the two groups of men. For example, the entrepreneur is likely to have less education; he typically comes from a family without roots in large organizations. Most importantly, entrepreneurs seem to be more in-

---

[4]Orvis Collins and David G. Moore, *The Organization Makers* (New York: Appleton-Century-Crofts, 1970).

dividualistic, thus seeking to become entrepreneurs as an escape from the organizational constraints of a large concern. In other words, they find outlets for their creativity and drive by creating their own business. What does this mean for those who may be contemplating a career in small business? Various studies have found that certain personality qualities or characteristics are essential to the successful management of a small business. According to Dr. H. B. Pickle, the characteristics significantly related to entrepreneurial success are:

1. *Drive,* comprised of responsibility, vigor, initiative, persistence, and health.
2. *Thinking ability,* comprised of original thinking, creative thinking, critical thinking, and analytical thinking.
3. *Human relations ability,* comprised of ascendancy, emotional stability, sociability, cautiousness, personal relations, consideration, cheerfulness, cooperation, and tactfulness.
4. *Communications ability,* comprised of verbal and written communications.
5. *Technical knowledge,* all-encompassing know-how related to the business.[5]

Thus, we can conclude from these studies that the successful small business manager is a man who possesses drive, superior ability in communications, creative and analytical thinking, human relations ability, and outstanding technical knowledge of his field. In addition, he is an individualist who has little regard for authority figures and the highly structured goals of established organizations.

Other studies and/or experts have categorized the traits of the successful entrepreneur somewhat differently. For example, L. T. White, a noted businessman who was active in the training and education of small business owners and managers, characterized the successful entrepreneur in these terms:

1. *Perception.* He has curiosity. He must look out and ahead. He's never quite satisfied or content. There's always a better way.
2. *Boldness.* He must act. He must do more than dream. He wastes no time blaming others. He is without fear or worry. He takes risks.
3. *Persistence.* This man keeps trying and trying. He doesn't make the same mistake twice. He tries something different until he hits the right combina-

---

[5] Hal B. Pickle, *Personality and Success: An Evaluation of Personal Characteristics of Successful Small Business Managers* (Washington, D. C.: Small Business Administration, 1964), p. 34.

tion. There is a fancy name for this. It's called pragmatic. When you are trying to sell something to somebody, think of this story. "You're the fifth insurance man who tried to get in to see me this week." "That's right. I'm all five of them."
4. *Persuasion.* Owners must influence bankers to supply money, employees to work harder and smarter, suppliers to furnish materials at lowest cost, and customers to buy and to remain friends.
5. *Ethics.* Business is disciplined usefulness. It's a social process. A high moral code is the source of the businessman's desire to help by selling, by being diligent, and by accepting self-denial in saving for further expansion.[6]

Introspection and Self-Selection

After recognizing the disadvantages, as well as the advantages, of establishing his own business, the prospective entrepreneur must realize that he will be the most important employee in his organization. It is imperative, therefore, that he carefully analyze his weak points as well as his strong points. For as Louis L. Allen pointed out, "there's something very special about the selection of the owner of a small business: *They have selected themselves.*"[7]

This means that the final decision of whether or not to start a business rests with the individual. Hopefully, he will know how to select himself as a potential entrepreneur. Unfortunately, the high failure rate of small businesses suggests that the entrepreneur too often makes his decision on the basis of "dreams" and desire rather than on objective, critical evaluation. All too frequently, the author has heard the comment from marginal small businessmen, "if only I had more capital." But money isn't everything; in business, success depends on more than possessing adequate capital. It is at least equally important that the owner-operator of a smaller firm possess certain personal traits, managerial skills, and business experience. As the head of a company which specializes in making loans to small business remarked, ". . . I become more and more impressed with the fact that this self-selection process is far more important to the success or failure of the company the man is starting than the monetary aspects of our negotiations."[8] Each person considering self-employment should carefully consider whether he has what it takes.

The sad truth is that there are individuals who simply are not cut out to be owners or managers of small businesses. The first step for a prospective

---

[6] From Joseph C. Schabacker, "The Special Case of Small Business as L. T. White Saw It," *Journal of Small Business Management* 8 (October 1970), pp. 12–13.
[7] Louis L. Allen, "Executive Self-Selection in Small Businesses," *Management of Personnel Quarterly* 4, No. 2 (Summer 1965), p. 3.
[8] *Ibid.*, p. 4.

entrepreneur, therefore, is to get to know himself. To assist you in gaining self-awareness, Table 2–1 (p. 22) lists ten traits considered important for the person operating his own business. Try to rate yourself objectively. After you have rated yourself, ask someone to have several people who know you rate you anonymously. The rating scale cannot be reduced to a single score. However, it may give you insight into your overall strengths and weaknesses.

In addition, there are three key points, suggested by Louis L. Allen, to be considered by those thinking of starting their own business:

1. "there is nothing to be obtained without paying the price." Sacrifices will be necessary in order for your business to succeed.
2. "self-select only experienced men to start a new enterprise." Don't run your own business if you don't know that business extremely well.
3. "ask yourself whether you can accept personal inconvenience." You may have to make choices such as temporarily reducing your living standard or moving to an area in which your business will have the best chance of success.[9]

As an additional step in your self-analysis, you can benefit from objectively answering the following questions:[10]

(Under each question, check the answer that says what you feel or comes closest to it. Be honest with yourself.)

1. Are you a self-starter?
   _____ I do things on my own. Nobody has to tell me to get going.
   _____ If someone gets me started, I keep going all right.
   _____ Easy does it, man. I don't put myself out until I have to.
2. How do you feel about other people?
   _____ I like people. I can get along with just about anybody.
   _____ I have plenty of friends—I don't need anyone else.
   _____ Most people bug me.

---

[9] *Ibid.*, p. 6.
[10] Adapted from "Checklist for Going into Business," *Small Marketers Aid*, No. 71 (Washington, D. C.: Small Business Administration, 1971).

Table 2-1. Rating Scale for Evaluating Personal Traits Important to the Proprietor of a Business.

Instructions: Place a check mark on the line following each trait where you think it ought to be. The check mark need not be placed directly over one of the guide phrases, because the rating may lie somewhere between the phrases.

Initiative	Additional tasks sought; highly ingenious	Resourceful; alert to opportunities	Regular work performed without waiting for directions	Routine worker awaiting directions	
Attitude toward others	Positive; friendly interest in people	Pleasant, polite	Sometimes difficult to work with	Inclined to be quarrelsome or uncooperative	
Leadership	Forceful, inspiring confidence and loyalty	Order giver	Driver	Weak	
Responsibility	Responsibility sought and welcomed	Accepted without protest	Unwilling to assume without protest	Avoided whenever possible	
Organizing ability	Highly capable of perceiving and arranging fundamentals in logical order	Able organizer	Fairly capable of organizing	Poor organizer	
Industry	Industrious; capable of working hard for long hours	Can work hard, but not for too long a period	Fairly industrious	Hard work avoided	
Decision	Quick and accurate	Good and careful	Quick, but often unsound	Hesitant and fearful	
Sincerity	Courageous, square shooter	On the level	Fairly sincere	Inclined to lack sincerity	
Perseverance	Highly steadfast in purpose; not discouraged by obstacles	Effort steadily maintained	Average determination and persistence	Little or no persistence	
Physical energy	Highly energetic at all times	Energetic most of time	Fairly energetic	Below average	

3. Can you lead others?
   _____ I can get most people to go along when I start something.
   _____ I can give the orders if someone tells me what we should do.
   _____ I let someone else get things moving. Then I go along if I feel like it.

4. Can you take responsibility?
   _____ I like to take charge of things and see them through.
   _____ I'll take over if I have to, but I'd rather let someone else be responsible.
   _____ There's always some eager beaver around wanting to show how smart he is. I say let him.

5. How good an organizer are you?
   _____ I like to have a plan before I start. I'm usually the one to get things lined up when the gang wants to do something.
   _____ I do all right unless things get too goofed up. Then I cop out.
   _____ You get all set and then something comes along and blows the whole bag. So I just take things as they come.

6. How good a worker are you?
   _____ I can keep going as long as I need to. I don't mind working hard for something I want.
   _____ I'll work hard for a while, but when I've had enough, that's it, man!
   _____ I can't see that hard work gets you anywhere.

7. Can you make decisions?
   _____ I can make up my mind in a hurry if I have to. It usually turns out O.K., too.
   _____ I can if I have plenty of time. If I have to make up my mind fast, I think later I should have decided the other way.
   _____ I don't like to be the one who has to decide things. I'd probably blow it.

8. Can people trust what you say?
   _____ You bet they can. I don't say things I don't mean.
   _____ I try to be on the level most of the time, but sometimes I just say what's easiest.
   _____ What's the sweat if the other fellow doesn't know the difference?

9. Can you stick with it?
   _____ If I make up my mind to do something, I don't let anything stop me.
   _____ I usually finish what I start—if it doesn't get fouled up.
   _____ If it doesn't go well right away, I turn off. Why beat your brains out?

10. How good is your health?
    _____ Man, I never run down!
    _____ I have enough energy for most things I want to do.
    _____ I run out of juice sooner than most of my friends seem to.

If most of your checks are beside the first answers, you probably have what it takes to run a business. If not, you're likely to have more trouble than you can handle by yourself. Better find a partner who is strong on the points you're weak on. If many checks are beside the third answer, not even a good partner will be able to shore you up.

If your objective evaluation is positive so far, consider the following general questions that should stimulate some thought about your proposed business venture.

1. How about your business background?

    Have you worked in a business like the one you want to start?
    Have you worked for someone else as a foreman or manager?
    Have you had any business training in school?
    Have you ever read a book on management?
    Do you want to own your own business badly enough to work long hours without knowing how much money you'll end up with?

2. How about the money?

    Do you know how much money you will need to get your business started?
    Have you figured out how much of your own money you can put into the business?
    Do you know how much credit you can get from your suppliers—the people you will buy from?
    Do you know where you can borrow the rest of the money you need to start your business?
    Have you figured out what net income per year you expect to get from the business?
    Can you live on less than this amount so that you can use some of it to help your business grow?
    Have you talked to a banker about your plans?

3. How about a partner?

    If you need a partner with money or know-how that you don't have, do you know someone who will fit—someone you can get along with?
    Do you know the good and bad points about going it alone, having a partner, and incorporating your business?
    Have you talked to a lawyer about it?

4. How about your customers?

    Do most businesses in your community seem to be doing well?
    Have you tried to find out whether businesses like the one you want to open are doing well in your community and in the rest of the country?
    Have you talked to potential customers about the product or service you plan to sell?

Whether or not to go into business for yourself is a major decision that warrants considerable and careful thought. Chapter 1 pointed out why some small businesses fail and offered some suggestions for overcoming these failures. Experience has shown that poor management is common to most business disasters. Basic to the problem of poor management in smaller firms is the lack of preparation and forethought given to starting a business. It is the author's belief that not everyone has the personal qualifications to strike out on his own. For most people, the American Dream of owning their own business should be just that—a *dream*. All too frequently, an individual with a little money and an idea jumps into a business opportunity only to become a mortality statistic by the end of the first year of operation.

Recognizing the shortcomings of any self-analysis checklist, this chapter has tried to offer the potential entrepreneur some things to consider before making his decision. In some cases it may merely reinforce your convictions about the likelihood of success. In some cases it may discourage an ill-conceived project. Hopefully, in all cases it has encouraged careful consideration of going into business for oneself. The balance of this book will present managerial concepts and practices that are important to the small firm.

Incident 2: The Future Winner

I know that it can be done, Pete thought, as he scribbled on the paper. It just can't be that tough. But then, that's what Sam's brother-in-law thought, too. I wonder what he did wrong?

Martha came in from the front room. "What are you so absorbed in there?"

"I'm still messing around with the idea of having our own business, baby. I think we can do it."

"Of course, you can. Pete, you know you're a good body and fender man. And you certainly see through Martin's bad management."

"We've got $755 in the bank, Martha, and as near as I can figure, we'll need maybe $3,400."

"We can always borrow it, Pete."

"Where?"

"Well, my father . . ."

"I know he's got it, Martha, but I hate to ask him. He doesn't think all that much of me anyway. Now if I had continued with college, like he was always telling me to, maybe he'd listen."

"Dad's up tight about money, Pete. If you wanted money for a car or something, he'd really blow his stack. But for business, well, he'd do it. I know he would."

"Yeah, you're right. He would. But boy, even with plenty of money it's one thing to think about it and another to really do it. I keep wondering if I have what it takes."

"I *know* you do, Pete."

"Yeah, but you're my wife—how about the guys who wreck cars? Will they believe it?"

"The only way to find out is to try."

"Martha, will you stick with me through it? I mean, if I quit my job and all that?"

"Of course."

1. Pete never took any courses in small business management. What are you learning in your class that he might need to know? Why? What are you learning that has nothing to do with business? Why?
2. List the personal characteristics Pete should have before he jumps into his own business. Does he have them, or can he learn them? Why or why not?

Discussion Questions

1. How do you explain the American Dream of going into business for oneself?
2. Discuss the advantages of self-employment.
3. How would you respond to the statement that the main advantage of self-employment is that you can be your own boss.
4. It was suggested in the chapter that the salaried manager or professional in a large organization has a strong need for belonging and association with his peers. Don't entrepreneurs have the same need?
5. Is job security greater as an entrepreneur or as a salaried employee?
6. What is the major advantage of entrepreneurship for the business-school graduate?
7. Is there such a thing as an "entrepreneur type"? Explain.
8. List and discuss the characteristics related to entrepreneurial success uncovered by Dr. H. B. Pickle.
9. Do the characteristics of the "entrepreneur type" differ from L. T. White's characterization of the successful entrepreneur? Explain.
10. What does Louis L. Allen mean when he says that the owners of small businesses have selected themselves?
11. Discuss the three key points suggested by Louis L. Allen for those thinking of starting their own business.
12. Do you agree that not everyone should strike out on his own? Why or why not?
13. Prepare a chart summarizing the personal qualifications necessary for entrepreneurship.

Suggested Readings

Baty, G. B., "So You Want to Start a Company?" *Machine Design* XXXVI (March 12, 1964), 122–131.

Beam, Jerome C., "Essential Personal Qualities for Small Store Managers," *Small Marketers Aids Annual No. 5.* Washington, D. C.: Small Business Administration, 1963. Pp. 9–16.

Bostrom, Karl, "Independent Venture Management—Its Nurture and Development," *Journal of Small Business Management* I (February 1963), 1–4, 6–8.

Building A Future in a Business of Your Own. New York: American Petroleum Institute, 1965.

Collins, Orvis, *The Organization Makers.* New York: Appleton-Century-Crofts, 1970.

Collins, Orvis F., Moore, David G., and Unwalla, Darab, "The Enterprising Man and the Business Executive," *Business Topics* XII (Winter 1964), 19–34.

Donnelley, Robert G., "The Family Business," *Harvard Business Review* XLII (July–August, 1964), 93–105.

Klatt, Lawrence A., ed., *Managing the Dynamic Small Firm: Readings.* Belmont, Calif.: Wadsworth, 1971. See "The Entrepreneur," pp. 1–25.

Morse, Fred C., *Going into Business for Yourself.* Austin, Texas: Fred C. Morse, 1965.

Small Business Advisory Service, "Opening Your Own Business," *Small Business Reporter* VII. San Francisco: Bank of America, 1966.

Pickle, Hal B., *Personality and Success: An Evaluation of Personal Characteristics of Successful Small Business Managers,* Small Business Research Series No. 4. Washington, D. C.: Small Business Administration, 1964.

"Should You Go into Business for Yourself?" Series of six articles in *Changing Times,* the Kiplinger Magazine (October 1959–March 1960).

Weston, J. Fred., "The Position of Small Business in the American Economy." In *The Financing of Small Business,* edited by Irving Pfeffer. New York: Macmillan, 1969.

Part Two

Management: The Key to Successful Entrepreneurship

Setting Goals

Chapter 3

During the earlier periods of industrial development, when unlimited opportunities and vast resources were available to the ambitious entrepreneur, formal planning was relatively ignored. The entrepreneurs were likely to be hard-driving men of action who met day-to-day problems with impulsive but imaginative reactions.

With the closing of frontiers came increased competition and a complexity of economic and technological changes, and impulsive decision making became a costly substitute for real planning. Today the businessman realizes that effective planning is a faster, less disruptive approach to the rapidly changing conditions of modern society. Furthermore, available evidence suggests that planning will become the determining survival factor for all but the very smallest firms. One reason is that the small business does not have the necessary strength to survive many mistakes; thus, the entrepreneur must carefully determine where he wants his business to go and how to get there.

The Planning Function

Most large corporations have a full-time planning staff, but a small firm cannot afford this luxury. Consequently, the owner–manager's ability to plan will determine whether he runs the business or whether the business runs him. Planning is looking ahead. It includes not only setting down objectives and establishing guidelines for achieving these objectives, but also the development of an orderly, carefully considered strategy for operating the business.

Planning involves not only predetermining a

course of action but also the mental searching for future problems that might appear. A modern business operates in a constantly changing environment; the modern manager must continually anticipate changes that may require him to discard old ways and adopt new ones. Thus, planning—both long- and short-range—is probably the most important managerial task in initiating a new firm and/or directing the present and future growth of an existing firm. While planning covers a wide range of activities, it boils down to deciding what will be done in one's business, by whom, and at what time. In brief, the entrepreneur tries to make a good decision that will result in the correct action at the right time.

Steps in Planning

Basically, all effective planning involves the following format:

1. *Establish objectives.* The first step is to clearly indicate (preferably by writing it down) what is to be accomplished and where the primary emphasis is to be placed.
2. *Formulate basic assumptions or premises.* Major assumptions should focus on:
   a. *Noncontrollable conditions.* Circumstances the firm cannot control, such as business cycles, competitive price levels, and population growth.
   b. *Semicontrollable conditions.* Those events the firm cannot control but can influence to some degree, such as the firm's share of the market, the company's price policy, and employee productivity and turnover.
   c. *Controllable conditions.* Policy matters that management can decide largely for itself, such as whether to expand into new markets, selection of a new site for the firm's location, and major remodeling of the business. Because the future is so complex, and the entrepreneur's time so limited, premises must, as a practical matter, be limited to those *most likely* to influence the operation of an objective. Otherwise, the planner risks wasting his time developing an infinite list of premises.
3. *Search for alternative courses of action.* Seldom is there an objective for which several alternatives do not exist. Frequently, after careful thought, an alternative that is not obvious proves to be the best.
4. *Evaluate alternative courses of action.* List pros and cons of each alternative and evaluate them by weighing the factors against objectives and premises. For example, one alternative may be more profitable but too risky; another may be less risky but incompatible with one of the firm's major goals. Some alternatives may require additional information before you can

evaluate them. In some cases you may have to hire an outside consultant to provide the facts.
5. Put the plan into action. Although the entrepreneur takes a reasonable time to consider the issues, he must be a man of action. He cannot postpone taking action merely because uncertainties and unknowns exist. In addition, subordinate plans must be formulated in order to carry out the major overall plan. If the situation allows it, it is wise to arrive at both a primary and an alternate decision to be used if something changes the primary plan.

It is important to recognize that the actual sequence of steps in planning may deviate from this model. For example, the entrepreneur may find an initial objective to be unrealistic or too low and may have to change it after examining various alternatives. The exact sequence to be followed and the depth of analysis employed will depend on the nature of the problem, long-range goals, and the amount of help available to the businessman.

Time Period

Any consideration of planning raises the question of how long a period of time one should plan. Or, in other words, when does short-range planning become long-range planning, and vice versa? For example, should one's long-range planning encompass 2, 5, or 7 years? The answer varies according to industry and firm, and any time classification of plans is necessarily arbitrary. At the same time, there must be some rationale for selecting a time range for planning. As a general rule, since planning is costly and time-consuming, a potential entrepreneur should not plan for a longer period than is economically justifiable.

Some management authorities suggest that the correct planning period should be based on the "commitment principle":

> What the commitment principle implies is that long-range planning is not really planning for future decisions, but rather planning the future impact of today's decision. In

other words, a decision is a commitment, normally of funds, direction of action, or reputation. And decisions lie at the core of planning. While studies and analyses precede decisions, any type of plan implies that some decision has been made. Under these circumstances, then, the astute manager will recognize the validity of gearing all planning into present decisions.[1]

---

[1] Harold Koontz and Cyril O'Donnell, *Principles of Management*, 4th ed. (New York: McGraw-Hill, 1968), p. 101.

Thus, one should carefully consider the long-range results of current decisions. This criterion suggests that the logical time period for a plan, and the forecasting required for it, should realistically allow enough time to accomplish the desired action. To arbitrarily jump into a 4- or 5-year plan without preliminary thought and analysis will surely result in a superficial plan. Long-range plans should also be revised annually to take into account objectives or forecasts that have changed since the last revision.

Objectives

Most successful small businessmen determine their business objectives, purposes, or targets at least in a general way before they start out. However, all too frequently these objectives are merely vague ideas in the mind of the founder, such as "to increase profits," or "to reduce costs." Seldom are objectives set forth explicitly so that the other owners, managers, or employees can share in the understanding and realization of them.

Large firms have many pressures to formalize their objectives. Typically, the large firm will spend considerable research time and money to prepare its objectives and to get them down in writing. These statements then become the starting point for policy formulation, company planning, and the development of operating procedures designed to build profits. The small firm may not feel this pressure, especially during its formative stage; nevertheless, the need is there. Formulating company objectives and writing them down need not be a costly or tedious task, but it does require careful thought about where the business is going and how it can get there.

Evidence suggests that the hardest task is getting started on formulating one's objectives. To overcome this barrier the small businessman might ask himself a series of basic questions: Why did I decide to go into business? Which of my goals can be achieved through this business? What is my place in the industry? How can I carve out a better competitive niche? What share of the market do I want? Next month? Next year? Do I have any plans for new product development or acquisition? What are my specific goals for profit improvement? Peter Drucker has suggested eight areas in which company objectives have to be set: "market standing; innovation; productivity; physical and financial resources; profitability; manager performance and development; worker performance and attitude; and public responsibility."[2] Of course, some of these areas are more important to the small firm than others, and many objectives in different areas will overlap. For example, worker performance has a direct bearing on productivity, and both of these affect profitability. Thus,

---

[2] Peter F. Drucker, *The Practice of Management* (New York: Harper and Brothers, 1954), p. 63.

since most firms have multiple goals, each goal must be established in view of the others. It would be inconsistent, for example, to establish an objective of increasing the share of the market that might negatively affect profits. Similarly, while objectives should be optimistic and cause the entrepreneur and his employees to "reach," they should also be realistic and reasonably attainable.

Policies

Once the objectives of the business are set down, policies for the achievement of these objectives must be established. Policies are guides for making decisions. The objectives state the broad goals; the policies provide the guidelines for achieving these goals. Since policies establish the ground rules for meeting objectives, it is important that the policies be related to the objectives. If the entrepreneur changes his objectives, he must be sure to review his policies as well.

For example, if a retailer decides to sell high-quality, fashionable men's apparel, then a decision to sell suits with a $75 price tag would probably be inconsistent with the objective. In this case it would be necessary to review pricing policies in light of the "high-quality, fashionable" objective.

Frequently, an entrepreneur will remark, "We don't have any policies. Our decisions have to be made quickly—we don't have time to look up policies." This is faulty reasoning, for policies in fact enable the businessman to make a prompt decision whenever a problem arises. The manager or employee simply applies the general guideline of the policy to each new situation and does not have to reformulate an analysis each time a problem comes up. Therefore, a clearly stated policy also encourages the delegation of decision making. For example, a credit policy might require employees to obtain approval for credit sales exceeding $200. This means that employees will have to check with management on large sales, but at the same time it clearly permits employees to make their own decisions in sales under $200 without having to worry if they have the authority to do so.

Policies, then, not only save time but also guide other members of the firm so that they do not require detailed supervision by the manager. In addition, policies provide consistency of action, which is desirable for good employee and customer relations.

The astute manager should consider the following policy guidelines:

1. Policies should reflect objectives and be understood by all members of the firm.
2. Policies should be consistent and placed in writing.
3. Policies should be stated in definite but broad terms so as to encourage employees to accept responsibility for their own decisions.

4. Policies should be relatively stable but subject to periodic review by management.

Once the basic objectives have been set forth and the policies established, planning for the operation of the business can begin.

Long-Range Planning

A successful entrepreneur must be able to forecast to some degree the technological, economic, and social changes that will affect his business and be prepared to use available resources to attain his goals under changing conditions. Most everyone can recall instances of businesses that have failed to recognize and respond to change: once-prosperous business sections of the city now run-down, closed, and customers shopping elsewhere; small plants losing out to firms using automated equipment; neighborhood grocery stores giving way to the supermarket; motels bypassed by superhighways, and so on.

Unfortunately, some people respond to such examples with "There are certain things you simply can't do much about." On the contrary, there is much that the entrepreneur *can* do something about. He can expect change, plan for it, and turn it into a positive advantage through long-range planning.

Such planning recognizes that as incomes increase, populations grow, and people move, products and production methods must be modified, locations shifted, and operations directed toward profitability. Long-range planning, therefore, means that the entrepreneur must concern himself with trends in income levels, industry developments, market size, product or service usage, merchandising and/or manufacturing methods, and business location. He must forecast whether he will have an adequate volume of sales to justify the high initial cost of a new product or service. He must make sure that he will have a reliable future source of parts or raw materials and that he will have alternative courses of action should he lose a major customer due to changes in needs, traffic, or competition.

Short-Range Planning

Short-range planning covers a more immediate time period of 3 to 6 months, a coming merchandise season, or at most, a year. Although short-term planning deals with the future, it does not involve a total restructuring or redirection of the firm. For example, if an entrepreneur is in the retail business and must order his merchandise a year ahead of the time he expects to sell it, his planning period should be at least a year. If he sells merchandise requiring only a few months' commitment, then his planning period might be 6 months or less.

Short-term planning is very important to the day-to-day operations of the firm because it allows the manager to solve specific problems and make decisions that cannot be anticipated in long-run planning. As short-run plans develop, the vague, unrefined areas of the long-run plan begin to take shape. Obviously then, part of effective goal setting is to establish short-range plans that contribute to and fit in with long-range plans.

Two of the most widely used short-term plans are budgets and production schedules, both of which will be dealt with in some depth in later chapters. We shall also see that short-term plans are the first step in establishing controls to insure that long-terms goals are accomplished.

Planning and Objectives

A discussion of planning and objectives frequently leaves the uninitiated somewhat bewildered. At times it appears that objectives are the result of planning; at other times, it appears that the objectives are the goals toward which the planning is directed. Many people are left wondering which comes first, plans or objectives? In fact, there is a close interdependence between plans and objectives. Objectives result from and at the same time are essential for proper planning. In one instance, the entrepreneur will set objectives through planning. At other times, he will plan in order to determine how to achieve his objective.

To illustrate this interdependence, consider the case of a small retailer who has a goal of expanding operations to include a suburban branch within the next 5 years. His long-range planning will attempt to forecast important changes in local population shifts, spending habits, purchasing power, competitive trends, government constraints, and financial requirements. Obtaining projections on these factors may lead him to consider other alternatives, such as modernizing his current store or even closing up the current store and moving to a new location. If so, one of these alternatives now becomes a new objective to plan for. On the other hand, if the future looks favorable for a branch store in 5 years, he will need to plan in order to meet this commitment. Specifically, the retailer may need to change the breadth and depth of lines of merchandise and drop others, initiate a manpower training program for the new store, start a promotion campaign, and update customer services.

The following is a brief description of an actual comprehensive planning program for a firm with about 100 employees and less than $2,000,000 annual sales. The plan was prepared by the company president and his four department heads.[3]

---

[3] © 1967 by The Regents of the University of California. Reprinted from George A. Steiner, "Approaches to Long-Range Planning for Small Business," *California Management Review* X, No. 1, 12–15, by permission of the Regents and the author.

**Corporate Long-Range Plan
for Magnetic Design, Inc.**

I. *Corporate Purposes:* the fundamental purposes of MDI. Two basic purposes are given, which is about standard. The four modifiers, however, are a little unusual.
   A. Two prime objectives of MDI are:
      1. To improve earnings through productive effort primarily applied (but not limited) to the manufacture of magnetic devices and power supply equipment.
      2. To conduct the business in a manner that is constructive, honorable, and mutually profitable for stockholders, employees, customers, suppliers, and the general community.
   B. These objectives are amplified further:
      1. To earn a reasonable return on investment with due regard to the interests of customers, employees, vendors.
      2. To expand sales while increasing profits.
      3. To support the military effort of the United States by producing top quality products.
      4. To grow at a steady rate.
   C. Departmental purposes: Administration, marketing, production and engineering, and finance. It is a little unusual for departmental purposes to be specified at this point in a plan; they are usually blended into specific goals set for their operations. Following are the objectives of the production and engineering department:
      1. Manufacture and design quality products with cost and delivery schedules which will be attractive to prospective customers.
      2. Stay alert to developments that promise new and improved company products.

II. *Basic Corporate Five- and Ten-Year Sales and Profit Objectives:*
   A. The five-year annual sales and profit objectives are:

	Sales	Pretax Profits	Pretax (%) Profit	Federal Tax	Posttax (%) Profit
First year					
Second year					
Third year			(Specified in dollars and percentages.)		
Fourth year					
Fifth year					

   B. The ten-year sales and profit objectives are: After taxes, sales will be $5,000,000 and earnings will be $750,000.

III. *Basic Premises:* forecasts of future markets, technology, competition, and evaluations of internal strengths and weaknesses. A framework of premises, with illustrations from the MDI plan, follows:

Setting Goals

A. External projections and forecasts:
    1. Survey of general business conditions, including Gross National Product forecast.
    2. Survey of the market for company products, based upon general economic conditions for industrial products and estimates of government spending for company products.
    3. Forecast of company sales based on the above two forecasts. (MDI made forecasts for each of the next five years. Since the company is in the Midwest, government spending for its products in the Midwest was estimated. Included were the Department of Defense, the National Aeronautics and Space Administration, and the Federal Aviation Agency.)
B. Competition: Because competition is keen for most companies, objective estimates of its strength are important. After looking at what its major competition was likely to do, the firm looked at itself.
    1. Several advantages have placed MDI several years in advance of competition in the magnetic devices equipment field. These are cryogenic magnets for commercial applications and high reliability power supplies for long-endurance military application.
    2. However, in order to realize fully the growth commensurate with the above advantages, several weaknesses must be overcome by developing an ability to construct crystals as well as developing more sophisticated test procedures:
C. Internal examination of the past and projections: Analyses of various parts of the enterprise, e.g.,
    1. Product line analysis:
        a. Product(s) performance (i.e., sales volume, profit margin, etc.).
        b. Customer class served.
        c. Comparison with major competitors' product(s).
        d. Comparison with substitutes and complementary performance.
        e. Possibilities for product improvement.
        f. Suggestions with regard to new products.
    2. Market analysis:
        a. Important factors in projected sales changes: product success; marketing organization; advertising; and competitive pressures.
        b. New markets to be penetrated (i.e., geographical areas and customer classes).
    3. Financial analysis:
        a. Profit position.
        b. Working capital.
        c. Cash position.
        d. Impact of financial policy on market price per share.
        e. Prospects for future financing.
    4. Production analysis:
        a. Plant and equipment (maintenance and depreciation).
        b. Productive capacity and productivity.
        c. Percent of capacity utilized.

    d. Suggestions for: productivity improvements; cost reduction; utilizing excess capacity; and planning expansion.
  5. Technical analysis:
    a. Research and development performance.
    b. Suggestions for improving research and development effectiveness.
  6. Employees:
    a. Employment and future needs.
    b. Technical manpower deficiencies.
    c. Appraisal of employee attitudes.
  7. Facilities:
    a. Evaluation of current facilities to meet new business.
    b. Machine replacement policy and needs.

IV. *Basic Objectives, Policies, and Strategies:* This covers every important area of the business, but most companies concentrate on A through F of the following:
  A. Profits.
  B. Sales.
  C. Finance.
  D. Marketing.
  E. Capital additions.
  F. Production.
  G. Research.
  H. Engineering.
  I. Personnel.
  J. Acquisitions.
  K. Organization.
  L. Long-range planning.

This list can be expanded. As noted elsewhere, the more concrete the specification here can be, the easier it usually is to implement the plans. It is especially important for a small businessman to know precisely what he is seeking and the method to be employed to get there. For example, MDI marketing objectives were set forth as follows:

1. Increase sales of magnetic devices 100 percent in the next five years. Increase sales of power supply equipment 200 percent during the next five years.
2. Increase the total volume of industrial sales from today's 25 percent to 50 percent of total sales at the end of five years.
3. Penetrate the western market to the point where the company will control 10 percent of it at the end of five years.
4. Enter the foreign market within five years by a licensing agreement, a joint venture, or manufacturing facility.

For each of these objectives, the company prepared a detailed series of strategies ranging from a strategy to "sell custom designs directly to prime contractors in geographic regions where their main plants are located" to details such as special services to selected specified customers, training programs for employees, and top management meetings with customers.

Further strategies which might be included in this section of the plan, with special regard to marketing, are organization, use of dealers, possibility of distributing products manufactured by others, salesmen's compensation plans, and pricing policy.

Drawing a proper line of demarcation between the strategic plans and the detailed operational plans is difficult. Ideally, the two blend together in a continuous line. This was the case with MDI, where those making the strategic plan also were the ones to implement it.

V. *Detailed Medium-Range Plans:* more detailed plans growing out of the above. For MDI these plans were developed for each of the succeeding five years:
   A. *Pro forma* balance sheet, yearly.
   B. Income statement, yearly.
   C. Capital expenditure schedule, yearly.
   D. Unit production schedule for major products, yearly.
   E. Employment schedule, yearly.
   F. Detailed schedule to acquire within three years a company with design capability in solid state magnetic devices.

VI. *One-Year Plans:* the next year's budgets. The first year's budgets for items A through N were, in the aggregate, the same for the first year of the five-year plan, but broken into quarterly time periods. In addition, MDI had other budgets, principally purchasing schedules for major components and raw materials and typical detailed administrative budgets covering such things as travel and telephone.

Some Final Comments on Establishing Goals

A small business operates in a dynamic, ever-changing world. Consequently, goals formulated several months ago may be in need of revision to accommodate changing conditions. For example, a consumer-durables manufacturer had the goal of making his company an industry leader. To do it, he needed to achieve a certain share of the market within a designated time period. Unfortunately, during periodic review it became clear that the company was not capturing the additional share of market on which sales goals were based. Although the quality product was priced competitively and marketed aggressively, the product was styled *above* mass tastes.

Fortunately, the owner–manager realized that he had failed to adequately research his consumers' tastes. Reviewing goals showed him the need for replanning. His new plans included a market study, and the results of the research showed that buyers were looking for something quite different from his product.[4]

Similarly, there is a basic need to study the "big picture" when formulating goals. For example, consider the following case of a small plant manager:

---

[4] Example from T. Stanley Gallagher, "Sound Objectives Help Build Profits," *Management Aids Annual No. 11* (Washington, D. C.: Small Business Administration, 1965), pp. 1–7. Reprinted in Lawrence A. Klatt, ed., *Managing the Dynamic Small Firm: Readings* (Belmont, Calif.: Wadsworth, 1971), pp. 52–58.

Andy Goforth (name disguised) decided that in a climate of strong competition and tightening profits his best chance was in a continuing expansion of sales. His confidence in this approach was inspired by his selling background. He had been an expert salesman before going into business for himself.

Then, too, in the short time he had been an owner–manager, he had seen other small firms failing because of declining sales. So he set his goal for increased sales. By working hard, he began achieving it.

However, as sales expanded his need for money increased. Soon he did not have enough working capital to carry the increased inventories and the accounts receivable which came from his increased sales. When he needed money in a hurry and tried to borrow, he found that he had to pay a high rate of interest. His young company had not had time to build a performance record which would qualify it for a less costly loan.

The high interest practically wiped out his net profit on the increased sales. And several times before he worked out of this dilemma, he thought he might go broke even though his plant was filled with orders.

What did Mr. Goforth learn from this experience? He learned three things:
1. He had hurt his firm by working without proper planning.
2. His improper planning was the result of his one-sided view—his failure to see all aspects of his business.
3. His attempted growth was not sound because it was one-sided.

He decided that, if he had studied the possible effects increased sales might have on his total operation, he could have planned for a somewhat slower expansion in sales. He told himself he could then have planned to get the necessary working capital over a longer period of time allowing for more negotiation to keep his interest rate down.

He decided to study the big picture when he was planning. He jotted down three vital questions to ask himself:
1. What is my business goal?
2. Can I do what I am trying to do, and, if so, how?
3. What is the future of my business?[5]

Incident 3: The Plan Emerges

Pete Smith has been working at his plan of action for his new body and fender shop. During his planning, he went to an antique car show near his city. The show opened up a whole new set of business possibilities to him.

Pete found that thousands of collectors of antique cars lovingly restore these vehicles to "like-new" condition. They might find a 1929 Ford Model A in a barn in disreputable condition and then completely take it apart and rebuild it. They would then repaint the vehicle to match the new (or better) condition of the original car.

---

[5] Adapted from Bruce E. De Spelder, "Management Planning for Sound Growth," *Management Aids Annual No. 9* (Washington, D. C.: Small Business Administration, 1963), pp. 8–15.

As a good body and fender repairman, Pete noted that much of the work on the antique cars was not very well done. Pretty good cars looked great sitting alone, but when lined up with beautifully painted and restored machines, they looked rather amateurish.

In talking to owners, Pete found out that many did their own work, which in part accounted for the ripples and waves and blotched paint on otherwise good-looking old cars. But he also found out that there was a shortage of good professional restorers. A good shop had a backlog of perhaps 2 to 3 years work, and since most of the work had to be done by hand, it was difficult to expand output. Moreover, few body and paint men were skilled enough to do a first-class job on an older car—the craftsman had to have special knowledge, such as the composition of older steels, how to weld in new metal on rusty surfaces, and how to smooth out the most complicated curved surfaces.

Pete knew he was good, and close inspection of some of the vehicles convinced him that he could do better. He also knew that Sam Brown was a better painter than most and that he could do a better job than most paint jobs he saw at the show.

Indeed, Pete got himself a job at the show. In chatting with one owner, Pete found himself working on a 1927 Essex, which had extensive front-end damage. The owner had been looking for someone to do the job, and when he saw that Pete knew what he was talking about, the owner offered him $150 to fix up the car.

A few days later, Sam wandered by while Pete was working on the Essex. He watched Pete carefully heating and working the left front fender.

"Hey, Pete, are you already in business?"

"Sort of, Sam. Nice car, isn't it?"

"Right now it looks like a pile of junk. What kind of nut was willing to pay you to fix it?"

"He's no nut, and the car is worth maybe two thousand—or it will be when it's finished," Pete said.

Sam wandered around it, looking at the gutted interior, the rusty body, and the grease-soaked engine. "Boy, I never would have believed it, although I've heard that these old cars can be worth up to thirty-five thousand or more. How did you get the job?"

Pete explained what had happened.

Sam began to get excited. "You mean that there are guys out there who are willing to pay big money to get junkers like this all fixed up?"

"Sure. And this fellow will need a really good paint job. I gave him your phone number—he may be in touch."

Sam sat on the running board. "You know, Pete, I'd like to work on this sort of thing. I bet the guy would pay to have a top-notch job done. I hate to work on those quicky jobs, where you slop paint on and to hell with it. This thing could be a real challenge."

Pete carefully finished off the fender, turned off his torch, and nodded. "Me too. You can't do this kind of car the easy way. Here I have a chance to do some really good work. I don't think any junkyard these days has a front end for a '26 Essex, so I have to work the old metal back into shape." He patted the fender. "When it's done, it will be just like new. Fifty hours of work, but it's worth it."

"Is there enough work in this stuff to pay, Pete?"

"This fellow said that there were over two hundred thousand Model A Fords from nineteen twenty-eight through thirty-one around alone. And there are thousands of others."

"I bet that a guy who owns a thing like this doesn't mind paying."

Pete wiped his hands. "Most of the guys I talked to seemed pretty well off—and boy, did they love their cars. No, Sam, I think that this sort of work just might pay off."

"Where does a fellow get this work done around here?"

"The nearest specialist is a hundred forty miles from here, in Central City. No one does it here."

"Pete, why don't you make your business this sort of specialty? There are dozens of body and fender shops around, and most of them are probably going broke. Here you could be a specialist and get high prices."

"That's what I'm thinking, Sam. Are you interested in joining me?"

Sam wandered around the Essex, eyeing it professionally. "I make five dollars an hour, Pete—what do you make, four bucks?"

"Four twenty-one."

"Do you think that we could set up a shop and make more money than that? If we could, I just might want to go in with you."

"I think so, Sam. Boy, I hope so, because this kind of work is great."

1. Pete and Sam are now starting to plan this new venture in some detail. Help them out by sketching a plan for them that will work. Include in your plan all the necessary marketing, finance, production, and other information they will need to have before they get started.
2. How could Pete and Sam find out about possible market demand? What sources of information would you suggest?
3. Is there a good way here for Pete and Sam to test their idea without committing all their time and resources to this project?
4. What appear to be Pete's objectives in this venture? Why?
5. What basic policies might emerge here for this venture? Why?
6. What is missing in the basic plan so far, as suggested by this incident?

Discussion Questions

1. Comment on the following quote: "This country was built by hard-driving men of action who had no time for planning. The entrepreneur today ought to imitate these men of action and avoid wasting his time planning while the world passes him by."
2. Explain the concept of planning.
3. Identify and explain the major steps in planning.
4. What is the value of identifying and categorizing your basic assumptions or premises when planning?
5. What is the correct time period for a plan?
6. Differentiate between objectives and policies.

7. Do policies hasten or slow down the decision-making process? Explain.
8. What is the difference between long-range and short-range planning?
9. Which come first, plans or objectives? Explain.
10. Why is "goal setting" not a one-time affair?
11. Develop a list of planning problems unique to small businesses.

Suggested Readings

Drucker, Peter, *The Practice of Management.* New York: Harper and Brothers, 1954.

Gallagher, T. Stanley, "Sound Objectives Help Build Profits," *Management Aids Annual No. 11.* Washington, D. C.: Small Business Administration, 1965.

Golde, Roger A., "Practical Planning for Small Business," *Harvard Business Review* XLII (September–October 1964), 145–55, 158, 161.

Klatt, Lawrence A., ed., *Managing the Dynamic Small Firm: Readings.* Belmont, Calif.: Wadsworth, 1971. See "Setting Goals," pp. 51–89.

Kootz, Harold, and O'Donnell, Cyril, *Principles of Management,* 4th ed. New York: McGraw-Hill, 1968.

Levinson, Robert E., "Checking Your Management Methods," *Management Aids Annual No. 11.* Washington, D. C.: Small Business Administration, 1965. Pp. 8–14.

McConkey, Dale, *How to Manage by Results.* New York: American Management Association, 1965.

Newman, William H., Summer, Charles E., and Warren, E. Kirby, *The Process of Management.* Englewood Cliffs, N. J.: Prentice-Hall, 1967.

Reilley, Erving W., "Planning the Strategy of the Business," *Advanced Management,* December 1965, pp. 8–12.

Steinmetz, Lawrence L., Kline, John B., and Stegall, Donald I., *Managing the Small Business.* Homewood, Ill.: Richard D. Irwin, 1968. Ch. 9.

Thompson, Stewart, *How Companies Plan.* New York: American Management Association, 1962.

Wingate, John W., and Helfant, Seymour, *Small Store Planning for Growth.* Washington, D. C.: Small Business Administration, 1966.

Chapter 4

Implementing Goals

While setting objectives and goals is not an easy task for the average small businessman, detailing plans to accomplish an objective is surely a more difficult task. It is only difficult, however, because many of us have not practiced sitting down and thinking analytically about *how* to accomplish a given thing or goal. A plan or action program is simply a step-by-step explanation or description of what must be done in order for a goal to become an accomplished fact. A description of "what must be done" should be associated with time intervals, and priorities should be set for each step along the way. Most action steps are sequential; some steps must be accomplished before others can be considered. For example, in building a structure, the concrete must be poured before the walls can be placed into position. However, you cannot wait until the foundation is completed before ordering the materials for construction of the walls, or if the walls are to be prefabricated, before starting construction of the walls themselves.

Thus, when an objective is formalized in writing,[1] the next logical phase of planning should take place—that is, to formalize in writing the step-by-step procedure for achieving the desired

---

Note: This chapter was written in collaboration with M. Godfrey Parsons, senior partner, Organization Program Dynamics, Inc., Ypsilanti, Michigan.

[1] There are certain advantages to formalizing objectives and plans by putting them in writing: (1) it lends authority to the objective or plan; (2) there is no need to rely on memory; (3) written work can be reviewed by the entrepreneur and read by others; (4) it can encourage the use of the "system" concept in other areas of the business. For example, in the areas of personnel hiring and evaluation—two often neglected areas in the average small business—a formal system can be of great value both in dollar savings and in sustaining long-run relationships with employees.

objective. Although this advice is easy to give, the actual task of thinking through the procedure takes time and effort. Furthermore, as was the case with stating objectives, the businessman all too frequently conceives programs (plans) to carry out his objectives in some orderly fashion, but he fails to record them or at least to get them down in some sequential manner. Of course, if the objective and the program to achieve it are basically simple (easy to achieve with few alternative courses of action to consider), then mental recording may be suitable. For example:

Objective: To create a memorable evening for a girl friend, mistress, or wife.

Action Program	Time of Completion
1. Contact girl and extend invitation.	Now
2. Phone for reservation at Candlelight Restaurant.	Just after "now"
3. Purchase orchestra seats for best-reviewed play.	Not much later
4. Take clothes to cleaners.	7:30 A.M.
5. Order flowers from florist.	9:00 A.M.
6. Wash car and fill with gas.	12:00 noon
7. Have liquor brought to apartment.	1:00 P.M.
8. Shave, shower, and dress.	6:00 P.M.
9. Pick up girl.	6:30 P.M.

(This program progresses to 29 steps and can be completed as desired.)

The men among us have planned this action program enough times in the past that we do not need to commit it to paper. However, some people find that a written note to augment their memory is a must, even if the action program is no more complicated than the "memorable evening" objective. Therefore, we ought to be easily convinced that as the objective, and thus the action program also, become more complicated, we must use more sophisticated means to insure that the job will be done. Because the author is devoted to an applied and practical philosophy, he encourages every businessman (experienced and prospective) to use the easiest method to achieve results. If the potential entrepreneur can mentally retain the array of "steps" to be accomplished in an action program, then by all means he should consider no other method. However, in achieving most business objectives, a system can assist a person's mental capacity to recall. In the following section, several methods of "formalizing" the planning process will be considered.

File-Folder Method

The easiest way to systematize the planning process is to use simple manilla or hanging file folders. As you agree on or "firm up" each business objective, write it down at the top of a plain sheet of paper and file it in a folder labeled *Objectives and Plans*. At any time you have thoughts about your business objectives and how you will implement them, take out your folder and jot down your planning ideas on the appropriate "objective sheet." When you realize you must act on all or one particular goal or objective, then take a look at your planning ideas. You can then detail the step-by-step procedure and arrange the steps in order of priority for accomplishing each specific goal. When you use the file-folder approach, do not concern yourself at the beginning with ordering or judging the importance or level of your objectives. As you use this method, it will eventually become quite apparent that certain objectives are critical in terms of time while others are critical in terms of importance. For example, you might have the following objectives in your folder:

a. Make 20 percent return on my investment next year.
b. Enlarge the selling space of my store by 5,000 square feet.
c. Build the managerial level of my staff by employing a qualified industrial accountant.
d. Modernize the employee rest room and lunch area.
e. Develop an advertising theme to be used for the next 3 to 5 years.

It is obvious that objective *a* takes precedence over the others, because it is of the highest level—that is, the completion or achievement of all the other objectives will contribute to the accomplishment of the prime or *a* objective: Make 20 percent return on my investment next year. In other words, selling space, managerial level personnel, employee comfort, and advertising theme are objectives that, when accomplished, will greatly contribute to the accomplishment of your objective of making 20 percent return on investment. "Return on investment" is usually considered a 1-year, or annual, goal. In other instances, your prime objective may encompass a longer period, meaning that your objectives, and therefore your written plans, will take on a hierarchical arrangement. Your plans will fall into at least three levels—less than a year, 1 year, and over 1 year. At this point, all your plans must be coordinated. This task will not be difficult if you have written plans, because priorities can be set within and between plans when they can be visualized all together.

Planning-Forms Method

Planning forms range widely in size and complexity. A planning form should have the following characteristics:

a. Space for statement of objective, planning details, time intervals, person responsible, and cross-referencing codes to other objectives and files.
b. Sufficient size to accommodate the written statements of objectives and plans in an orderly layout pattern (from several square feet to the major portion of an office wall).
c. Areas for which planning is imperative, such as the often-used standard list of management areas:

>Financial
>Sales
>Building and Equipment
>Personnel
>Purchasing
>Production
>Administration and Office

or the list of planning areas suggested by Drucker and mentioned in Chapter 3:

>Marketing Standing
>Innovation
>Productivity
>Physical Resources
>Financial Resources
>Profitability
>Manager Performance
>Manager Development
>Worker Performance
>Worker Attitude
>Social Responsibility[2]

Some planning-form frames are constructed so that small magnets can be used to hold the typed planning forms. These frames allow easy removal or changing of individual plans. Some forms are placed behind a sheet of glass so that a grease pencil or other marking instrument can be used to indicate changes, progress, and so on. The use of the planning-forms concept gently forces the entrepreneur to consider the full array of business areas for which objectives and plans should be developed. It also provides an organized and visual planning method. One small businessman explained that the formal planning process meant very little to him until he saw the planning forms used by a business acquaintance.

---

[2] Drucker's list covers all the areas, except "Administration and Office," in the standard list but he adds two areas—"Innovation" and "Social Responsibility." However, the specific and clear-cut way in which he has delineated them makes his list preferable in the thinking of many businessmen.

Implementing Goals

```
                        PLANNING FORM

    BUSINESS AREA
                                        Completion Date

    Objective:                          _____

    Plan (How to Achieve Objective):

        1.                              _____
        2.                              _____
        3.                              _____
        4.                              _____
        5.                              _____
        6.                              _____
        7.                              _____
        8.                              _____
        9.                              _____
       10.                              _____
       11.                              _____


    Person Responsible: _____
    Cross-Reference Code: _____
```

Figure 4–1. Example of a Planning Form (From Daily, James M., and Parsons, M. Godfrey, *A Guide for Developing Business Objectives and Operating Goals*, Columbia, Mo.: C & M Publishing, 1966, p. 3).

PERT Method

While the PERT method (Program Evaluation and Review Technique) is more commonly known and used as a technique for control, it is basically a method of planning for the accomplishment of nonrepetitive objectives. It has contributed to the planning of projects as vast as the Apollo mission to the moon and for goals as small and simple as cocktail parties. PERT gives the small businessman a planning device that enables him to think through a plan in great detail. It points up trouble spots, time delays, and helps resolve these difficulties. PERT, which was developed approximately 12 years ago for use in defense projects, had its origins in network theory that had been used for many decades by production managers. PERT is simply a planning map—the step-by-step procedure shown over time.

There are *two* vital definitions to be understood in PERTing.

Event: A specific accomplishment that will occur at a specific time; represented in a PERT network as a circle or square with an appropriate number written inside it: ① or ☐.

Activity: The effort or work required to complete an event; represented by a line and arrowhead: ⟶

For example, "start foundation" would be an event, as would "complete foundation," while the actual work of building the foundation would be an activity. Thus, "start foundation" would be Event 1, and "complete foundation" would be Event 2; and the actual work of digging the earth, putting in the forms, leveling the earth, and pouring and finishing the concrete would be the activity and would be represented in PERT terms as:

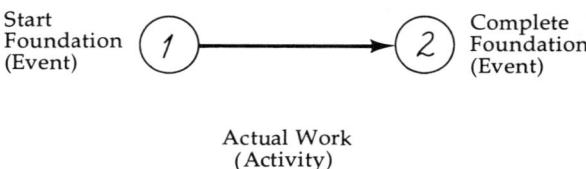

Start Foundation (Event) ① ⟶ ② Complete Foundation (Event)

Actual Work (Activity)

Thus, the start and finish are *events*, and the work required to finish or complete an event is an *activity*.

The first step in PERTing is to list the steps that must be completed to accomplish the desired goal. The next step is to decide which are events and which are activities and to mark them as such. Finally, you must represent each event and activity in a network diagram taking care to put the network together after considering time periods and how events are related to each other. Consider the following example of the PERT method:

Objective: Build addition to store.

Planning Steps

a. Complete building plans.
b. Complete concrete foundations and slab.
c. Complete rough carpentry.
d. Complete electrical work.
e. Complete plumbing.
f. Complete finishing carpentry.
g. Complete furnishing.
h. Complete building addition.

PERT Events and Activities

Event 1: Start building plans.
Activity: Draw up building plans.
Event 2: Complete building plans.
Event 3: Start concrete foundations and slab.
Activity: Dig, build forms, pour and finish concrete.
Event 4: Complete concrete work.
Event 5: Start rough carpentry.
Activity: Frame, stud, rafter, sheath, and roof.
Event 6: Complete rough carpentry.
Event 7: Start electrical work.
Activity: String wire, put in outlets, connect lights.
Event 8: Complete electrical work.
Event 9: Start plumbing.
Activity: Lay pipe, connect sewer, install equipment.
Event 10: Complete plumbing.
Event 11: Start finishing carpentry.
Activity: Plaster, trim doors, windows, and baseboards.
Event 12: Complete finishing carpentry.
Event 13: Start furnishing.
Activity: Install shelving and fixtures.

Event 14: Complete furnishing.
Event 15: Complete addition to store.
(Complete objective.)

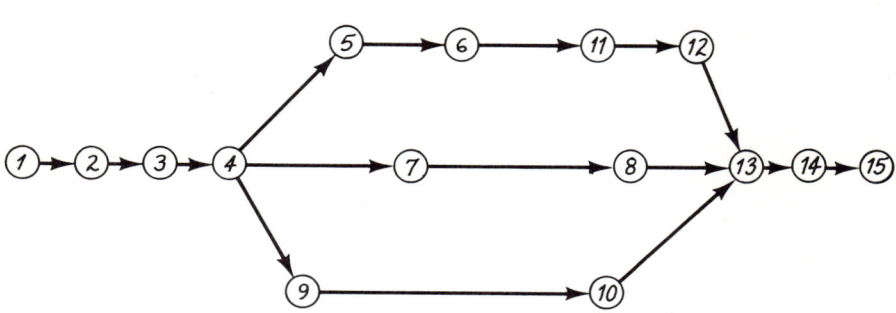

Figure 4–2. The PERT Network.

Explanation   You know that the beginning plumbing work (9) must be started shortly after the rough carpentry work (5) is started, but before its completion—that is, some pipe must be laid before walls are erected. You also know that some electrical work (7) can begin before rough carpentry work is completed (6). It is also true that all finish work must be completed (12) before furnishing begins (13). And, that once furnishing is completed the objective has been met.

This example is oversimplified, but it does point up the procedure for PERTing an objective. As you go more into planning detail, the PERT network becomes more complicated. But the important fact is that this method can give you a more sophisticated way of getting on with the job of planning.

The next step in the PERT planning method is the determination of the critical path based on the time to accomplish each of the activities. The appendix to Chapter 13 contains a more detailed approach to the PERT method. You will also want to examine and read one or several of the references given in the bibliography for a more detailed explanation of the PERT method.

There are many different systematized planning approaches used by individual businessmen, but the three presented here are representative and give you a choice. The benefits to you in choosing one will greatly outweigh the difficulty of starting.

Decision Making and Planning

According to Drucker, "Whatever a manager does he does through making decisions."[3] Indeed, the planning process involves making one decision after the other. A decision is a choice from among a number of alternative courses of action that at the time offer a solution to a problem. A decision "not to decide" or "do nothing" is as much a decision when made consciously as is a choice for a positive alternative.

Man is a decision-making animal, but the businessman *specializes* in decision making. Some years ago a psychologist estimated that each individual makes literally tens of thousands of decisions in the normal course of a day. He included, of course, all the decisions we make in moving our bodies and activating our minds in one way or another. Most decisions of this nature are made with little or no conscious awareness. They are simply responses to stimuli—where the alternatives are few. But the businessman has more varied and complex decisions to make.

It is almost impossible to set forth a step-by-step procedure for making a decision. Even with the most simple problems—for example, what brand of detergent to purchase—we are enabled to decide very quickly because past experience comes in to aid in the decision-making process. How the individual uses past experiences and combines them with current facts and opinions is largely unknown. However, we often find that following some process or sequential procedure can be beneficial. At the least, such an approach can give us a better understanding of how we reach a decision in a particular instance.

Decision-Making Process

1. Define the problem. It is often said that "If you identify the problem you have it half solved." Indeed, until the problem is clearly identified and stated there is little chance for a solution. Frequently a problem is defined in such broad terms as to make it unwieldy. For example, if one states a problem "the firm's net profit is too low," it is too big to handle. But if one asks "what are the determinates of net profit?" it is easier to reduce the problem to manageable proportions. The determinates of net profit are sales and costs. Now the problem becomes "how can we increase sales without an undue increase in costs?" and "how can we lower costs generally?" Each of these problems can be divided further by asking the questions, "what are the determinates of?" until we have

---

[3] Drucker, *The Practice of Management* (New York: Harper and Brothers, 1954), p. 351.

reached the point at which analysis can reveal the real problem. The problem of low net profit may be "excessive personnel costs"; it can now be handled.

2. List alternative solutions. If the problem is properly and clearly delineated, there is a good chance that a number of alternatives will suggest themselves immediately. In lowering personnel costs two solutions are apparent: (a) lower total hours worked by reducing the average hours worked per person, or (b) lay off sufficient people to reduce costs. If, in this instance, these two solutions are the only ones that can be considered, then the implications of each produces a problem—how to implement either decision with a minimum impact on others, in this case, hard feelings among employees and the public. This problem should generate a large number of alternative solutions. It is then necessary to practice creative thinking in order to develop a large list of possible solutions, hopefully some that have not been considered before. Some techniques of creative thought will be discussed in the next section.

3. Choose the best alternative. This step must be the most difficult in the decision-making process for most people. When an array of possible decisions lies in front of some people, their immediate desire is to flee from the area. Yet a distinguishing aspect of management talent is the ability to decide with a high degree of confidence. Alternative solutions must each be considered in the light of such factors as profitability, social responsibility, market position, employee and public relations, costs, and the future. In cases in which only a few alternatives seem possible, the choice may be relatively easy. In other cases, it may be possible to test alternatives and then judge the results, which in turn may suggest alternative solutions that can be "costed up" in dollars and cents. Sometimes the best choice will be that made by several people in your organization and not the decision of the entrepreneur alone. In increasing numbers today, small businessmen are recognizing that it is highly beneficial to morale, and frequently to productivity, to involve their employees in the decision-making process. Participatory management can contribute greatly to developing employees for their assumption of greater responsibility.

Although it seems obvious, the only problem in decision making, and therefore in planning, is that decisions affect only the future, and the future is uncertain. It is not possible to make a decision that affects a previous time. Thus, the alternatives available, or rather those we recognize as possible alternatives, are yet to occur and whether or not they do occur and in which way is a matter of uncertainty. Mathematically all matters of uncertainty can be associated with some probability of occurrence. We always consider the probabilities of alternative courses of action even though we do so intuitively. For example, it is important for an entrepreneur to decide on an inventory system to be installed. He discusses the matter with three salesmen from firms manufacturing different inventory systems. Each system requires a different training period for employees, each system requires a different amount of installation time, and so on. Even though he may not mathematically calculate the probability of the success for each component of each system, he intuitively sums up "subjective" probabilities for each system and makes his decision about which inventory system to invest in.

It is important to understand that each decision has some probability of success, even though it may not be easy to calculate it. Modern decision-making techniques are oriented toward mathematical calculations of success probabilities and then, obviously, to the selection of the decision with the highest probability of success.

Creativity in Planning and Decision Making

We have seen that the processes of planning, problem solving, and decision making are highly interrelated and that they are all important in the solution of problems. Business problems, whether in the context of planning or decision making, ought to be approached in a creative or imaginative way. Even old problems that keep coming back—such as personnel recruiting, training salesmen, or motivating employees—cry out for new solutions. Even a prudent man would be willing to bet that each successful business has a unique or creative feature that is primarily responsible for its success. In some cases, this uniqueness will be location, or advertising theme, message or media used, or store decor, or menu served, or service(s) rendered, or politeness of salespeople, or product feature, and so on. There is always something that separates a successful business from the rest of the pack and secures its success. So it is with all the major decisions that the successful manager makes—he strives to differentiate his decisions, his objectives, and his plans from his competition. In this way he assures himself of some uniqueness in the market for the goods or services he offers. It seems that everyone, no matter what traditional values they hold most closely, appreciates and is intrigued by the new and the innovative. Newness by itself does not guarantee validity or usefulness. But the new idea that is appropriate as a real solution to a problem is applauded, whether by customer or general public.

Creative thought is simply getting new ideas, a definition that does not get us anywhere unless we define what we mean by new idea. A new idea is a combination of *previously* known elements that forms something heretofore *unknown*. For example, the cigarette lighter was a brand new idea in the 1920s that contained the following elements or ideas that had been known for many years: wheel and axle, cotton to hold fuel, flint and steel, lever principle, threaded screw, small portable container, ratchet, metal washer, metal spring, wick, nonrusting metal, shape (snuff box), and flame snuffer (candle snuffer idea). It was the combination of these ideas that created the cigarette lighter. For us, the significance and usefulness of the definition of a new idea lies in the term "combination." Any difference in combination produces another *new* idea. All we need do is change some element or feature of any "old" idea to produce a wholly new one. It is possible, of course, to generate a completely new idea, but in most instances new ideas are taken from old concepts or from old applications outside the business or industry.

How Can We Become More Creative?

Researchers over the past two decades have been unable to find significant relationships between education, sex, intelligence, age, nationality, or race and creative ability. There is no proven direct relationship. Although there are highly creative people among us — businessmen, artists, diplomats, actors — each of us possesses creative ability to some degree or extent. The problem is how to increase the ability we now possess.

Develop the ability to change. We all drift into habit patterns that we repeat time and again with no thought of doing otherwise. Habit is easy, comfortable, and safe; however, it must continually be challenged if we are to strengthen our ability to accept change. Some people have found that doing a new thing every day helps them more readily accept change in other things, whether that new thing is eating rhubarb for breakfast or taking a new route to their place of work. But opening one's mind to accept others' ideas is a step in the right direction of accepting change. Too often an idea of a fellow worker or close associate is given tentative acceptance: "that's a great idea, but . . ." And the "but" statement simply means that the idea will not be used and that changes will not take place. The creative person is flexible and accepts change readily.

Set up the best creative thinking environment. It is often difficult to attack problems creatively in an environment that is not conducive to creative solutions. For most people, constant interruption, noise, or movement of people does not allow them to concentrate as they must. Thus, time and place are important considerations. If an entrepreneur finds the best time of the day and the best place to do his thinking, he will have solved the important aspects of the environment problem. Each person has a best time at which he or she is most creative. For some the early morning hours are best; for others, midday; and for still others, late at night. Similarly, each person has a place in which he is most likely to come up with new ideas. For some the office may be best, while for others a library, conference room, or den may be the place in which he can best concentrate. Sir Conan Doyle, who created the famous character Sherlock

Holmes, generated his most creative insights during concerts performed in the late evening hours.

Practice with problems and solutions. Each of us can involve ourselves more in the creative solution of problems and thereby build our fluency with problems so that solutions can come more easily. In many cases, a problem may not have been on one's mind recently. But if ideas have been written down in the past, even though their future use was unclear at the time, they can be useful at the most unexpected times. A highly organized entrepreneur will set up an idea file for constant reference. Such a file can be organized by classifying ideas as business and personal or by breaking down the business section into sales, personnel, production, planning, and so on.

When facing a problem that demands a creative solution it is always best to set a goal of how many new alternative solutions are to be generated and the time to be spent achieving that goal. In addition, it is always wise to keep separate the tasks of idea generation and idea judging. It is important to first let one's mind range and quest for possible solutions to a problem before allowing any judging to take place. Premature judging seems to destroy creativity to a large degree. Creative thinking requires a free-wheeling, exploratory attitude while judging requires sober reflective thought. This is not to say that one must not judge one's own ideas, but rather that one should employ each thinking process separately so as not to hamper either.

Make a start toward improving your creative ability. As is true in any area of self-improvement, you must make a start to be successful. Personal motivation is the key, and personal motivation is almost always a matter of how much benefit can be derived in either pleasure or profit. The importance and benefits derived from creative thought in decision making, problem solving, and planning should be enough for every small businessman to motivate himself toward improving his creative ability.

Creative Techniques

Brainstorming. In the late 1930s Alex Osborn[4] developed a method designed to help individuals or groups build up a large list of alternative solutions to problems. He called it brainstorming. A brainstorming group should generally not be larger than eight nor smaller than four persons. The group should,

---

[4] Osborn, Alex F., *Applied Imagination* (New York: Charles Scribner's Sons, 1957).

if possible, sit around a table, select a secretary to record the ideas, and select a chairman to keep the ideas flowing. The chairman states the problem and asks that everyone throw out his ideas for solution. The group is required to obey the following brainstorming rules:

1. Throw out as many ideas as you can. Quantity is desired; it is assumed that some quality will be there.
2. Do not put forth negative or judgmental thoughts. Negative comments and judgments, whether good or bad, hinder creativity.
3. Say what you're thinking. If you hold back on an idea, it is difficult if not impossible to create more.

While this technique can help in the generation of a large number of ideas it is not a substitute for the kind of hard-headed thinking required in many cases to refine a decision. However, brainstorming can and should be used as both an exercise in creativity and for developing a large number of ideas when needed. Evaluation of these alternative solutions must be careful, because a negative attitude on the part of the evaluator(s) can result in his discarding truly good ideas.

Some other techniques that can be used to creatively plan and solve problems are discussed below.[5]

Reverse Brainstorming   Sometimes useful prior to a brainstorming session. It consists of being critical instead of suspending judgment. (a) List all the things wrong with the operation, process, system, or product. (b) Systematically take each flaw uncovered and suggest ways of overcoming it.

Check-List Technique   A system of getting idea-clues or "leads" by checking the items on a prepared list against the problem or subject under consideration. The objective is to obtain a number of general ideas for further follow-up and development into specific form.

Free Association   A method of stimulating the imagination to some constructive purpose. (a) Jot down a symbol—word, sketch, number, picture—which is related in some key way to

---

[5] The following is reprinted by permission of the publisher. From M. O. Edwards, "Solving Problems Creatively," *Systems and Procedures Journal* 17, No. 1 (January–February 1966), pp. 16–24.

some important aspect of the problem or subject under consideration. (b) Jot down another symbol suggested by the first one. (c) Continue as in Step 2—AD LIB—until ideas emerge. The objective is to produce intangible ideas, advertising slogans, designs, names, etc.

Forced Relationship A method which has essentially the same basic purpose as free association, but which attempts to force association. (a) Isolate the elements of the problem at hand. (b) Find the relationships between/among these elements. (similarities—differences—analogies—cause and effect) (c) Record the relationship in organized fashion. (d) Analyze the record of relationships to find the patterns (or basic ideas) present. Develop new ideas from these patterns.

Input-Output Technique A method for solving dynamic-system design problems. (a) Investigate direction (input, resources, etc.). (b) Establish measures for testing. (c) Develop methods. (d) Optimize a structure. (e) Accomplish a structure. (f) Convince others of its value. The objective is to produce a number of possible solutions which can then be tested, evaluated, and developed.

Inspired (Big Dream) Approach A "breakthrough" approach which sometimes leads to spectacular advancements. (a) Think the biggest dream possible—about something to benefit mankind. (b) Read, study, and think about every subject connected with your big dream—and do so regularly, persistently, continually. (c) Drop down a dream or so, then engineer your dream into reality. The objective is to make the greatest possible achievement for human benefit.

Edisonian Method An approach consisting principally of performing a virtually endless number of trial-and-error experiments. A "last-ditch" approach, to be resorted to only: (a) When other, more systematic methods have completely failed to produce the desired results and/or (b) When one is knowingly and necessarily delving into the unknown in areas of basic research.

Kepner-Trigoe Method A method particularly calculated to isolating or finding the problem and then deciding what to do about it. A systematic outline is made to describe precisely both the problem and what lies outside the problem but is closely related to it in order to find possible causes of the problem and facilitate decision making.

Value Analysis (or Engineering)	A specialized application of creative problem solving to increase value. It may be defined as an objective, systematic, and formalized method of performing a job to achieve only necessary functions at minimum cost. Six questions are evoked concerning each part: (a) What is it? (b) What must it do? (c) What does it do? (d) What did it cost? (e) What else will do the job? (f) What will that cost?

In summary, the previous chapter has pointed out that setting goals is not easy for the average small businessman. This chapter has pointed out that setting up an action program is even more difficult. Therefore, we have examined three approaches to systematizing an action program. Since each step in carrying out a goal or plan requires a decision, we have examined the decision-making process as well. It was also noted that the entrepreneur, to remain competitive, must approach decision making in a creative way. We have analyzed creativity in some depth and, finally, surveyed several creative techniques. In the following chapter we shall consider the additional management functions performed by the manager in attempting to reach his goals.

Incident 4: Writing It Down

Pete has been thinking pretty deeply about his new business, and now he finally thinks that he has enough money to make the move to independence. His father-in-law is lending him $3,400, and he has saved $2,500. He figures that he will go into the antique auto restoration business. He will start by renting a shop, buying the necessary equipment (mainly hand tools), and doing a bit of advertising. He already has five jobs lined up for complete restoration, so he figures that he will be busy for at least the first 10 weeks. He will average around $3,200 per job, and he will be paying out around $800 per job for parts and materials. The rent for the shop he plans to obtain is $375 per month, and he will pay all his own utility bills and insurance.

1. Help Pete out by writing down an action program for him for the next 6 months. Indicate clearly in your plan just what critical decision points Pete will face as he gets into business.
2. What kinds of written plans do you think Pete should develop and continue to revise as his business works out?
3. What specific marketing plans should Pete be making right now? How could he tell if he were achieving these plans?
4. Pete doesn't know much about legal problems or insurance. What kinds of written plans should he have in these areas?

Discussion Questions

1. What is meant by an action program?
2. What is the primary advantage to using some systematized approach to the planning process?
3. Describe in your own words the PERT method of planning. What are its advantages?
4. Explain the relationship between planning and decision making.
5. Outline and explain the decision-making process.
6. What role does the future play in the decision-making process?
7. What is a "new" idea? How do "old" ideas become "new" ideas?
8. What steps can the entrepreneur take to become more creative in his approach to planning and decision making?
9. How does brainstorming differ from the logical or more traditional approach to problem solving?
10. Is brainstorming a substitute for the "hard-headed" thinking required in many cases to refine a decision? If not, what problems lend themselves to brainstorming?
11. Creativity is an attribute that some people are born with. Therefore, the only way to increase creativity in a firm is to find people who have it. Do you agree?
12. If you were interested in reducing your production costs by 10 percent, how would your approach to generating ideas differ using the reverse-brainstorming technique and the value-analysis technique?

Suggested Readings

Crawford, Robert P., *The Techniques of Creative Thinking*. New York: Hawthorne Books, 1959.

Drucker, P. F., "The Effective Decision," *Harvard Business Review* 45, No. 1 (January–February 1967), 92–98.

Edwards, M. O., "Solving Problems Creatively," *Systems and Procedures Journal* 17, No. 1 (January–February 1966), 16–24.

Goldner, B. B., *The Strategy of Creative Thinking*. Englewood Cliffs, N. J.: Prentice-Hall, 1962.

Kepner, C. H., and Tregoe, B. B., *The Rational Manager*. New York: McGraw-Hill, 1965.

Klatt, Lawrence A., ed., *Managing the Dynamic Small Firm: Readings*. Belmont, Calif.: Wadsworth, 1971. See "Carrying Out Goals," pp. 90–119.

Miles, L. D., *Techniques of Value Analysis and Engineering*. New York: McGraw-Hill, 1961.

Miller, D. W., and Starr, M. K., *Executive Decisions and Operations Research.* Englewood Cliffs, N. J.: Prentice-Hall, 1960.

Newman, W. H., and Summer, C. E., Jr., *The Process of Management.* Englewood Cliffs, N. J.: Prentice-Hall, 1967. Ch. 14–16.

Osborn, Alex F., *Applied Imagination.* New York: Scribner's, 1957.

Stryker, Perrin. "How to Analyze That Problem," *Harvard Business Review* (May–June 1965).

Taylor, Jack, *How to Create Ideas.* Englewood Cliffs, N. J.: Prentice-Hall, 1961.

Williams, Frank E., *Foundations of Creative Problem-Solving.* Ann Arbor, Mich.: Edwards Bros., 1960.

Reaching Goals

Chapter 5

Like his counterpart in a large business, the manager of a small business must perform certain general functions of management to reach his goals: planning, organizing, actuating, and controlling. Chapters 3 and 4 were concerned with the process of planning. This chapter will focus on the concepts of organizing, actuating, and controlling as related to the small businessman's operations. While we will discuss each function separately, keep in mind that all are closely interrelated.

Organizing

Organizing is the management function of allocating tasks and delegating authority in order to accomplish objectives effectively. It is the means by which an entrepreneur makes his plan meaningful to each of his employees. To organize effectively the entrepreneur must:

1. Prepare a list of all activities that must be performed to accomplish the desired plan.
2. Group together related activities, and form them into jobs or positions.
3. Fill those positions with competent individuals.
4. Keep the organizational structure flexible to allow for development of individual employees and activities.

Note: Parts of this chapter are taken from the author's article: "Management Self-Analysis," *Photo Marketing* 46, No. 6 (June 1971), pp. 2–4, 22.

Essentially, then, the entrepreneur must set up a work team that can function efficiently and profitably. One of the best ways for him to appraise his effectiveness in performing this function is to examine his existing organizational structure. The entrepreneur might ask himself such questions as: Am I willing to delegate authority and to build the skills and experience of others? Have I clearly defined department functions and responsibilities? Does every employee know to whom he reports and who reports to him? Is there true communication between employees and supervisors?

Organizational Structure

Of course, there is no form of organization that can be universally used by all types of businesses and in every type of industry. The "proper" organization for reaching a firm's objectives must evolve from the special considerations and problems of the firm, from the personalities and abilities of its management and employees, and from the historical designation of authority and responsibility ("the way we've always done it").

Although there is no uniform way of organizing a business, there are general guidelines and principles that the entrepreneur can apply to his specific situation. For example, a typical introductory management book will devote considerable discussion to the different forms, shapes, and methods of organization. (The reader might want to consult one of the books listed at the end of this chapter.) In practice, however, the entrepreneur starting a new, small business hires men as required by the business. When he reaches a point at which he cannot manage more employees, he groups the workers into one or more sections according to some logical classification (all salesmen, all clerical personnel, and so on) and appoints a supervisor or manager for each group. As the company grows and as additional employees are hired, he will add more sections. When the entrepreneur can no longer manage the growing number of subordinate managers, he will group them into departments and appoint a manager for each department. At this point, three organizational levels exist, and the entrepreneur will be further removed from his nonmanagers.[1]

Peter Drucker has suggested three ways to determine the kind of structure needed for a particular business: activities analysis, decision analysis, and relations analysis. That is, Drucker suggests that a business be examined to determine its actual activities rather than relying on preconceived generalized headings such as "production" or "selling." He stresses that by rigorous activities analysis, management can find out what work has to be performed, what work belongs together, and how each activity should be emphasized in

---

[1] Harold Koontz and Cyril O'Donnell, *Principles of Management*, 4th ed. (New York: McGraw-Hill, 1968), pp. 237–238.

the organizational structure. Accordingly, decision analysis determines what kind of decisions are needed, where in the organization they should be made, and how each manager should be involved in them. Relations analysis involves finding out the contribution each manager must make to programs, with whom he works, and what contribution other managers must make to him.[2]

Organization in Practice: A Case Study[3]

Abe Little, like most small merchants, was a jack-of-all-trades. He did all jobs in the store as the need arose, or he assigned tasks to employees on a random, nonspecialized basis. In a sense, employees were extensions of the owner–manager, and they carried out tasks he lacked the time to attend to himself. Initially, Abe did not set up distinct functions and lines for the flow of authority, nor did he select specialists to handle each function. As the store grew, however, Abe recognized that a new type of organization was necessary.

Abe had read that one can introduce specialization of tasks or specialization of people. Specialization of tasks narrows a person's activities to simple, repetitive routine. Thus, a relatively untrained employee can quickly become proficient at a specialty and turn out more work with fewer mistakes. (However, as we shall see in a later section on motivation, overspecialization negatively affects worker productivity.) Specialization of people involves developing a person to perform a certain job better than someone else can. That is, through training and experience, he improves the quality and quantity of the particular type of work performed.

Abe knew that in small businesses, most specialization is of the second type; but in a larger business there is a growing need for task specialization. Recognizing that his was a small growing store, Abe's first need was to develop people who were specialists in handling a major function or a certain grouping of merchandise.

As a first step, Abe reviewed the many jobs performed each week. He found that he could group them into classes, each demanding a certain combination of skills for good performance:

1. *Merchandising.* Buying and managing inventory for different groups of merchandise.
2. *Direct and general selling and adjustments.* Customer contact.
3. *Sales promotion.* Advertising and display.

---

[2] Peter Drucker, *The Practice of Management* (New York: Harper & Row, 1954), pp. 194–201.
[3] Adapted from John W. Wingate and Seymour Helfont, *Small Store Planning for Growth* (Washington, D.C.: Small Business Administration, 1966), pp. 27–28.

4. *Accounting and finance.* Records, correspondence, cash handling, insurance, and credit.
5. *Store operation.* Supervising problems related to the building, equipment, and safety measures.
6. *Merchandise handling.* Receiving, marking, storing, and delivering.
7. *Personnel.* Employment, training, employee benefits, and personnel records.

Because no one function was a full-time activity in Abe's small business, he recognized that he did not need a specialist for each function. Thus, he combined some functions and delegated them to an employee, giving him more than one job for a while. Others he continued under his own direct supervision.

As the business continued to grow, Abe departmentalized the store and set up merchandise department managers in charge of each. He made them responsible for inventory management of their departments and for supervision of the salespeople assigned to them. In addition, he used them as salespeople and as assistant buyers. Abe continued for a time as chief buyer, but before long he was able to free himself of this responsibility and act as merchandise manager only.

About the same time that Abe selected the department managers, he assigned one man to supervise both store operation and merchandise handling. During busy times of the day, he too performed the sales function. For a while, accounting was handled by a part-time accountant, but as the firm grew, a full-time employee was hired for the job of office manager; he handled correspondence, accounting records, routine reports, payroll and other personnel data, and credit records.

In sales promotion, the first step toward specialization was to hire a part-time display man (on a contract basis rather than as an employee). At the same time, Abe needed to employ a part-time advertising man. Before long, the growing store probably would need a sales-promotion man to handle advertising and publicity and to supervise a display man and sign writer.

When the store has grown more, Abe intends to develop or employ a specialist to devote at least part of his time to employment, training, welfare, and the maintenance of personnel records. While the store is still relatively small, Abe can share this personnel function with the office manager and the merchandise department managers. Figure 5–1 is a chart depicting the planned organizational growth of Abe's store.

If the business in this case had been a partnership, the partners might have shared the ownership responsibility according to their interests and abilities. For example, one partner might act as merchandise manager, supervising the department managers and sales-promotion manager as well as handling merchandise budgets. The other partner could act as store manager,

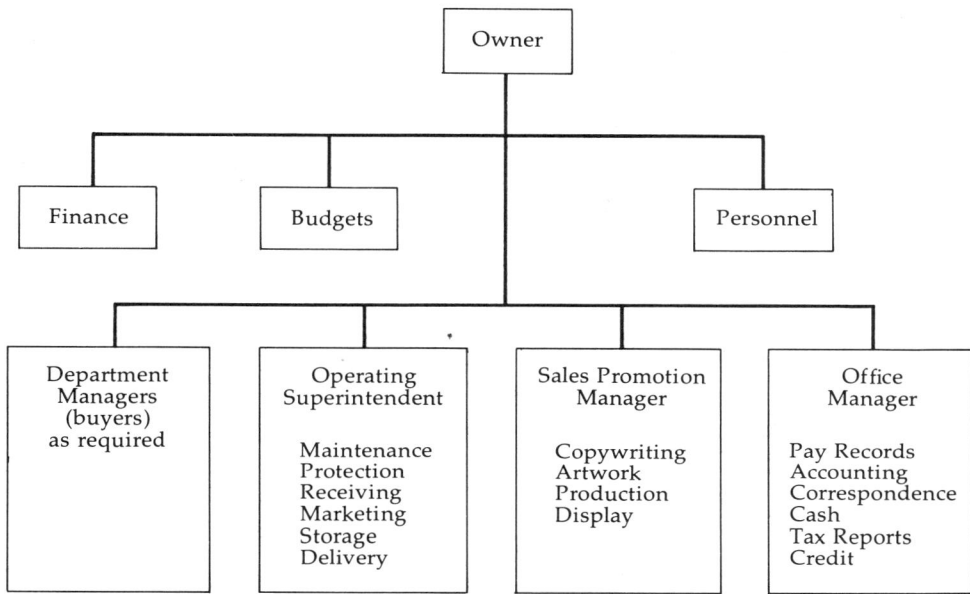

Figure 5–1. Organization of the Growing Store.

supervising the operating superintendent and the office manager. He could also handle the expense budget and personnel matters.

Principles of Organization

Numerous principles have been enumerated to aid in establishing an organization necessary to reach established goals. It is important, however, to recognize that these principles are only "rules of thumb" and should be used with recognition that:

1. Organization is inevitably the result of a series of compromises.
2. Organization is a living, moving, fluid force.
3. Organization represents people who react and respond to stimuli that escape precise definitions. "Principles" therefore should be regarded as "considerations" which, under normal circumstances, provide general questions for the organization planner to answer for specific situations with which he is dealing.

Some major principles or considerations of organizing a business are listed below, followed in each case by some of the factors that must be weighed carefully in using them.

I. The number of individuals reporting to a supervisor should not be more than can be effectively coordinated and directed.
   A. A given supervisor's span of control is not the same in each situation.
   B. Among the factors to be considered in determining the span of control in a given situation are the extent to which the work is routine and repetitive, whether or not the work is homogeneous, and how qualified the manager and employees are for the job.
II. Authority and responsibility for action should be decentralized to the greatest extent possible.
   A. Some considerations in determining the extent to which delegation is desirable are:
      1. Authority and responsibility for an activity cannot be delegated until policies can be spelled out so as to assure uniform administration.
      2. Certain matters (requests from important customers, and so on) take on top importance because of the potential repercussions if the case is mishandled.
      3. The importance or size of an item may have a bearing on the extent to which performance can be delegated—for example, the owner may feel that credit sales beyond $200 should be approved by the credit manager.
III. The responsibilities assigned to each unit or individual should be clear-cut.
   A. There is nothing that encourages confusion, recrimination, and jurisdictional conflict more than vague assignments of responsibility.
   B. On the other hand, too specific definitions of responsibility leave the way open for not doing things because they were not specifically defined; broad definitions of responsibility encourage initiative and resourcefulness.
IV. Throughout the organization, each member should know to whom he reports and who reports to him.
   A. A clear understanding of the lines of command and accountability is essential for everyone.
   B. However, it is important to recognize that:
      1. Interrelationships exist outside of the line of command that require reporting to and working with many other people for effective work.

2. The line of command need not be the line of communication for effective teamwork. More will be said about this point in the section dealing with communication.

Committees

A committee is not commonly shown on the organization chart and is frequently over-looked by the small businessman when he is mapping out the organization of his firm. The essential purpose of the committee—sometimes referred to as a board, task force, or team—is to apply group action to some matter entrusted to it. Too frequently, the entrepreneur is likely to run his business with little consultation with his management personnel or employees. He may feel that he always maintains an "open door" policy and that his personnel will come to him if they have ideas or problems, but in reality this is seldom the case. While a business may be small and relationships among members of the organization may be informal, barriers between different levels in the organization, or between various functional areas (for example, between the sales manager and the production manager) are likely to exist.

Committees can be formed to overcome these barriers to communication as well as to bring the collective judgment of people from different areas or levels to bear upon problems or activities that cut across several business specialties. For example, if a budget committee composed of all top managers were formed, not only would the business benefit from having several experts contributing knowledgeable inputs into the final budget, but it would also benefit from the improved relations resulting from key employees sharing work and information.

An entrepreneur may form temporary committees to solve specific problems or permanent standing committees to keep abreast of long-range problems and goals. Some small firms consider formal committees as part of the organizational structure, with specifically assigned duties and authority. An owner–manager of one successful small company has an executive committee consisting of himself and his four managers. They meet each week at a designated time to discuss general business problems and problems unique to their areas. They also suggest improvements and engage in brainstorming sessions to develop new ideas.

If the firm is incorporated, it is legally required to have a *board of directors*. Unfortunately, rather than view this group as a helpful committee, the typical small corporation considers a board of directors a meaningless legal requirement. Seldom is this group called upon to perform an active role.

The wise president of a small corporation will select people to serve on his board who will complement his own abilities. He will draw upon people such as local bankers, attorneys, retired businessmen, business professors, and accountants. He will meet regularly with them (perhaps monthly) and make use of their combined talents to solve major problems or obtain advice on policy issues. While some directors may require a nominal fee or a small share of the stock, many individuals are willing to serve for the challenge.[4]

Informal Organization

A discussion of organization would be incomplete without some reference to informal organization. This type of organization cannot be seen; it does not show up on the organization chart, yet it can most definitely be felt by the small businessman.

In a sense, the informal organization starts when the entrepreneur first brings a group of new employees together. Suddenly placed in a formal organizational structure, the employees begin to interact with one another, which of course gradually yields many sentiments or attitudes among co-workers. These sentiments lead to a number of activities not specified by the job description or formal organization, such as getting together for lunch, finding ways to "beat the system" and shortcutting jobs, "covering" for each other when someone has to leave early, and so on. Eventually this interaction builds strong bonds of identification, and the group of workers becomes more than a collection of people—it becomes an organization in itself.[5]

Underlying the workers' association with this informal organization is the fact that social needs are strong motivators to action, as we shall see in a following section on motivation. Thus, with a strong need to be accepted by his peers, the employee either consciously or unconsciously is drawn into membership in these informal groups, which in turn exercise a strong influence on his work behavior and attitudes toward management and the company. In fact, in many instances these informal groups may exercise stronger control over the attitudes and performance of the worker than does management.

The astute small business executive should recognize that since he can only reach his goals through his employees, he cannot ignore the existence of the informal organization. Therefore, he should try to identify and understand this social organization in his business. He should attempt to tactfully use its leaders as sources for communication and to positively orient employee behavior. To do so will make him a much more effective leader and in turn will facilitate his job of implementing goals.

---

[4] H. N. Broom and Justin G. Longenecker, *Small Business Management*, 3rd ed. (Cincinnati: South-Western Publishing, 1971), pp. 244–246.
[5] See George Strauss and Leonard R. Sayles, *Personnel: The Human Problems of Management*, 3rd ed. (Englewood Cliffs, N.J.: Prentice-Hall, 1972), p. 75.

Actuating

Actuating, the third fundamental function of management, literally means "moving toward action." Through this process, the entrepreneur guides the actual performance of subordinates toward company goals.

In order to carry out the planning and organizing functions, the effective manager must initiate and continue the necessary actions for moving employee performance toward company goals. What actions he takes will depend, of course, on what activities are to be done, the qualifications of the workers, and his own style of leadership. As a leader, the manager must be careful to create a work climate that fosters loyalty and efficient teamwork. Adequate pay, good working conditions, fair treatment, opportunities for advancement, and proper matching of jobs to workers' interests and abilities all contribute to this work climate. Much research has been done on effective ways of actuating workers. The manager can ask himself the following questions to get an idea of the findings:

1. Do I study my subordinates to find out the most effective way of motivating each one?
2. Do I let my employees know where they stand?
3. Do I use committees and meetings effectively for harmonious action?
4. Do I allow employees to participate in decisions that directly affect them?
5. Do I criticize and reprimand in private, but praise promptly and in public?
6. Am I careful not to perpetuate a paternal relationship with my immediate associates?

A manager who answers "yes" to all of the above is probably doing a good job of actuating employee performance. Keep in mind, however, that actuating is a never-ending task. Motivating employees to maximum achievement is a continuous challenge to the small business manager.

Motivation

Good pay is simply not enough to motivate employees. Motivating workers to achieve a high level of productivity and to accept the goals of the business has been a problem throughout modern times. From the beginning of the industrial revolution to the emergence of large, powerful unions, the common philosophy was predominantly one of negative sanctions: fear and punishment. With the growth of unions, tightening of the labor market, and the growing influence of a democratic approach in this country, the old system of motivating became unsuccessful. During more recent times, managers have relied greatly on the use of such economic rewards as higher pay, benefits, and so on.

Recent behavioral science findings, however, have shown us that the employee is not merely an "economic man" who responds to economic incentives. Research findings have shown that the modern employee is a "complex man" and that the human factor, including the various physical, social, and psychological needs of human beings, is a vital part of motivation. Unfortunately, managers in small as well as large businesses have made certain incorrect assumptions about man's nature whenever they have attempted to consider the human factor. One of the men who has questioned our assumptions about managing workers is Douglas McGregor.

Theory X and Theory Y. In his book *The Human Side of Enterprise* (1960), McGregor pointed out two opposite approaches to leadership styles: autocratic and permissive. He then set forth explicit statements of the assumptions about human nature and behavior underlying each theory.[6]

The autocratic, or "Theory X," manager makes the following assumptions:

1. The average human being has an inherent dislike of work and will avoid it if he can.
2. Because of this universal dislike of work, most people must be coerced, controlled, directed, and threatened with punishment to get them to work toward the achievement of organizational objectives.
3. The average human being prefers to be directed, wishes to avoid responsibility, has relatively little ambition, and wants security above all.

At the opposite extreme, the permissive, or "Theory Y," manager assumes that:

1. The expenditure of physical effort and mental effort in work is as natural as play or rest.
2. External control and the threat of punishment are not the only means for motivating people. An employee will exercise self-direction and self-control in achieving objectives to which he is committed.

---

[6] Douglas McGregor, *The Human Side of Enterprise* (New York: McGraw-Hill, 1960). Reprinted with permission.

3. Commitment to objectives is a function of the rewards associated with their achievement.
4. The average human being learns, under proper conditions, not only to accept but to seek responsibility.
5. The capacity to exercise a relatively high degree of imagination, ingenuity, and creativity in the solution of organizational problems is widely distributed in the population.
6. Under the conditions of modern industrial life, the intellectual potentialities of the average human being are only partially realized.

Of course, few managers neatly fit into one or the other category. The small businessman, however, can examine his own leadership style in view of the above assumptions. In other words, he should question whether or not the assumptions he has made about the behavior of his employees are correct.

Basic motivation concepts. A quick review of two other theories dealing with motivation should be helpful to the entrepreneur seeking insight into ways of more effectively motivating employees. One of these theories was expounded by Abraham Maslow in his book *Motivation and Personality*. Maslow believed that human beings have a hierarchy of needs, going from the lower order to the higher order as follows:

1. Basic physiological needs, such as hunger.
2. Safety and security needs.
3. Love or social needs.
4. Esteem and self-respect needs.
5. Need for self-fulfillment and accomplishment.

The theory maintains that the higher-order needs do not become important until the lower-order needs are relatively well satisfied. At the same time, once a lower-order need is satisfied, it ceases to act as a motivator. Thus, since the employee's physiological and security needs are pretty well met by most jobs, we can assume from this theory that he will be motivated by the next higher order of needs—that is, social needs. Once his need for social interaction is satiated, he will be motivated by the need for self-fulfillment (that is, the desire to become more what he is—to become everything that he is capable of becoming). The lesson for the small business executive is to recognize that there is a higher order of needs to which he must try to appeal in attempting to motivate his employees to higher levels of productivity—needs for psychic *as well as* monetary rewards.

Another theory of motivation was set forth by Frederick Herzberg, a noted social psychologist. Herzberg suggested that man's needs are divided into five job dissatisfiers and five job satisfiers. He lists job dissatisfiers as company policy and administration, supervision, salary, working conditions, and interpersonal relations. His job satisfiers are achievement, recognition, work itself, responsibility, and advancement. The reader will note that his job satisfiers correspond to Maslow's higher-order needs—social and esteem needs and the need for self-fulfillment. However, in contrast to Maslow, who claimed one need must be satisfied before another is challenged, Herzberg maintains that all needs are pursued at the same time and come in no particular chronological order.

Furthermore, Herzberg found in his studies that the five dissatisfiers, or hygienic factors as he called them, can prevent job dissatisfaction but cannot create true job satisfaction. In other words, Herzberg would say that maintaining the hygienic factors at adequate, or even high levels won't make the employees more effective, but failing to maintain them may cause the employees to become less effective or even to quit. On the other hand, given the hygienic factors, employees can be motivated by the "job satisfiers." To the small businessman, this might mean that once he feels that the hygienic factors in his firm are comparable to other similar firms, or at least are perceived as fair by his employees, he should become more concerned with how to make the jobs in his business more challenging and meaningful. For example, he might emphasize more job autonomy and responsibility and encourage advancement and rewards for achievement on the job.

Communication

Goals, policies, and operations developed by the executives of a small business have no value until put into action. However, before they can be actuated, they must be transmitted to other levels of employees in the business. This transmission and interpretation of information is called communication. While we are discussing communication under the general heading of actuating, keep in mind that all managerial functions involve communication problems. In fact, it is through communication that all management functions are brought together. At the same time, the essence of actuating management goals is the ability to communicate. For the best plans, organization and control would be meaningless without proper communication.

Fortunately, a manager of a small firm has a distinct advantage over the big business, for in a small organization the "chain of command" is short and most communication is likely to be face to face. In a very small firm the owner-manager can talk directly with employees, and he does not have to rely on written instructions passed down through channels. At the same time, he can immediately answer any questions that arise. He can watch reactions and consider comments and ideas from the employees at the time they are made.

Thus, a smaller organization provides unlimited opportunity for effective communication. However, effective communication doesn't "just happen." A manager must become communication-minded. He must understand the basic ideas underlying effective communication, must be aware of the value of good communication, and, most of all, he must be sure that everyone else in his organization also sees the value.

Understanding communication. Communication in an organization can be categorized into three groups: vertical, horizontal, and informal. Vertical communication takes place when the owner or manager gives orders to others further down in the organization structure. The organization chart shows this type of downward, vertical flow of communication through the chain of command. At the same time, upward, vertical flow of communication takes place as employees send reports, suggestions, feedback, and so on, back up through the hierarchy.

Horizontal communication takes place between managers or employees on the same level of the organization. This type of communication is every bit as important as vertical communication in that it facilitates the coordination of efforts and speeds up the decision-making process. For example, two managers at the same level can work out a problem among themselves without having to go through the "proper channels."

The third type of communication, sometimes referred to as the "grapevine," exists as part of the informal organization and serves the social needs of the members in the organization. The "grapevine" is an amazingly effective way by which information, rumors, and gossip spread throughout the organization. A significant number of employees consider the grapevine their prime source of information about company affairs. In fact, since the grapevine is perceived by workers as a personal type of communication and since it encourages feedback, it often has a stronger impact on the recipient than do the more formalized types of communication.[7]

Effective communication. As mentioned earlier, good communication doesn't "just happen." To develop more effective communication in his organization the entrepreneur might consider the following principles:

---

[7] See Lawrence A. Klatt and David L. Kurtz, "The 'Grapevine' as a Management Tool," *Akron Business and Economic Review* I, No. 4 (Winter 1970), pp. 20–23.

1. *Be a good listener.* Listen to ideas and suggestions as well as complaints. Often, procedures that save time or money are first suggested by employees "down the line." Listening is a two-edged tool for a manager. It gives him essential facts and greater understanding, and it gives the employees a feeling of participation and heightens their interest in their work.
2. *Keep employees informed.* Pass along to employees information on matters that affect them. Let them know ahead of time if changes are to be made in policies or procedures. Give them advance notice about contemplated changes in working hours or wage rates. Above all, explain why changes are necessary or policies are being adopted.
3. *Encourage two-way communication.* In addition to being a good listener and passing along necessary information to subordinates, a manager should encourage two-way communication throughout his organization. Employees should feel free to discuss problems with supervisors. Effective job performance depends upon the continuous upward and downward flow of communication.
4. *Let subordinates take a part in decisions.* Give employees a chance to take part in discussions before final decisions are made on matters that will affect them. This is a "Theory Y" approach. Employees will be likely to back the "majority" decision more strongly than one handed down arbitrarily.
5. *Use the grapevine for information instead of misinformation.* Grapevine news travels fast. Much of the news is disturbing to employees, and much of it is false. Rumors often start because someone misunderstands an instruction or announcement. Or rumors may start because management is withholding information. A manager should learn what the grapevine is saying. Then he can stop rumors and spread accurate information informally.
6. *Create a climate of trust and confidence.* Effective communication thrives in a climate of confidence. By reporting facts honestly and by keeping promises, a manager establishes a reputation for truthfulness and sincerity and inspires employee confidence.

Controlling

This managerial function consists of measuring and correcting performance so that goals are accomplished as planned. Controlling is closely related to planning. In fact, a control is used to check that plans are carried out as needed. It is this controlling function that lets the manager know whether or not things are working out as he planned them.

The manager must establish standards, compare operating results to these standards, and then take prompt remedial action when results are significantly below par. Control is particularly important in the areas of sales, quality, profits, output, costs, and labor relations. The cornerstone of control, especially in the smaller business, is the budget. In appraising how well he does in this area of controlling, the manager should consider the following two questions raised by the Small Business Administration:

Do I express my plans in the form of a budget covering sales, stocks, markups, and expenses? If the answer is "no," you may be headed for trouble. For the goals expressed in a budget give you something definite to shoot for; and if the budget is carefully made, you can achieve a balance among your various factors.

Do my key employees have a voice in formulating budget plans concerning them? Hopefully, yes. Normally a standard or a budget will be more effective when it includes the thinking of those who are to be guided by it rather than when it is solely the product of the owner or manager.

Controlling through Planning

The small businessman can benefit from viewing the control function as an outgrowth of the planning function. In the large firm, controlling operations can be assigned to many work sections where sophisticated methods can be used. This is not possible for the small entrepreneur, but it is possible for him to achieve a high level of control by combining his control systems and his formal planning. The purpose of administrative control is to assure that the performance in any area conforms as closely as possible to the established objectives. The control process consists of the following steps:

1. *Setting objectives or standards.* A standard for employee performance or financial performance, such as a percentage return on sales or investment, is actually a goal that a manager hopes to achieve as well as a guideline. Thus, standards and objectives or goals should be considered synonymous.
2. *Measurement of performance.* For example, if the entrepreneur has set a sales objective of $200,000 over a 1-year period, then he will want to know at the end of that year the sales figure for the year.
3. *Comparison of actual performance with the objective.* Control requires that a constant check be made of its effectiveness, and its effectiveness is measured by how closely the final results resemble the original objective or goal.

4. *Instituting corrective action.* There are only three possibilities:
   a. If the comparison between actual performance and a desired objective shows both to be the same, then the manager can probably applaud himself on both the objective and the performance.
   b. If the comparison shows actual performance to be greater than the objectives, then there are two possibilities—first, the manager may have set his objective or standard too low, or second, the performance may have been outstanding.
   c. If the comparison shows that actual performance was lower than the objective or standard, then the business is in trouble unless the objective was simply set too high. In any case, the manager must investigate *why* performance did not come up to the objective and then take corrective action.

By simply formalizing the comparison between actual and planned performance, the manager challenges himself to determine causes for noncompliance and is then in a position to remedy the situation for the next time period. It is most important in controlling operations that he attempt to shorten the time period over which he measures performance. For example, if he waits until the end of the year before he measures sales against his goal, he has no time in which to remedy a poor performance. Thus, he should break down an annual goal, for instance, into twelve monthly goals, considering the seasons involved as he does so. For example, in December retail sales will always be larger than any other month because of the impact of Christmas purchases.

Common control systems should cover such areas as inventory, production, quality, employee performance, and major expense items. Financial objectives or standards, while initially difficult to formulate, can often be established by reference to average performance figures for the industry as collected and published by the industry trade association. The method of presenting comparisons of results with standards or objectives must be given some consideration. The reader who has attempted to interpret large masses of data can appreciate the problem. In general, the simplest and most direct method is desired. For example, graphs or charts provide one way of visualizing important relationships without cluttering details.

Basic Control Problems

In devising effective controls in a small business, the entrepreneur must cope with two basic problems. First, to be of practical value, his system must not be very costly since a small company cannot afford to be burdened with excessive personnel and overhead charges. Thus, the control system should be simple, requiring limited manpower.

Second, he must face the fact that almost everybody not only resents the idea of being controlled but also objects to being judged. More often than not, the targets of a control system are regarded as personal report cards. According to several studies, standards and budgets can be highly unpopular. Many supervisors dislike them. They feel, for example, that standards put more pressure on employees and overemphasize past performance. Furthermore, supervisors often feel that while standards don't show why the goal wasn't reached, they do strengthen the idea that supervisors have to be constantly goaded into greater efficiency. Consequently, a control system should be installed with patience and tact so as to be accepted by those who will operate under it. Otherwise, it may not have much success.[8]

Incident 5:   Getting Organized

"Here's your coffee, Pete," Sam said, as Pete emerged from under the Stutz fender. "Hey, let's get a coffee urn in here, or something—I'm tired of running four blocks for coffee."

"OK, maybe next week, when we get paid for this job," Pete said.

"When will you finish up? I can't paint until you get done."

Pete wiped his hands. "Maybe two, three hours. Are you done with the Bentley?"

"It's drying—can't touch it 'til tomorrow."

Pete looked around. "The place looks a bit dirty."

Sam sighed. "I know. I'll clean up. But Pete, paying five bucks an hour for a sweeper isn't very good business."

"It's better than having you sit on your can doing nothing."

"Sure, sure." They sipped their coffee.

"You know," Pete said, "it's hard to believe that I really have this business. And it's good, too—already we've done seven cars. Now that Martha's keeping the books, I think I even know how much we're making. But somehow it keeps leaking away. We should be doing better than we are."

"So far, my checks haven't bounced," Sam said, "so I'm no worse off than I was before. But I notice that Martha's still working, and that you look a bit seedy—I bet you're not even making as much as old man Martin used to pay."

"Not yet, Sam—but just wait. It will take a while to get this organized."

"What's our next job? We've got these two, and then what?"

"I don't know yet, Sam. I'm hoping that Mr. Baxter—you know, the fellow who owns the Bentley—will send us some friends. So far, all we have are satisfied customers."

"So far. But how far is far? I mean, how many of these old cars are there?"

Pete waved his hands. "Lots. All we have to do is do good work, and they'll come."

---

[8]See also Edward L. Anthony, "Effective Control for Better Management," *Management Aids* (Washington, D. C.: Small Business Administration, 1962).

"They'd better come soon. We'll be through with these two in about a week. And I wonder how many owners have the thousand bucks or so to get this kind of work done."

"Don't worry, Sam. Remember, I'm the boss. I'm supposed to worry."

"The boss pays my wages, so I'm worried." Sam leaned back and drank his coffee. "I've never had it so good, Pete. Here I can do the work I want to do. It's a real challenge, and I get a kick out of seeing the customers' reactions when they see the finished product. But, boy, we'd better figure out how to keep it coming in."

Pete was plenty worried, but he didn't want to tell Sam about it. He had been trying to drum up some new business, but times were tough, and not as many people as he had thought were willing to spend big money for old cars. Pete figured he could get the business if he got out and talked to owners, but someone had to do the bodywork. He also found that lots of owners wanted high-skill mechanical work done at the same time, and while he and Sam could do simple tasks, they didn't have the machinery to do complicated mechanical work. And he spent more time than he wanted looking for old parts and sheet metal.

He was having trouble on his estimates, too — something that looked simple in straightening out a fender turned out to be complicated, and ended up taking longer than he figured. So far he was earning about two dollars an hour. He was learning fast, but for a while it would be tough.

Pete figured that he needed a good mechanic/machinist to help out. And if he could offer spare parts, he could do still better. He had found out that many spare parts for older cars were now being manufactured by small companies and that they sold at good markups. Other items came on the market from time to time as new old stock — that is, stocks of new parts from long ago, which someone had found in an old abandoned Packard agency or maybe in a barn. Customers would pay well for these parts. However, he had never had any retail experience, and he knew the business took a lot of time and skill. Still, it was an interesting idea — people kept wandering in asking for such parts, and Pete knew fairly well already what would sell.

All of this would take money, too. He had used up his father-in-law's $3,400 in leasing the shop and buying equipment, plus $500 of his own. A good parts inventory would cost maybe $20,000, of which $4,000 would have to be cash.

Pete knew that Jack Simmons, an old school friend, was a top-flight mechanic and knew enough about auto machinists' work to do that too. Maybe he would come in on that side . . . Pete decided to talk to him about it.

And all the business details were a lot more complicated than he had figured. The technical side was easy, but he had found out the hard way that he had to have insurance; that the city zoning commission was dubious about his location (he would have to show up and argue his case next Tuesday evening); that even with Martha helping, bookkeeping was a mess, to say nothing of banking; and that sometimes he had to carry a customer's account for quite a while before he got paid. The Stutz would mean $2,000 in a week, but he already had $472 of his cash tied up in parts and paint. And a tax man had showed up the other day, asking questions about whether he had paid his sales tax to the state. Unfortunately he hadn't — there went another $750 he didn't have.

When he finished the Stutz fender, he would be free for a while. He knew an old fellow who had a 1926 Chrysler that he might be willing to have completely restored — that job would bring $5,000 at least. He planned to go talk to him later in the afternoon.

1. What planning and control issues do you see in this incident? List them for Pete to study.
2. What goals does Pete have now? Are they workable ones? Why or why not?
3. Does Pete have an organization problem? Why or why not? If he does not, indicate why. If he does, what is it, and how might he improve his operations?
4. What standards should Pete now set? Why? Suggest how he might set up a set of standards that he can use.

Discussion Questions

1. What is the primary objective of the management function of "organizing"?
2. How would an entrepreneur go about "organizing" his newly formed business?
3. Is there an ideal form of organizational structure for a firm? What influences the "proper" organization for reaching a firm's goals?
4. Explain how you would determine the kind of structure needed for a particular business using Peter Drucker's approach.
5. What reservations or cautions would you point out to someone attempting to apply principles of organization?
6. What points should an entrepreneur consider when assigning responsibilities to his employees?
7. In what ways can a committee be useful to a small business?
8. Explain how a board of directors might effectively be used by a small business organization.
9. How does the informal organization differ from the formal organization? How should the owner or manager of a small business view the informal organization?
10. Define the "actuating" function of management. How does it relate to the planning and organizing function?
11. Do you agree that good pay is not enough to motivate employees? Why or why not?
12. How do Theory X and Theory Y relate to the practice of management?
13. In what ways might Maslow's and Herzberg's theories be of practical value to the owner–manager of a small business?
14. Define communication. In what ways does the manager of a small firm have a distinct advantage over the big organization when it comes to communication?

15. Distinguish among vertical, horizontal, and informal communication.
16. How might the entrepreneur go about developing more effective communication in his organization?
17. At what point in management does the control function begin?
18. Outline the basic steps of the control process.
19. What are some areas or items for which an entrepreneur should have a control system?
20. What practical advice could you offer to the small businessman for devising controls in his business?

Suggested Readings

Anthony, Edward L., "Balanced Skills: Measure of Effective Managers," *Small Marketers Aids Annual No. 4*. Washington, D. C.: Small Business Administration, 1962. Pp. 48–54.

_____, "Effective Control for Better Management," *Management Aids Annual No. 5*. Washington, D. C.: Small Business Administration, 1959. Pp. 32–38.

Blomstrom, Robert L., and Fearon, Harold, "An Analysis of the Functional Work Assignments of Managers in the Small Manufacturing Firm," *Journal of Small Business Management* III (January 1965), 3–15.

Charm, Sumner D., "Organizing the Owner–Manager's Job," *Management Aids Annual No. 7*. Washington, D. C.: Small Business Administration, 1961. Pp. 16–23.

Communications and Control, Administrative Management Course Program, Topic 9. Washington, D. C.: Small Business Administration, 1965.

Drucker, Peter, *The Practice of Management*. New York: Harper & Row, 1954.

Katz, D., and Kahn, R. L., *The Social Psychology of Organizations*. New York: John Wiley, 1966.

Klatt, Lawrence A., "Management Self-Analysis," *Photo Marketing* 46, No. 6 (June 1971), 2–4, 22.

_____, *Managing the Dynamic Small Firm: Readings*. Belmont, Calif.: Wadsworth, 1971. Pp. 90–120.

Koontz, Harold, and O'Donnell, Cyril, *Principles of Management*, 4th ed. New York: McGraw-Hill, 1968.

Krentzman, Harvey C., "Reducing Management Waste," *Management Aids Annual No. 10*. Washington, D. C.: Small Business Administration, 1964. Pp. 47–54.

Levinson, Robert E., "Checking Your Management Methods," *Management Aids Annual No. 11*. Washington, D. C.: Small Business Administration, 1965. Pp. 8–14.

Maslow, A. H., *Motivation and Personality*. New York: Harper & Row, 1954.

Massie, Joseph L., *Essentials of Management*, 2nd ed. Englewood Cliffs, N. J.: Prentice-Hall, 1971. Ch. 6, 7, 8, 11.

McGregor, Douglas, *The Human Side of Enterprise*. New York: McGraw-Hill, 1960.

Newman, W. H., Sumner, Charles E., and Warren, E. Kirby, *The Process of Management*, 2nd ed. Englewood Cliffs, N. J.: Prentice-Hall, 1967.

Raines, I. I., *Better Communications in Small Business*, 2nd ed. Small Business Management Series No. 7. Washington, D. C.: Small Business Administration, 1962.

Saxenian, Hrand, "Effective Communications in Small Plants," *Management Aids*, No. 163 (April 1964). Washington, D. C.: Small Business Administration.

Schleh, Edward C., "How Is Management Related to Company Size?" *Advanced Management Journal* XXX (January 1965), 59–65.

Serif, Med, "Pointers for Developing Your Top Assistant," *Small Marketers Aids*, No. 101 (April 1964). Washington, D. C.: Small Business Administration.

Part Three   Starting the Business

Two Paths to Entrepreneurship

Chapter 6

There are two distinct paths to entrepreneurship: buying an established business, or starting a new one. The most common route to small business ownership is purchasing an existing business.

Buying a Small Business

Buying a business is a complicated transaction. The potential entrepreneur must locate opportunities, evaluate existing opportunities, and close the deal in a safe, legal, and equitable manner. Above all, he must do a great deal of preliminary work, attempting to maintain an objective attitude so that he will not allow excessive enthusiasm to cloud the disadvantages. Obviously, there are several advantages to buying an existing firm:

1. When starting a new firm, the entrepreneur must spend a great deal of time and money to determine the feasibility of alternative locations, but even with great precaution, the wisdom of his choice will not be apparent until the business has been in operation for a period of time. When one buys an existing business, however, it can easily be determined whether or not the location is desirable.
2. When purchasing an existing business, the entrepreneur also purchases an established clientele. Thus, the going business gives him a head start by keeping him going until his income starts to come in more quickly. He will also need less working capital to meet the bills during the initial period.
3. Buying a going business eliminates much time, effort, and cost that would be needed

to launch a new one. Since the seller has already accumulated those assets (including inventories and manpower) necessary to run the business, the uncertainty of the future success of the business is somewhat reduced.
4. A final advantage is that a business may be available at a bargain price. Of course, the value of the business must be carefully verified to make sure it is a bargain. For example, the price may appear low, but the owner might have lost a prime contract or may have been notified that his franchise is being withdrawn. On the other hand, the price may be reduced to settle an estate or because the owner wishes to retire and is willing to "sacrifice" in order to make a quick sale.

At the same time, there are a couple serious disadvantages to buying an existing firm:

1. The previous owner may have been a poor manager. His inventories may be outdated, his equipment poorly maintained, or his customers alienated and intent on staying away from the business. If such conditions exist, it may be extremely costly and difficult to change them.
2. Some locations are so bad that regardless of how effectively a new owner manages the business, he is doomed to failure. Frequently a business in a poor location sells as what appears to be a real bargain. But a failure at any price is no bargain.

Evaluating the Business

At this stage, the entrepreneur faces the problem of determining a fair price for a business opportunity. The business may already be on the market with a value attached, or a prospective buyer may make an offer for a business he thinks is promising. In either case, the seller is likely to have an emotional attachment to the business that may cause him to place a higher value on the business than is merited by an objective evaluation. Therefore, a prospective buyer's careful analysis of a business should consider the reason(s) the business is for sale, the profitability (past and potential) of the business, assets (tangible and intangible) and liabilities, and several other factors to be discussed below.

Reason for selling. The reasons given by the seller are frequently different from the reasons known to the business community, which in turn may be different from the facts. The seller commonly cites ill health or retirement as the primary reason for giving up his business. Closer investigation may reveal that the seller intends to open a competing business at a more favorable location; or that long-term trends, such as plans to build a shopping center, rerouting traffic, or condemnation of property by the city, bode ill for the success of the business; or that products or services offered by the business will soon become obsolete; or that receivables are impossible to collect; and so on.

In order to uncover the real reason(s) for selling the buyer may want to talk to the local bank, previous owners, customers, suppliers, employees, and possibly even a competitor. Knowing the reason for selling will enable him to evaluate the business more realistically.

Profitability of the business. The determining factor in evaluating a business is its profit potential. To estimate the potential earning power of the business, the buyer must find out about past profit, sales, and operating ratios for each of the preceding 3 to 5 years. If the seller does not have audited business records, these data can be obtained from his federal and state tax returns. If the seller will not provide the necessary information, the buyer should beware. An honest seller should be willing to provide the information that will allow an accurate evaluation of his business.

The buyer should see that the following questions about profitability are answered to his satisfaction: Are profits satisfactory? If not, what are the chances of increasing them? Are profits in line with similar businesses? What is the profit trend? What are the reasons for the trend? How do operating ratios compare with industry averages?

The major concern of the buyer, of course, is the future of the business. Therefore, on the basis of past records, he must estimate sales and profits for the next year or two. If he is not familiar with accounting and tax records, it is wise to have an independent accountant familiar with the type of business evaluate them for him. Of course, the fact that past profits are not favorable need not discourage him from buying the firm if the business is inherently sound. Poor earnings is a common reason for selling a business. The buyer's analysis may indicate that the poor earning record was brought about by a condition he can correct — poor management, poor pricing policies, and so on.

Assets and liabilities. An independent appraisal is usually desirable to verify that the fixed assets (equipment, building, fixtures, and so on), which are normally carried on the books at cost less depreciation, are fairly valued and representative of current worth. The buyer should also take a physical count of the inventory to determine its reasonable value. He will need to determine if the stock of goods consists of fresh salable, balanced selections of materials or merchandise and how much of it will have to be sold at a loss.

If accounts receivable are included in the sale, the buyer should examine them carefully. They should be aged by period of time outstanding to determine how many of them are unlikely to be collected — the longer the period, the less the value of the account.

The intangible as well as the tangible assets should be cautiously evaluated to estimate their worth and to make sure they are transferable along with the business. For example, will key employees continue to work for the new management? If not, would this adversely affect the profitability of the business? Along the same lines, are any exclusive franchises or contracts transferable to the purchaser? Probably one of the most troublesome intangible assets to value is goodwill—the amount the seller is asking for the favorable public attitude he has developed toward the business. The buyer must be realistic in evaluating how much this intangible asset is worth. A recommended way for the buyer to judge the value of goodwill is to approximate the additional income he will receive through buying the business rather than by starting a new one.

The assistance of a lawyer is usually necessary to determine what liabilities, if any, the buyer will be assuming. A lawyer can find out, for example, if there are any back taxes, unpaid bills, liens against assets, mortgages, pending suits, or other creditors' claims. The liabilities to be assumed should be put in writing and their value should be subtracted from the value of the assets to arrive at a net amount to pay.

Other factors. A number of additional factors should be given attention by the prospective buyer. For example:

1. Are there any zoning restrictions or health-code requirements that may come into effect with the change of ownership?
2. What are the future trends of the industry, business, community, and location?
3. What is the total amount of capital necessary? Will there be enough for working capital, repairs, modernization, new inventories, opening expenses, cash to carry accounts receivable, and an adequate allowance for unforeseen expenses?
4. Are any special licenses required? Is the lease transferable to the buyer? Is anything being taken for granted?

Determining the Price

Determining the worth of a business as a going concern is probably the most difficult part of buying a small business. As the previous discussion has suggested, there are two basic ways of determining the price. The first, which is the preferred method, is based on expectations of future profits and return on investment. This approach is known as *capitalizing future earnings.* Accordingly, the capitalized value is one that would bring the stated earnings at a specified rate of interest. The rate of interest used is usually the current rate of return for investments involving similar risk. The capitalized value then is found by dividing the annual profit by the specified rate of return expressed as a decimal.

For example, assume that the projected profits for business are $20,000 annually. If the investment were as safe as an investment in a blue-chip corporate stock, earning 10 percent in price and dividend increase, the buyer would want to use a higher rate. As a rule of thumb, 20 to 25 percent is considered adequate. Thus, if the business earns the projected rate, the buyer would be willing to pay between $80,000 and $100,000 for the business. He would recover his investment (aside from tax considerations) in 4 or 5 years.

The second method, which is the most commonly used, is based on the value of the *asset appraisal*. While it is easier to use, it is less desirable because it pays little attention to the future of the business. Using this method, the buyer and seller agree on the assets to be included in the transaction. Normally these assets will be sales and office supplies, inventories, accounts receivable, fixtures, equipment, and goodwill. A price is then negotiated based on the value of the assets.

A third approach to determining the price of an established business combines elements of the previous two methods and introduces another consideration—the present earning power of the purchaser. It involves capitalizing the excess earning power of the business (that is, the average net profit of the business minus the purchaser's present earning power) and adding this figure to the adjusted tangible net worth, Table 6–1 (p. 94) illustrates this method.

This last approach assumes that the purchaser will be quitting his job to become the owner–operator of the business. Also, since the present earning power (line 4) will vary depending on the prospective purchaser, the fair price will vary. Or, to state it another way, the "fair" price may be a different figure for each prospective purchaser. And, of course, the "fair" price for the seller may be different from that of the purchaser. In either case, the final selling price will be modified through negotiation between the buyer and seller.

Determining the Profit

The previous discussion pointed out that the past profitability of a firm is an important consideration in purchasing an existing business. Unfortunately, the purchaser will frequently take the past profit figure at face value without giving proper thought to how the figure was determined. The following is intended to aid the potential entrepreneur in determining the true profitability of a business.[1]

---

[1] Adapted from Frederick G. Disney, "Are You Kidding Yourself about Your Profits?", *Small Marketers Aids*, No. 25, Washington, D. C.: Small Business Administration, 1971.

A good first question to ask is "What actually is the true profit?" You must realize that a final answer to this question is not necessarily indicated by the figure of "Net Profit" shown on the profit-and-loss (P and L) statement. To make sure that you are not being misled by this figure, you must analyze the basis of it.

Table 6–1. An Example of the Combined Method of Determining the Price of an Established Business.

1.	Adjusted tangible net worth (appraised value of tangible assets less liabilities)		$100,000
2.	Normal earning power at 7% (what buyer could get by investing $100,000 in corporate bonds)	$ 7,000	
3.	Salary for owner–operator (whatever buyer is making now)	$15,000	
4.	Present earning power of buyer (without buying the business)	$22,000	
5.	Average net profit of business (over the past 3 to 5 years)	$25,000	
6.	Excess earning power of business (line 5 less line 4)	$ 3,000	
7.	Goodwill (as determined by this formula: for a well-established business, five times excess earning power; for a moderately well-established business, three times)		$ 15,000
8.	Fair price (tangibles plus goodwill, or profit potential)		$115,000

Analyzing the basis of net profit. An orderly procedure is to start at the top of the P and L statement and compare every item with its counterpart in several other operating periods. It is important to maintain a questioning attitude about each figure on the statement so that you can evaluate the true situation. You should not accept figures at their face value but rather look behind each one to ferret out any hidden meanings.

A word about profit and loss statements. There are two principal methods of reporting income and expenses on the P and L statement—the cash method and the accrual method. The cash method shows only the actual receipt of cash (income) and the actual expenditures of cash (expenses). The accrual method reflects business transactions that took place during the reporting period, whether or not any money changed hands. These two methods can convey totally different pictures of profit.

The cash method is usually not a reliable picture of income and expenses for the period covered by the P and L because credit business comprises over 90 percent of all commercial transactions. Thus, a P and L reflecting only cash transactions will not account for much of the business applicable to the period. The accrual method, however, can account for all activities, cash or credit, completed during the period.

Sales. Some accounting procedures do not include the determination of net sales (generally the gross sales less returns and allowances). Try to make sure, therefore, that "sales" figures reflect the actual, final sales that took place in the period covered by the P and L.

Cost of goods sold and inventory valuation. Cost of goods sold, which follows "Net Sales" on the P and L, is determined by subtracting the inventory at the end of the period from the total obtained by adding the inventory at the beginning of the period to purchases made during the period. (Note: Beginning inventory and purchases are often referred to as "merchandise available for sale.") Sometimes this method of inventory valuation can be the cause of significant distortion in the profit picture. If, for instance, the closing inventory were valued high, the cost of goods sold would be lower and profits would be higher. Thus, the cost-of-goods-sold figure can easily be distorted by any change in the method of inventory valuation, or by failure to observe sound valuation methods.

Therefore, you should review the inventory procedures to determine, first, what basis is used, and second, if this basis reflects the most realistic value of the stock on hand.

Depreciation. One of the most critical areas in the overstatement or understatement of profits is depreciation. In this area, you can be misled by what appears to be a sound and accurate accounting procedure. For one thing, the depreciation account can show a record of depreciation down to the exact penny and thus give the impression of absolute accuracy. You can easily lose sight of the fact that the human judgment that established the original depreciation rate could have been in error—sometimes in gross error.

For example, the decision to depreciate some store fixtures over a period of 10 years by one company proved to be unrealistic since it was found that these items had actually reached the limits of their usefulness and needed to be replaced at the end of 6½ years. Hence, for 6½ years the owners of that company had been kidding themselves about the amount of their profit.

You should carefully review depreciation policies in light of your past experience, good judgment, and the experiences of the trade. The tax rules of the Internal Revenue Service can be a useful guide because they inform you of legal limitations and serve as a basis for the determination of a realistic depreciation policy.

The Final Transaction

Before closing the deal, it is important that the buyer get a lawyer to help him in a final check of all vital points. The sales agreement or contract should be drawn up by a lawyer, for the assets to be transferred need to be specifically listed in the agreement, as well as the liabilities that are to be assumed and those that are not. Also spelled out in the contract are when the buyer will take over the business, who is to get the money from sales while the business is in escrow, and how real-estate taxes and insurance premiums are to be prorated.

Starting a New Business

While the more common route to entrepreneurship is to buy an existing business, some small businesses prefer to start from scratch for a number of reasons. Some of these reasons are:

1. Starting his own business allows the entrepreneur to choose his own location, products, services, employees, equipment, and merchandise.
2. He is not bound by the old firm's policies and practices and therefore has more freedom to innovate and organize.
3. If his capital is limited, the owner can start at any scale he wants. He can also build and design facilities to meet the needs of his new business.
4. In some cases, there are no established businesses of the type the entrepreneur desires, or there are none that adequately serve a particular market.

Of course, any investigation of the feasibility of initiating a new business must include an evaluation of existing competition to determine their approach and success in doing business, as well as the consideration of the possibility that it would be wiser to buy an existing business. The entrepreneur must keep in mind that there are basically only two situations in which another business similar to an existing business is justified: (1) There are not enough firms to serve a permanently expanded market; or (2) poorly managed existing firms are not adequately serving the market.

Thus, in investigating a new business opportunity the entrepreneur must determine: (1) What products or services are needed by a particular community or communities; and, (2) whether he can supply them at a price and volume that will give him a profitable return on his time and invested capital. The rest of this chapter will be devoted to pointing out some of the key factors that should be thoroughly investigated before opening the doors of a new business.

Feasibility Study

Because prospective entrepreneurs have a natural tendency to be overly optimistic about the opportunity for their proposed venture, they should be sure that they base their decision on a careful market study. A useful market study will include objective data about the potential in the target area and the strength of the competition and should include the following considerations:[2]

Population. For most businesses, the total population is less important than certain segments of the population. For example, an entrepreneur contemplating a mobile-home development for senior citizens will naturally be interested in a particular age group.

The permanency of the population must also be considered. In markets in which employment is seasonal or cyclical, a large part of the population may be transient. Rapidly growing communities will have a larger-than-average percentage of young families, while areas with static or declining population will have a larger percentage of older employees.

The SBA suggests some of the following questions when analyzing population:

1. What has been the change in total population in the market area over the past 10 years? (A comparison of census figures will answer this question. Many city and county governments compile population figures on various geographical bases.)
2. What is the current age-group distribution in the market? How has this distribution changed? (In most areas, the age distribution of the population has been changing dramatically.)

---

[2] Most of this section is based on an excellent SBA publication: Verne A. Bunn, *Buying and Selling a Small Business* (Washington, D. C.: Small Business Administration, 1969), especially Chapter 12.

3. What is the average family size? (In many consumer-goods businesses, such as a child's clothing store, the size of the average family unit may be more important than total population.)
4. What percentage of the total population or family units are potential customers for your kind of business? (An analysis of the market for specialized goods and services may be the key to evaluating the future of your business.)
5. Will you be depending on a few large-scale buyers? (For example, if you will be selling a product or service to the industrial market, could the loss of one or two large-scale buyers win your volume?)

Income. Income is important in market analysis because changes in income are reflected in the demand patterns for goods and services. Some of the income considerations are:

1. What is the total spendable income within the market area? What is the per capita income? What is the distribution of income by income class? (A high-income area is not desirable for all consumer goods and services. For example, one of the largest family-restaurant chains has found that a market area with a mixture of income classifications — low, medium, and high — is better than an area with either low or high incomes.)
2. If you will be selling consumer goods or services, do the consumers in the trading area have a pattern of income and expenditures that will support a high level of business activity? (You need to study past trends and make future estimates.)
3. What is the level of unemployment in your target area? Is it decreasing? (Unemployment is important because of the direct effect it has on purchasing power and the psychological effect of possible unemployment.)

Competition. There is competition in one form or another in almost every market. You need to size up your competition and obtain as much knowledge as possible on their strengths and weaknesses. You need a sound basis for concluding that your new business will operate at least as efficiently as existing or potential competition. Therefore, you should make a detailed analysis of competition, determining the state of competition, the relative strength of the business within the market, and the general patterns of development and change. According to the SBA, you should ask yourself:

1. How many competitive businesses are there within the market area of the business? Where are they located? (The market area in this sense is

the trade area in which the business operates. In a retail, wholesale, or service business, this trade area may be rather narrowly defined. For example, the greatest percentage of the total sales volume for a carry-out restaurant will come from a radius of approximately 1 mile. On the other hand, in a manufacturing or mail-order business, there may be a number of markets—regional, national, and even international.)
2. How many competitive businesses have opened in this market area within the past year? (What is the reason for any increase? Can the market support all these businesses?)
3. What other kinds of businesses are in indirect competition—that is, deal to some extent in the same kind of goods or services? (The pattern of competition changes rapidly as businesses continue to add lines of merchandise, expand services offered, and create new products and services.)
4. Does poor management of existing firms lead you to believe that you can take away a sufficient part of their business? (This requires firsthand familiarity with such factors in the local situation as high prices, extensive out-of-town purchasing, slow service, high business turnover, poor workmanship, unattractive appearance of business, and high incidence of customer complaints.)

Sources of Information

The entrepreneur must recognize that every proposed business is unique and that a market analysis must therefore be designed to fit that business and the information that is economically available. For example, appraising the market potential for a manufacturing firm would be quite different from a study for a proposed retail store. The industrial market, as opposed to the consumer market, covers a wide range of purchasers, including manufacturers buying raw materials, supplies, and manufactured goods for resale or their own use, institutions, wholesalers, retailers, and governments. It is necessary, therefore, that the entrepreneur be able to clearly define his market, know its characteristics, and determine its size.

A wealth of data that will assist entrepreneurs with their business-potential analysis is available free or at a nominal cost. The annual *Statistical Abstract of the United States* is filled with national statistics covering everything from population and income expenditures to business population and turnover. The *Survey of Current Business* contains a monthly summary of the business situation, monthly business statistics on a wide range of businesses and products, and special articles on income, purchasing, buying habits, and so on. The *County and City Data Book* has data by counties and cities with over 25,000 population. It contains information on everything from the number of business establishments and their sales in a small city to the number of occupied dwellings.

In addition, various government agencies collect and publish useful market information. For example, the Bureau of Labor Statistics has data on employment, wages, and hours. The Bureau of Mines and the Department of Agriculture have data on raw materials. Entrepreneurs will also find that most trade associations and local chambers of commerce have information about geographic locations, consumer expenditures, populations, incomes, and local business conditions. Of course, if a contemplated business will be entirely new or involves a new type of product or service, direct contact with prospective customers will be an essential part of the investigation. An entrepreneur who intends to produce a component to be used by manufacturers must see that his market analysis includes comments of prospective industrial buyers about the proposed project.

The above discussion should suggest that a great deal of thought, planning, and investigation needs to be undertaken by the entrepreneur to determine the feasibility of a proposed venture. As a popular small business text notes:

> The preliminary consequences of inadequate investigation and planning are (1) poor business location, (2) inadequate sales potential, (3) unplanned or ill-planned distribution procedures, (4) working capital shortage, and (5) crushingly strong competition. . . . The ultimate consequence to be expected is business failure.[3]

Incident 6: What's It Worth?

Pete Smith was trying to get out of his bank inconspicuously when Bill Weston, the branch manager, called him over. It was embarrassing, because one of Sam's payroll checks had bounced, and Pete had had to do a bit of scrambling to cover it. He thought he had enough cash in the account, and only because a customer had been willing to make a $500 deposit on some work had he been able to cover it.

"Yes, Mr. Weston?" Pete said.

"Sit down, Pete. I'd like to talk to you."

Oh, boy, Pete thought, here it comes. Is writing a bum check a felony? The embarrassment of it was that it was his fault. He had just added up the column wrong. "Yes, sir?"

"Pete, you've been in business now for over a year, right?"

"Yes, sir, about fourteen months."

"You've never asked us for credit."

---

[3] K. N. Broom and Justin G. Longenecker, *Small Business Management*, 3rd. ed. (Cincinnati: South-Western Publishing, 1971), p. 144.

"Well, I really didn't need it. That is, I didn't see how I could qualify."

"Your account has been active enough. Apparently you've been doing pretty good business."

"Sure, the gross is great, Mr. Weston, but the profits are not so hot. Somehow, the minute I start doing well, some expense seems to wipe it all out."

"Have you ever been in business before, Pete?"

"No, and sometimes I wish I wasn't in it now."

"Why?"

Pete felt that it might be good to talk to Mr. Weston about his business worries. "Well, I'm a body man, and a good one. I started this business because I could see that a real craftsman could make money by restoring old cars. And I was right—we charge good prices for our work, and after a shaky start, we have plenty of work. But somehow, no matter how much I make, we always seem to come out behind."

"Pete, I'm a banker, not a technician, but I may be able to help out on the business side. How much did you gross last year?"

"Oh, around thirty-eight thousand."

"Around? Aren't you sure?"

Pete sighed. "I work in the shop, and my wife tries to keep our records. But she's working, too, and we never seem to have enough time to get our books in shape."

"Do you have a profit-and-loss statement?"

"Well, sort of."

"How about a balance sheet?"

"Well, I'm not too sure how to do one."

This time Mr. Weston sighed. "I don't suppose that you have a budget for this year?"

"No, Mr. Weston, we just try to spend less than we get—and that's tough enough."

"How much equipment do you have?"

"Oh, maybe it's worth five thousand—I'm not sure."

"Did you take depreciation last year on it when you filled out your tax form?"

"You know, Mr. Weston, I wanted to ask you about that. When I filled out the form, I noticed that line, and there was a big section in the rules about it. But I never quite figured out what it was all about. So I took two hundred dollars and hoped that the government wouldn't notice."

"They wouldn't, Pete." Mr. Weston leaned back. "Look, Pete, one thing we make money on is lending money. I like to find new, solid companies to lend money to—it's my job. But you're not very solid right now, even though you seem to have found a pretty good thing. Can you drop by my house tomorrow night? Bring along your records. Maybe I can help out by showing you what a bank expects from a businessman. If you can get your business in shape, not only will you make money, but maybe we will too. It would be nice to know that you are going to be rich, fat, and happy—to say nothing about the money we just might make if you get into good shape."

1. Attachment 6-1 shows the records Pete took over to Mr. Weston the next night. Put them in good shape as one would expect a firm to have them.
2. In the discussion with Mr. Weston, Pete figured that he would gross $47,000 next year and that to do this, he would have to hire one extra man at $140 per week (for 50 weeks). He also expected to spend about $1,500 more than last year for parts, paints, and supplies. Make up a cash budget for Pete and show what he might earn.

Gross revenue – $38,072 (cash)

Receivable – $2,126 (maybe $427 is a bad debt??)

Wages to Sam $10,060
{ Social Security taxes (not paid yet) $256
  Employers

State Sales Tax (paid) $1,326

Bought a paint sprayer for $628 – paid cash

Rent $300 Month

80 hours a week for this?!!

Legal fee on that zoning problem – $600

Utilities – Gas & Electricity – $86 per month

Tools owned – maybe $4,250 worth new – most were used when we started. (Not counting new stuff bought during year.)

Sam needed a stripping outfit for $188 – bought it for cash in February.

Sandblaster – $772 – bought in May

Supplies, paint, and equipment – $12,357 (owe only $221 of bills – rest paid)

Bought a power body jack in January $1,342

Property Taxes – on equipment & such $401

Used wheel aligner (good deal) – paid $165 cash in May

Insurance – Fire, etc. $277 (paid)

Unemployment & Workmans Comp insurance – $196 (paid)

Repayment of loan – Martha's Dad $500 cash

Telephone bills for year – $210

Miscellaneous Expense – Postage, paper, forms, etc. $207

I kept the rest – what little there was of it!

Pete Smith

Attachment 6-1. Pete's Records

3. If you were interested in buying this business from Pete, what would you pay for it, given these records? Why?

Discussion Questions

1. State and evaluate the reasons for buying an existing business rather than starting a new one.
2. To what degree is risk minimized by buying an existing business?
3. Under what conditions would you prefer to start a new business rather than buy an existing business?
4. Outline and briefly explain the steps to take when evaluating a business for sale.
5. How would you determine the value of goodwill?
6. Distinguish between the asset-appraisal method and the capitalizing-future-earnings method of determining the price for a business. Which method is more desirable?
7. How would you go about determining the fair price for a business? What role, if any, would your present earning power play in your evaluation of the business?
8. List the various ways a seller could distort the amount of profit he actually has. What suggestions do you have for the buyer to overcome each of these?
9. What are some of the major items to include in the sales agreement?
10. Under what conditions can another business similar to an existing business be justified? Explain.
11. Outline the major items to consider in a feasibility study for a new business.
12. What questions would you want answered about competition for your new venture?
13. Can the same market analysis be used for different types of businesses. Why or why not?
14. Develop a list of information sources that would be helpful for an analysis of business potential.

Suggested Readings

Broom, H. N., and Longenecker, Justin G., *Small Business Management*, 3rd. ed. Cincinnati: South-Western Publishing, 1971. Ch. 7.

Bunn, Verne A., *Buying and Selling a Small Business.* Washington, D. C.: Small Business Administration, 1969.

Colley, Donald G., "Buying a Small Going Concern," *Small Marketers Aids Annual No. 2.* Washington, D. C.: Small Business Administration, 1960. Pp. 15–21.

Gould, G. H. B., and Coddington, Dean C., "How Do You Know What Your Business Is Worth?" *Management Aids,* No. 166. Washington, D. C.: Small Business Administration, 1964.

"How to Buy or Sell a Business," *Small Business Reporter* 8, No. 11. San Francisco: Bank of America, Small Business Advisory Service, 1969.

"How to Go About Buying a Business," *Changing Times,* The Kiplinger Magazine, February 1971.

Huff, David L., "Defining and Estimating a Trading Area," *Journal of Marketing* XXVIII (July 1964), 34–38.

Kelley, Pearce C., Lawyer, Kenneth, and Baumback, Clifford, *How to Organize and Operate a Small Business,* 4th ed. Englewood Cliffs, N. J.: Prentice-Hall, 1968. Ch. 5 and 6.

McKenna, Francis, *Starting and Managing a Small Drive-in Restaurant.* Washington, D. C.: Small Business Administration, 1972.

Metcalf, Wendell O., *Starting and Managing a Small Business of Your Own,* Vol. 1, 2nd ed. Washington, D. C.: Small Business Administration, 1962.

Robinson, Roland L., *Financing the Dynamic Small Firm.* Belmont, Calif.: Wadsworth, 1966.

Sanzo, Richard, *Ratio Analysis for Small Business.* Washington, D. C.: Small Business Administration, 1970.

Soloman, Martin B., Jr., *Investment Decisions in Small Business.* Lexington, Ky.: University of Kentucky Press, 1963.

Steinmetz, Lawrence, Kline, John B., and Stegall, Donald P., *Managing the Small Business.* Homewood, Ill.: Richard D. Irwin, 1968. Ch. 7.

Choosing a Location and Form of Organization

Chapter 7

The location of a business is usually a key element in its profitability. One real-estate expert has grouped the factors influencing business locational decisions into three catagories:

1. Cost factors: land, labor, material, and transportation.
2. Demand factors: extent of the market, location of competitors, sales potential.
3. Intangible factors: preferences for particular environment, security, other personal and family considerations.[1]

In addition, the various locational factors will vary significantly with the kind of business venture. For example, retailers and most service businesses need to be "where the action is" for maximum exposure and identity; wholesalers and manufacturers must be close to loading and unloading points. But all potential entrepreneurs, regardless of the kind of business, need to start their location analysis with an outline of their present and future needs. Once this is completed, the entrepreneur can set out to find a location that meets these requirements. Normally, the choice of a location depends on three major decisions: (1) selection of a town or city, (2) selection of an area within the town or city, and (3) selection of a site within that area.

---

[1] Paul F. Wendt, "Deciding on Location for a Small Business," *Journal of Small Business Management* (January 1972), p. 1.

Selecting a Town or City

Many small businessmen prefer to locate in their own hometown. This, of course, has certain advantages. For example, credit is easier to get, provided they have established good credit references. Similarly, friends and acquaintances can give them valuable word-of-mouth publicity and/or patronage. On the other hand, experience has shown that locating in one's hometown is no guarantee of success. Few people have a wide enough circle of influential friends to make a business succeed on that basis alone. At the same time, personal factors may limit the entrepreneur's range of choice to some specific region or city.

In choosing between a metropolitan area or a less densely populated area, the businessman might consider the following information gathered by the Small Business Administration:

Firms best suited for being in nonmetropolitan small areas tend to be those which:

1. Require fewer skills at the outset.
2. Are oriented more to the assembly of purchased parts than to the fabrication of those parts.
3. Are faced with low profit margins in their industry and, therefore, must keep out-of-pocket costs down.
4. Use mostly catalog-ordered or standard raw materials.
5. Have utility requirements that are not unusual in any way.
6. Do not find it necessary to have professional or technical men attached closely to the facilities.
7. Have customers who do not normally visit the business.

The businessman's knowledge of his product or service, and the information derived from his market analysis, will suggest certain things to consider when choosing a town or city. He will need to consider nearness to the market, nearness to the source of materials (especially important in manufacturing), availability of certain kinds of labor, wage rates and general labor environment, and population and income trends. He will also find that some local industrial-development groups, in an effort to attract new business (especially manufacturing or research), will offer tax concessions and financial assistance in building. Inducements such as tax breaks and free sites should be cautiously scrutinized if other factors in the city or town are unfavorable.

The importance of giving considerable time and effort to locating a business cannot be overemphasized. One intensive study of eighty-one small retail and service firms during their critical first 2 years of operation revealed that:

> The choice of location was frequently based on such reasons as vacancy of premises, nearness to home, familiarity with the neighborhood, and availability of a business for sale. Too often these reasons appeared to the owners as good and sufficient; they did not bother to make any objective evaluation of the locations' potential as business sites. Failing to do so, some overlooked the fact that the area was declining—that is, losing population or being bypassed because of new highway construction, or that it was unsuited for the type of goods or services offered. In some instances, the business was too specialized, and in others, the same goods or services were already adequately supplied by other firms.[2]

The study found that within 2 years, forty of the eighty-one firms under study had closed their doors and that others were "marginal closures."

Selecting an Area within the Town or City

The size of the town or city and the type of business will to a great extent determine the area to locate in. For example, if the town is very small and the business will engage in retailing or service activities, there may be little choice but to select a downtown area or a shopping center on the outskirts of town. Other constraints are availability of land and/or buildings that meet current requirements and provide for expected expansion; governmental restrictions, such as zoning laws, that prohibit establishing certain businesses in particular locations; and existence of local competition in the desired area.

When considering an area in which to locate his business, the entrepreneur should always take the future into consideration. For example, is there any possibility that the status of the location will change in the foreseeable future? Will there be urban-renewal programs, flood-control projects, military-defense uses, or rezoning that might reduce the feasibility of locating in a given area?

In selecting an area, the entrepreneur must be concerned with the kind of business he will be in and the amount and kind of traffic needed to sustain it. For example, let us assume an entrepreneur is in the process of selecting an area for a limited-menu "take-out" restaurant. He might begin by obtaining a map, preferably a population-density map (obtainable from the city-planning commission or the local chamber of commerce), or census-tract information (from the local post office), and research the area for adequate density. Next, he might mark off on the map the low-, medium-, and high-income residential areas and look for the areas of mixed income classes. (For this type of business, a mixture of low-, medium-, and high-income groups is more desirable than

---

[2] Kurt B. Mayer and Sidney Goldstein, *The First Two Years: Problems of Small Firm Growth and Survival* (Washington, D. C.: Small Business Administration, 1961).

either a low- or high-income area.) He will then seek out apartment complexes or high-density, single-residence areas in which many of the couples are young, with both husband and wife working—prime areas for "take-out" restaurants. Ideally, retail stores and office buildings should be nearby, since they generate necessary traffic. It will also be desirable for his business to be in an area of compatible (not competitive) types of food establishments rather than being isolated from existing food traffic. Few, if any, areas will have all of these characteristics, but the more there are, the more desirable the area.

Rental costs in the areas being considered are also important factors in the location decision. While a businessman may not be able to afford to overextend himself with an expensive lease in a "good" location, he should also avoid taking a poor location just because of low rent. Consider, for example, two locations for a retail establishment. One is a well-populated suburban community and easily accessible to the market area. Pedestrian and motor-vehicle traffic is moderately heavy. One site in the area has a large regional shopping center adjoining it, with a theater, department stores, and other smaller stores. The rent at this location, which contains 20,000 square feet of ground, is $1,000 a month.

About a mile away, there is another location of the same size. It is on a state road, and there is a small community business area nearby. This second site rents for $750 a month. The first location has projected gross sales of $25,000 a month; the second, $15,000. Which location would you choose?

The following table carries the analysis of the two locations a little further:

	First Location	Second Location
Rent per month	$ 1,000	$ 750
Projected gross sales per month	$ 25,000	$ 15,000
Rent as a percent of sales	4%	5%
Projected gross sales per year	$300,000	$180,000
Projected net income before taxes at 10 to 12 percent of sales	$ 30,000 to $ 36,000	$ 18,000 to $ 21,600

Another factor, of course, is the amount of money an entrepreneur can invest. Suppose he chose the first location. He would then have to build and equip a business large enough to handle the greater volume of sales. He must ask himself whether his market analysis indicates enough potential to attain this sales volume, as well as whether he will have enough money left to pay his business and personal expenses while building up his sales to this level.

Selecting a Site within the Town or City

After deciding to locate in an area within a given community, the entrepreneur's next decision will be to select a site within that specific area. It is at this point that expensive mistakes are frequently made. He must pay close attention to such things as comparative cost of construction or lease, zoning regulations, accessibility of inter- and intracity transportation, availability of proper utilities, and parking facilities. In each instance he needs to ask himself "What do I need? What is available? What can I afford?"

Usually it is unwise to buy an existing structure or to build a new one during the early stages of a business if there is a possibility of renting a building that is in a good location and if it can be remodeled to meet the requirements of the business. To buy or build requires a heavy drain on initial capital. Of course, if the business has some unusual requirements, it may be necessary to build. But even in this case, a real-estate company or a firm specializing in building investments will erect a building for lease by the new business.

The entrepreneur may want to obtain an expert to assist him in some technical aspects of site location. Also, he should not overlook valuable free assistance from such sources as area-development departments of banks, cities, utilities, and railroads, as well as the Small Business Administration. In the last analysis, however, the decision must be made by the entrepreneur. For he needs to determine a location most beneficial to his business as well as satisfactory for his personal life.

Businesses may be put into two general categories, for site selection. In one group are those firms, such as retail and service establishments, whose location must be customer-oriented. In another group are firms, such as manufacturers and most wholesalers, whose location decision is heavily influenced by nearness to certain required resources or by site-related costs (purchase and operating costs of a particular site) rather than by customer accessibility. Let us briefly examine some of the special considerations for each group.

Retail and service business. Unless a business has a product or service sufficiently in demand to attract customers, it must locate where the customer wants to shop. Service establishments, such as barbershops and real-estate offices, usually do well on inside locations, as do retail stores catering to patrons who shop around for baked goods, gifts, and hardware items. Drugstores and stores selling convenience items warrant, and are usually willing to pay, a premium rate for a corner location.

Some businesses—such as brokerage firms and optical, dental, and surgical supply firms—can be operated just as well from an office or showroom located above or below street level. Rents for such locations generally run from 40 to 50 percent lower than they do for street-level spaces. In general, off-street locations can be used where retail merchandising (in the usual sense) is a minor part of the operation or not a part at all. If a store offers unusual services or particularly attractive merchandise—furriers, jewelers, low-price clothing dealers, and repair shops—such locations may also be acceptable. Certain types of restaurants, coffeehouses, and nightclubs have found such locations advantageous because of the atmosphere of privacy or intimacy they may convey. In general, however, an above-street level carries greater prestige than a basement location.

For a retail or service business, including a restaurant operation, it is important to check the site for existing competition, traffic flow, parking facilities, street location, physical aspect of the building, type of lease, and the history of the site. The entrepreneur should ask the following questions about the site history: Has the building remained vacant for any length of time? If so, why? Have various types of businesses occupied it for short periods? If so, the site probably should be avoided. Moreover, vacant buildings are generally regarded as bad neighbors, so investigate the status of unoccupied buildings next door.

Consider the following directions given by a large "take-out" restaurant franchisor to its franchisees as an example of the importance of site selection to a large firm:

> Once you have selected the proper trade area, you must select the specific property within the area that will be large enough to allow the proper positioning of your building and allow adequate and uncrowded parking in the front or on the side of your building. Avoid "rear parking" only locations. No one, especially women, likes to "park in back." Adequate frontage is necessary so that cars can easily drive in and pull out onto the main thoroughfare. The store and sign should be easily seen from a distance—*do not even consider hidden locations*. A corner location is preferable, but good "inside" locations can be found. Generally, an inside location will require more frontage than a corner site in order to have good visibility and access. Beware of corner locations in high traffic areas that are "traffic bound" during your prime hours. Traffic that consistently backs up to block your driveways will discourage prospective customers.
>
> Seek locations that large numbers of people must pass going to and from home. It is easier to stop people en route home from work, from shopping, etc., than it is to draw them away from their accustomed routes. Generally, the better side of the street would be the "going home side" and the "afternoon shady side." The ability to make both a left and right hand turn from the major traffic artery into the property is most important for high volume. Beware of the one-way street or divided highway with no cross-over. The normal traffic speed at the site should be such that it is reasonably easy to get into your parking lot. You should be sure to study the traffic flow at your proposed site during the prime evening hours—5:00 to 8:00 P.M.

Wholesale and manufacturing businesses. Since many traditional wholesale functions have been absorbed as part of large-scale business operation, the typical small wholesaler is likely to be engaged in more specialized types of operations than past wholesalers. As a result, different types of wholesalers have somewhat different location needs. For example, small wholesalers who make truck deliveries or who have traveling salesmen have different site-selection problems from the wholesaler doing "store" business (that is, his retail buyers visit the warehouse). In the first case, the wholesaler needs to select a site near the center of the desired trading area in order to minimize the distance traveled by trucks and salesmen. A slight difference in the travel distance between two potential sites may very well be the deciding factor in selecting one location.

In many cities, central wholesale districts have developed as a result of proximity to transportation facilities. If accessibility to customers, suppliers, or transportation necessitates a central-district site, the wholesaler can expect to pay a higher rent than another wholesaler locating outside of the central district. In brief, while many factors may be mentioned for selecting a site, the small wholesaler should basically try to locate where his overhead will be low and where he can efficiently service his customer as quickly as his specialty may dictate.

While the small manufacturer must consider many of the same factors facing the wholesaler (transportation, suppliers, and so on), he has considerably more flexibility in his site selection. For one thing, small-scale manufacturing usually does not require a particular kind of location, which allows the manufacturer more freedom in choosing among buildings and plant facilities. A poor choice of location, however, may lead to a shortage of skilled manpower or high transportation costs for moving raw materials or finished products. On the other hand, a strategic location can give a substantial edge over competition.

When making a plant location decision, it is advisable to begin by writing down the exact requirements. This would include:

1. Current and future market. Where are major customers located, and what percentage of total cost is in freight?
2. Raw material requirements. Is frontage on a railroad siding necessary because of large shipping volume?
3. Labor needs. Will adequate skilled labor be available, and at a suitable wage?
4. Utility requirements. Is water used for cooling in the production process?
5. Present tax load. Are the local real-estate and property taxes on machinery and inventory favorable?

These factors, of course, are only general considerations in locating any type of manufacturing venture. Particular industries or situations may require other considerations. For example, a small electronics firm might well consider a location on the West Coast where the engineering and technical skills are concentrated. Similarly, a production process with unusual nuisance problems (odors or noise) might be excluded from desirable areas.

The complexity of factors involved in the location decision can be minimized by determining the comparative costs of the alternative locations. Basically, this process involves comparison of three major manufacturing costs:

1. *Cost of inputs.* The cost of materials at their source and the cost of transporting from that source.
2. *Cost of conversion.* Including operating costs and taxes. The operating costs include the total cost of labor, utilities, rent (or depreciation), insurance, and equipment costs.
3. *Cost of distribution.* The expense of maintaining and transporting finished goods.

The optimum or best location then becomes a compromise among alternatives. For example, a location in which both input and conversion costs are lowest may be rejected because of unusually high distribution costs.

There are a number of quantitative techniques that can be employed to aid the decision maker in evaluating some of the considerations in plant or warehouse location. One such technique, linear programming, is discussed later in this book. A small company, which serviced an area 15 miles wide and had sixty-five trucks, used linear programming in their plant-location decision. It was determined that a plant located only 3 miles off-center from the optimum site would result in an increase in distribution costs of $15,000 per year to the company.

Buying or Leasing Land for a Site

According to one expert, an entrepreneur considering a vacant site for his business should investigate the following aspects of the site:[3]

1. Is the land zoned, or can it be zoned, for commercial use?
2. If the land is zoned for commercial use, does the zoning permit your type of business?

---

[3] Adapted from Francis X. McKenna, *Starting and Managing a Small Business Drive-In Restaurant* (Washington, D. C.: Small Business Administration, 1972), pp. 19–20.

3. Are there any covenants on the land that would ban your type of business?
4. Do building restrictions require specific setbacks from streets and side lines?
5. Are electric signs permitted on the property? What regulations govern them?
6. Are there any easements on the land that would restrict its use?
7. Is any street widening planned that would reduce the size of the site?
8. Is the land at street level, above street level, or below street level? Customers prefer commercial property on a level with the street.
9. Can curbs be cut for driveway access to the site?
10. Are sewer, water, gas, electricity, police protection, and fire protection available?
11. If no sewer is available, is the soil suitable for a septic tank?
12. What are the real-estate, sewer, water, and other taxes?

If the site is unimproved, the entrepreneur has a choice: (1) He may be able to purchase or lease the land as it is, or (2) the owner may be willing to build the structures and improve the grounds and then lease the entire property to him. If the landlord wants to sell the land as is, the entrepreneur may want to look for a real-estate investor who would be willing to purchase the land, improve it to his specifications, and lease it to him. As mentioned earlier in the chapter, if he can lease improved property, the entrepreneur can avoid tying up his capital in real estate.

Source for Location Assistance

All too frequently, the entrepreneur "goes it alone" when confronted with the task of selecting a location for his business. This need not be the case since there are many sources of assistance. While some sources, such as consulting firms, may be expensive, other sources are available for a very nominal fee— or even free. The following is intended as a brief guide to some of these sources:

Trade associations. There are over 2,000 trade associations in this country, covering nearly every conceivable line of business. Most trade associations provide some sort of location assistance or information to their members. For example, the Oklahoma Restaurant Association has had computer-based mathematical models developed for evaluating restaurant sites. This service, which is available to anyone through the restaurant association in their state for a small fee, will project the annual gross sales of certain types of food-service operations within 5 percent, plus or minus, 95 percent of the time. The service can evaluate hamburger, general, specialty, drive-in, cafeteria, chicken carry-out, and taco-specialty restaurants.

Industrial-development departments.[4]   Most electric and gas utilities, railroads, and state development agencies have industrial-development departments. For no charge, these departments can provide the small manufacturer with the following types of information:

1. Data about a community or site, including such information as land costs, taxes, availability of raw materials and labor, topography, and market potential.
2. Special studies for industrial prospects, such as water studies for chemical plants and hardwood availability for furniture manufacturers.
3. Transportation, power, and communication facilities in the area.
4. Liaison with the necessary business and government people in the community to help find out how to get zoning changed or utility lines extended.

Chambers of commerce.   While many chambers of commerce have been criticized for "overselling" their communities, nevertheless, they can be one of the best sources of current community data. In addition, they are in a position to put the new small businessman in touch with necessary business personnel, such as local bankers or realtors.

Consultants.   The large firm frequently hires a consultant or consulting firm to assist with its location problems. While hiring a site-location consultant is likely to be expensive, it is not necessarily out of reach for the small businessman. For one thing, he can usually employ the consultant to undertake only part of his location project if his funds are very limited. Also, of the many sources of assistance available, the consultant is probably in the best position to give you an impartial recommendation.

Other sources.   Since they are acquainted with local markets, distributors and manufacturers can provide information about market potential for specific areas. University bureaus of business and economic research frequently en-

---

[4] See James H. Thompson, "The Small Manufacturer's Guide to Plant Location Services," *Journal of Small Business Management* (January 1972), pp. 5–10.

gage in business studies of the region or community they serve and can provide valuable data about the area. Many of these bureaus will "contract" with businessmen to provide a location study for a business.

Field offices of the Department of Commerce and the Small Business Administration, while typically understaffed, can help in selecting a location, or at least suggest other places to contact. Still other sources would include realtors, bankers, and other local businessmen.

Form of Organization

The legal form of a business affects taxes, the division of profits, risks, the amount of capital raised, and many types of managerial decisions. Basically, there are three forms of legal organization for the small business: the sole proprietorship, the partnership, and the corporation. There was a time when going into business involved little more than finding a location and hanging out a sign, but this was before the dawn of licenses, franchises, taxes, lease-back arrangements, capital gains, preferred stock issues, workmen's compensation, and large liability settlements.

Sole Proprietorship

This form of legal organization is the most common form for small businesses. It is the easiest way to get started and in many circumstances is the most efficient and most economical way of doing business. Starting a business as a sole proprietorship usually requires no more of the owner than that he find out if he needs a license and if he has to pay a state tax. The sole proprietor *is* the business. The proprietor's business and personal assets are the same for income-tax purposes; if the business is sued, he is personally sued.

This form of legal organization has several advantages for the small businessman:

1. It can be established quickly and with very little cost.
2. Decisions can be implemented quickly without having to clear them with partners or a board of directors.
3. The owner can avoid corporate reports, capital stock taxes, and the "double tax" when profits are distributed.
4. Business losses and other deductions can be offset directly against other personal income.
5. It has minimum legal restrictions and can be terminated as easily as it began.

Unfortunately, there are also a few severe limitations to the sole proprietorship:

1. It is usually more difficult to attract outside capital into this form of enterprise.
2. The entrepreneur is personally liable for all debts of the business; thus, his home, automobile, and other personal property is subject to creditors' claims.
3. A one-man business seldom has all the talents and resources necessary for a dynamic, growing enterprise. Similarly, serious illness or injury to the owner can mean the downfall of the business.

The Partnership

This form of organization is an association of two or more individuals who enter business to share in profits and losses. The most important feature of a partnership is that each partner can legally bind and obligate the other(s). Therefore, if an entrepreneur has any reservations about the integrity or ability of a potential partner, he should stay away from a partnership.

The partnership resembles the proprietorship more closely than it does the corporation, but it has certain advantages over both which make it more desirable for some businesses. Some of the advantages of partnerships include:

1. Like the sole proprietorship, it is relatively simple to establish or to terminate; business losses are deductible from the personal income of each partner; and government regulations are minimal.
2. If the partners are skilled in different phases of the business, they may complement each other and thus have a greater chance of success.
3. The combined financial resources of all the partners provide strong support for capital acquisition.
4. Since the personal assets of corporate owners are usually beyond the reach of creditors, and since there are at least two owners in the partnership, creditors have more collateral to support their loan under the partnership form. Therefore, in a new venture, partnerships probably enjoy the best credit rating.

There are, however, certain significant limitations to this legal form of organization:

1. By law, each partner can bind and obligate the other. Thus, each partner is personally liable for the actions or conduct of any one of the other partners.
2. Death or withdrawal of any of the partners can mean that the partnership must be dissolved and the business liquidated or reorganized.
3. Proper division of work and harmonious relationships between partners are often difficult to maintain.

The Corporation

The corporation is an independent legal and tax entity and, unlike the partnership and proprietorship, continues even if its officers and/or stockholders change. Being a legal entity, the corporation can sue and be sued and can enter into contracts. In many small firms, the officers, board of directors, and stockholders are all the same people. If one individual owns the majority stock, he can control the firm as effectively as if he were a sole proprietor.

Advantages of the corporate form are:

1. The liability of a stockholder is limited to the amount of stock owned.
2. Ownership interest, represented by the shares of stock, can be easily transferred.
3. The business continues to exist despite death or incapacity of other owners.
4. The corporate form lends itself to more efficient management. For example, management can be concentrated, or even in the hands of professional managers, even though ownership is widespread.
5. The corporation has various tax options available to it, and in some cases can even choose to be taxed as a partnership.
6. Since the corporation can offer the investor limited liability, flexibility in moving in and out of ownership, and continued life, capital is more readily obtainable.

At the same time, there are problems involved with the corporate form:

1. A corporation can be expensive to form. At the onset (when entrepreneurs are most in need of funds), the cost of filing (based on the value of the stock, franchise tax, and attorney fees) can amount to several hundred dollars.
2. The advantage of limited liability may not exist for the new or very small corporation since creditors may require major stockholders to guarantee all payables and loans.

3. If earnings are allowed to accumulate unreasonably, or if a large portion of the earnings is from investment income, the corporation may be faced with a larger special tax.
4. Minority stockholders, unless they can prove fraud or mismanagement, may have little to say about important managerial decisions.
5. The corporation is subject to more government regulations, more control, and more recordkeeping than any other legal form.
6. Corporate activities are limited to those specifically granted in the charter. Similarly, the geographic area of operations is limited to the incorporating state unless permission is obtained from other states. To obtain permission means additional licensing and regulations.

Choosing a Legal Structure

As already suggested, the entrepreneur has a wide range of considerations before deciding on the proper legal form of organization. In addition to personal tax situation, the Small Business Administration suggests six main points to consider:[5]

1. Costs and procedures in starting. Sole proprietorships are the easiest and cheapest to get started. Partnerships can also be started relatively simply. The corporation is the most complicated and costly form to initiate. It can be created only by following the strict legal procedures of the state in which it is incorporated. Owners who are unfamiliar with the procedure will have attorney fees as well as a franchise tax and filing fees.

2. Size of the risk. The degree to which investors in an enterprise risk legal liability for the debts of the business is a cardinal consideration. Regardless of legal structure, creditors are always entitled to be paid out of business assets before any equity capital is withdrawn. In cases in which those assets are insufficient, the extent to which owners can be compelled to meet creditors' claims out of their own pockets varies with the type of organization.

A sole proprietor is personally liable for all debts of his business to the extent of his entire property and cannot restrict his liability in any way. Similarly, each member of a partnership is fully responsible for all debts owed by

---

[5] The following is a condensation of Edward L. Anthony, "Choosing the Legal Structure for Your Firm," *Management Aids for Small Manufacturers*, No. 5 (Washington, D. C.: Small Business Administration, 1963), pp. 11–15.

his partnership irrespective of the amount of his own investment in the business. Corporations have a real advantage, as far as risk goes, over other legal structures. Creditors can force payment on their claims only to the limit of the company's assets. Thus, while a shareholder may lose the money he put into the company, he cannot be forced to contribute additional funds out of his own pocket to meet business debts. However, major stockholders in a new or very small firm may have to personally guarantee all loans.

3. Continuity of the concern. While sole proprietorships have no time limit on them by law, they are not fundamentally perpetual. Illness of the owner may damage the business, and his death ends it. Partnerships are perishable in the same general sense in that they are terminated by the death or withdrawal of any one of the partners. Corporations have the most permanent legal structure of all, for they have a separate continuous life of their own. Moreover, the certificates of stock, which represent investments and ownership in the business, may be transferred from one person to another without hampering the concern's operations.

4. Adaptability of administration. In the sole proprietorship, policy and operations reside in one individual. This situation can be good or bad depending on the managerial skills of the proprietor. In a partnership, the combined abilities and knowledge of several executives may be an advantage if harmonious relations exist. But the division of functional responsibility among the partners can also lead to fundamental policy disagreements that can be harmful to the business. In a corporation, the stockholders do not necessarily participate either in operations or in policy formulation, but they may. Often, however, those functions are centralized in a relatively small group of executives who own only a small percentage of the shares.

5. Influences of applicable laws. The sole proprietorship is the oldest and most widespread business legal structure. As a result, little doubt remains about the laws regulating its legal rights and obligations. Therefore, a private citizen working in Iowa can carry on business in Kansas without paying any greater taxes or incurring any more obligations in Kansas than do local Kansas businessmen. Broadly speaking, this situation is also true for a partnership.

Corporations, however, owe their legal life solely to the state in which they are organized. No other state is required to recognize them. To be sure, all states do permit out-of-state corporations to function inside their boundaries. Nevertheless, out-of-state corporations must always comply with special in-state obligations. Also, corporations are regulated by numerous laws within their state that vary considerably and have been interpreted differently in different places. Therefore, in running a corporation effectively, competent legal counsel is virtually indispensable.

6. Attraction of additional capital. Every business may require additional funds from time to time to carry on operations. And if it can't obtain adequate capital, it may well be headed for failure. In proprietorships, the owner may raise additional money by borrowing, by purchasing on credit, and by investing additional amounts himself. Since he is personally liable for all the debts of his business, banks and suppliers will look carefully at his personal wealth. Consequently, the funds he can get will always be limited by his own circumstances. For this reason alone, a business requiring large amounts of capital for successful operation should probably not be organized as a single proprietorship.

Partnerships can often raise funds with greater ease, since the resources of all partners are combined in a single undertaking. Corporations are usually in the best position to attract capital. For example, they can acquire additional funds by pledging corporate assets to borrow money. Also, they can sell securities to the public and attract a wide range of investors.

In summary, when choosing a form of business organization the small businessman must keep in mind that no one form is suited to each and every small business. In most cases, however, choosing among a sole proprietorship, partnership, or corporation is a two-way rather than a three-way choice. As one expert points out:

> If the promoter of a small business can supply his own capital, he can choose between a proprietorship or a corporation. If the promoter must bring in some outside capital, then he has a choice between a partnership or a corporation. In practice, the partnership is practical only between those with roughly equal net worths starting with some knowledge of one another. The corporation is almost the only way to attract investors not initially known to the promoter. If both alternatives are available in practice, tax considerations will dominate the choice made.[6]

Tax considerations are complicated and the entrepreneur would be wise to have a tax consultant or qualified attorney examine the tax consequences of alternative choices of business organization. Since almost every aspect of business taxation has an exception or modification, it would be meaningless to

---

[6] Roland S. Robinson, *Financing the Dynamic Small Firm* (Belmont, Calif.: Wadsworth, 1966), pp. 26–27.

attempt any generalizations on the tax consequences of the legal forms of organization. Much will depend on such factors as the income level of the business, the tax bracket of the owner, and the number and income goals of other owners.

Finally, when a legal form has been decided upon, the decision should never be viewed as final. The business will grow and its needs will change; the owner's goals and income may change; tax laws are ever changing; and new owners may buy the business. As these changes occur, the entrepreneur needs to reexamine the suitability of continuing under the existing legal form.

Incident 7: You Can't Get There from Here—Or Can You?

"Now what are you worrying about, Pete?" Martha asked.

Pete continued to figure on his scratch pad. "I'm wondering if we're in the right place. Somehow I think we're not."

"Why not? We have a nice shop."

"Yeah, but it used to be an ordinary auto repair shop that had to be close in to get business."

"What are you getting at?"

Pete scratched out some numbers. "We pay $300 a month rent. It's a high price for our space, but it's close in. Now, the way I figure, we could be almost anywhere—in fact, I'm not even sure we should be in town."

"Well, you sure get customers from all over."

"That's a fact," Pete agreed, "because the work we do is so special. Last week Mr. Perkins brought his Packard in from Chicago—over eight hundred miles. There aren't many shops like ours, and the customers are willing to go almost anywhere."

"But most of your business is local."

"So far. But we're planning to place those ads in national magazines, and if we do, we may get even broader business than we're already getting."

"So what are you thinking?"

"There's a shop for rent out in Swath Crossing for $150 a month, and it's bigger than ours."

"But honey, that's eighteen miles from here. And the place is dying."

Pete nodded. "Exactly. That's why the shop is cheap. But I'm beginning to think that we need more space, and this shop has it. Besides, there's lots of space around it for parking and storage."

"But Pete you mentioned that you were thinking of selling parts. How about that?"

"That's the part that has me worried. I just don't know how far old car owners will go to get what they want. If they're willing to go miles, it doesn't matter. But if they want convenience, then this new deal is a bad one."

"Well, I'll trust your decision."

1. Should Pete move? Why or why not?
2. Where do you think old car owners are likely to be? Why?

3. How far is an owner of a 1929 Chevrolet likely to go to find a badly needed part? Why?
4. How far is a man who wants his 1926 Chrysler restored likely to travel to get it done right, since he will spend between $1,000 and $5,000 for the job? Why?

Discussion Questions

1. What role should personal and family considerations play in the location decision?
2. How would you start your location analysis for your business?
3. List and briefly discuss any factors not mentioned in the chapter that should be considered in selecting a location.
4. Give several examples of firms best suited for locating in a nonmetropolitan small area. Explain.
5. Outline the steps you would take in selecting an area within a medium-size city for a "take-out" type restaurant.
6. Is it better to buy or to build a structure for a new business? Why?
7. How do site factors differ for a small industrial firm and a retailer? For a small wholesaler and a service firm?
8. What are some of the things any potential entrepreneur should consider before buying or leasing land for a building site?
9. How would the location assistance received from a utility company, a location consultant, and the local chamber of commerce differ? Explain.
10. Discuss the pros and cons of organizing a small business as a sole proprietorship.
11. Compare the three major forms of legal organization from the viewpoint of management control for the owner.
12. "The entrepreneur is always able to get more capital by organizing under the corporate form." Do you agree? Why or why not?
13. Briefly discuss the factors you would want to consider when choosing the legal structure for your business venture.
14. What is meant by the statement "Choosing between a sole proprietorship, partnership, or corporation is a two-way rather than a three-way choice"?

Suggested Readings

Anthony, Edward L., "Choosing the Legal Structure for Your Firm," *Management Aids for Small Manufacturers*, No. 5. Washington, D. C.: Small Business Administration, 1963.

Broom, H. N., and Longenecker, J. G., *Small Business Management*, 3rd ed. Cincinnati: South-Western Publishing, 1971. Ch. 8 and 10.

Choosing a Form of Business Organization, Administrative Management Course Program, Topic 11. Washington, D. C.: Small Business Administration, 1965.

J. K. Lasser Tax Institute, *How to Run a Small Business*. New York: McGraw-Hill, 1963.

Kahn, C. Harry, *Business and Professional Income under the Personal Income Tax*. Princeton, N. J.: Princeton University Press, 1964.

Kelley, Pearch C., Lawyer, K., and Baumback, C. M., *How to Organize and Operate a Small Business*, 4th ed. Englewood Cliffs, N. J.: Prentice-Hall, 1968. Ch. 10, 12, and 13.

Mertes, J. E., *Creative Site Evaluation for the Small Retailer*. Norman, Oklahoma: University of Oklahoma Press, 1962.

Metcalf, Wendell O., *Starting and Managing a Small Business of Your Own*, Vol. 1, 2nd ed. Washington, D. C.: Small Business Administration, 1962.

"Problems of Location and Real Estate" (Theme for the issue), *Journal of Small Business Management* (January, 1972).

Peifler, Ronald M., "Plant Location Factors for Small Industry," *Management Aids Annual No. 7*. Washington, D. C.: Small Business Administration, 1961.

Robinson, Roland S., *Financing the Dynamic Small Firm*. Belmont, Calif.: Wadsworth, 1966.

Small Business Location and Layout. Administrative Management Course Program, Topic 13. Washington D. C.: Small Business Administration, 1965.

Steinmetz, Lawrence L., Kline, J. B., and Stegall, D. P., *Managing the Small Business*. Homewood, Ill.: Richard D. Irwin, 1968. Ch. 4 and 17.

Weber, Fred J., Jr., "Locating or Relocating Your Business," *Management Aids for Small Manufacturers*, No. 201. Washington, D. C.: Small Business Administration, 1969.

Chapter 8
Getting Capital and Credit

One of the major causes of small business failures is inadequate financing. "If only I could get my hands on more money" is often heard from an owner of a dying small business. The short- and long-term capital needs of a business must be accurately forecast before the business venture is started. The entrepreneur must carefully estimate not only the capital necessary to promote and initiate the business but also the capital needed for operating the going concern.

In general terms, capital is purchasing power; it includes not only the funds invested by the owner but also the funds made available by creditors. Three types of capital are required for initiating a business: promotional or venture capital, working capital, and fixed-asset capital.

Promotional capital involves all the expenses of getting the business venture off the ground. It may include compensation payments to a promoter for his time and effort in bringing the various resources together; purchase or lease options for land or buildings, attorney fees, and utility deposits; and costs related to finding a suitable location and locating initial equity capital.

Fixed capital includes all funds needed for buildings, land, fixtures, and machinery. *Working capital* consists of cash and all assets that can be readily converted into cash, such as inventories and accounts receivable. Working capital is used to purchase materials, merchandise, and supplies and to pay off current obligations, such as rent and wages. The entrepreneur must be able to distinguish between these kinds of capital when estimating his capital needs. He should also realize that a reasonable period, usually from 3 to 9 months, will lapse before income will be sufficient to provide for his expenses. He must, therefore, include in his estimate of initial capital a minimum salary to provide for his living expenses.

Determining Capital Requirements

Experience has shown that an important contribution to a new firm's success is its ability to "hang on" until a break-even point is reached. It invariably takes longer for sales to reach the goal optimistically envisioned by the entrepreneur. Because of the high cost of capital for a small business, time becomes critical. For example, technologically based enterprises often experience delays, and a delay of a couple years can double the amount of capital needed to start the business. It is important, therefore, that the entrepreneur

Table 8–1. Florist Shop Initial Capital Requirements Worksheet.

Item	Average Dollars/Mo. on $70,000/Yr. Sales	Industry Ratio	Initial Cash Requirement for Two Months
Sales	$5,832.34	100%	
Cost of sales	2,713.66	46.52%	$2,713.66[1]
Gross Profit	3,118.68	53.48	
Fixed Expenses			
Rent[2]	140.00	2.40	280.00
Utilities	228.66	3.92	457.32
Insurance	58.92	1.01	88.38 (one
Taxes and licenses	51.34	.88	qtr.)
Interest	5.34	.12	
Depreciation	128.34	2.20	
Subtotal	$ 612.60	10.53%	
Controllable Expenses			
Gross wages	667.34	11.44%	1,334.68
Labor,[3] outside	68.84	1.18	137.64
Supplies	228.08	3.91	456.16
Repairs and maintenance	68.84	1.18	
Advertising	119.00	2.04	357.00 (one
Bad debt	210.60	3.61	qtr.)
Car and delivery	4.08	.07	8.16
Admin. and legal	67.60	.85	99.20
Misc. (all other expenses)	103.82	1.78	207.68
Subtotal	1,520.22	36.59	
Total Expenses	$2,132.82	36.59%	
Net Profit	$ 985.26	16.89	
Initial Cash Requirement (carry forward)			$6,128.26

[1] Inventory rate of turn: 24 times, or $1,576 every 15 days (ratios based on $50,000–$75,000 annual sales).
[2] Assumes rental of premises rather than purchases.
[3] Does not include owner's compensation.

give careful thought to the delays and uncertainties he is likely to face and provide for them when determining his capital requirements. He must always remember that time costs money.

Determining capital requirements is no easy task. It is impossible to come up with an average figure since requirements will differ widely depending on the kind of business, its location, the general state of the economy, whether it is an existing business with new ownership or has started from scratch, and so on. A recommended approach is to start with a forecast of expected sales. This is a logical starting point since the minimum amount of most assets is tied directly to the volume of business.

After establishing the sales figures as objectively as possible, the next step is to estimate fixed and controllable expenses by applying standard industry ratios to the sales figures. These ratios are available for most kinds of businesses from trade associations, bankers, and Dun & Bradstreet. Table 8–1 is an example of one type of worksheet that can be helpful. This table, which is worked out by the Small Business Administration for a small florist shop, is based on the assumption of $70,000 in annual sales. If the florist shop in Table 8–1 fits the industry average, the owner will have a need of $6,128.26 for the first 2 months to operate the business. In addition, he will have certain nonrecurring initial capital requirements, amounting to $10,928.98 (see below) for a total of $17,057.-24 required for just the first 2 months of operation, plus his family requirements.

Initial Cash Requirement		$ 6,128.26
Nonrecurring Initial Capital Requirements		
1.	Furniture, fixtures and equipment (if purchased on installment, includes down payment plus two installments).	6,000.00
2.	Inventory reserve of 35% (industry standard).	948.98
3.	Accounts receivable (50% of 30 days' sales).	3,000.00
4.	Initial advertising and promotion.	600.00
5.	Rent deposit.	180.00
6.	Deposits for utilities, sales tax, and so on.	150.00
7.	Reserve for petty cash.	100.00
	Subtotal	$17,057.24
	Family Income requirements for two months	
	Total Initial Cash Requirements	$

Another approach to estimating capital requirements is to select a profit figure and to work back from that figure. For example, if an entrepreneur plans on manufacturing widgets and would like to earn at least $20,000 annually, he would consult the industry standard ratios. Assuming the profit for sales in the widget industry is 5 percent, he would have to reach sales of 20 times his desired profit, or $400,000. If his widgets will sell for $10 apiece, he must sell 40,000 widgets a year, or an average of 800 widgets per week for 50 weeks. He must then ask himself questions such as: How much equipment will I need? How many machines and men will be required? What will materials, wages, rent, and other expenses add up to if I produce this number?[1] Since the entrepreneur will be dealing with industry averages, he may want to consult with someone in the industry, such as a supplier, to verify the estimates he has worked up, especially to get an idea of the feasibility of reaching his sales forecast in the desired span of time.

Two things must be emphasized about initial capital requirements. First, the entrepreneur must hold down his investment in fixed assets to a minimum. If too much capital is tied up in fixed assets, he may not have enough left for working capital. Also, heavy fixed costs resulting from overinvestment in fixed assets raises the break-even point and may become a burden during periods of falling prices or low sales.

Second, capital requirements must include a safe margin for working capital. A business depends on daily receipts to meet daily obligations. Therefore, a sudden decrease in sales or unanticipated increase in expenses could result in creditors' forcing the business into bankruptcy.

Sources of Initial Funds

A later chapter deals with sources for short- and long-term funds once the business is established. This section will emphasize possible sources for the initial financing phase for the promoter–entrepreneur. These sources include: (1) personal savings, friends, and relatives; (2) banks; (3) Small Business Administration; (4) Small Business Investment Corporation; (5) trade credit; (6) issuance of stock; (7) venture capitalists; (8) commercial finance companies; and (9) miscellaneous sources.

Personal savings, friends, and relatives. Typically, a large part of the equity capital in a new business comes from the promoter–entrepreneur's own savings. Due to the high rate of failure among small businesses, "venture capital" is expensive to borrow and difficult to obtain. Therefore, the entrepreneur should draw on his own savings to whatever extent is possible. Furthermore, most lending sources will not loan funds to new businesses unless the ownership equity in the enterprise equals a minimum of one-half to two-thirds of the total capital.

Friends and relatives have traditionally played an important role in providing venture capital for new enterprises. If this source is used for initial capital, it would be wise to provide for some type of repayment plan once the business gets off the ground. The close personal relationship that friends and relatives

---

[1] These two examples are from Wendell O. Metcalf, *Starting and Managing a Small Business of Your Own*, 2nd. ed. (Washington, D. C.: Small Business Administration, 1962), pp. 9–11.

share with the entrepreneur frequently leads them to attempt to "manage" the business, or more correctly, to interfere with managing the business.

Banks. The commercial bank is perhaps one of the most important sources of credit for the small firm. While most banks limit their lending to providing working capital, some initial capital will come from this source as well. It is important, however, to recognize important differences among banks as potential sources of funds:

1. Some banks follow more conservative lending practices than others. Marginal credit risks that might be unacceptable to a small localized bank might be accepted by a larger, more diversified bank.
2. Some banks have departments whose specific function is to provide loans to firms with growth potential. The personnel in these departments are often anxious to provide special counsel to the customer. This specialized credit service is most likely to be found in larger banks.
3. Banks differ in the extent to which they support their borrowers in bad times. Some banks display more loyalty to customers by "standing by" the firm and working with it to help it attain a more favorable condition. This quality is perhaps more often found in the small "personal" bank.
4. Banks differ in the degree of loan specialization they provide. Larger banks may have special departments to serve various borrowers, while small banks may serve specialized business sectors. A bank that is good for one firm may not be good for another.
5. It is imperative that relations with a banker be established before the loan is actually needed. Early visits with a bank loan officer about the plans and objectives of the firm will encourage a closer working relationship and may result in additional counseling service. Banks should always be provided with financial statements, including the source and application of funds statement, the cash budget, and the capital budget. If there is a seasonal need for financial assistance, a "line of credit" might be established so that each loan will not have to be separately negotiated. The main point to keep in mind is "don't wait till you need money to see your banker."

Small Business Administration. By law, the SBA may not make a loan if a business can obtain funds from a bank or other private source at reasonable terms. Credit requirements of the SBA are similar to those a bank would have for a term loan, except their application procedure is somewhat less stringent. SBA loans are usually secured by mortgages or by assignment of life-insurance policies, securities, and so on.

There are two basic types of SBA loans available to the entrepreneur: direct loans and participation loans. The SBA may *participate* in a loan in two ways: (1) by guaranteeing up to 90 percent or $350,000 of a bank loan, whichever is less (in this case, the SBA does not provide an outlay of cash; it merely guarantees the bank 90 percent or $350,000); or (2) by providing $150,000 as the SBA share of an immediate-participation loan with the bank.

On the other hand, the SBA may make *direct* loans to the business, subject to a $100,000 limit if the bank or other lending institutions decline to participate in an SBA loan. Direct loans by the SBA, however, may not exceed $100,000 and at times are not available due to federal fiscal restraints.

In addition to making and guaranteeing regular loans, the SBA administers an "economic opportunity" loan program to help minority and low-income people with business potential who cannot qualify for regular SBA loan assistance. When considering "economic opportunity" loans, the SBA relaxes its credit standards and emphasizes the character and potential of the applicant.

Small Business Investment Corporation. SBICs, which are either privately or publicly owned and operated, are licensed and financially assisted by the Small Business Administration. They are required to restrict their activities to providing equity capital, long-term financing, and advisory services to small business.

While SBICs can lend either funds or supply equity capital, most have heavily emphasized equity capital. In most cases they provide this capital by purchasing stock in the new company or by purchasing convertible debentures (that is, bonds that are converted into stocks at the option of the SBIC). The reluctance of many entrepreneurs to dilute their equity, and thus their control, in their business has limited the use of SBICs as a source for initial funds. The MESBIC (Minority Enterprise Small Business Investment Company) is a special type of SBIC that provides long-term funding and management assistance to minority small businessmen.

Trade credit. Credit extended by suppliers at the wholesale or retail level is another major source of funds for new firms. Manufacturers and distributors usually like to strengthen their sales with new customers who have growth potential. For example, equipment manufacturers, knowing that the typical small business is not able to pay cash for expensive installations, have liberal finance plans to increase their sales. Typically a down payment of only 25 percent is required, the balance to be repaid in monthly installments over a period of two or more years. Other plans allow the entrepreneur to lease equipment at reasonable rates—frequently with an option to buy the equipment at the end of a stated period.

Issuance of stock. If the entrepreneur has incorporated his business, he has the option of securing equity capital by selling stock to new investors. However, in distributing common stock to the public market, he will require the services of an investment banker. Unless the stock issue is relatively large, the fees of the investment banker make the sale of securities rather expensive. Because of the uniqueness of each case, an entrepreneur considering this source of equity funds should consult an attorney specializing in such matters.

Venture capitalists. R. Bruce Ricks has defined a venture capitalist as "an individual, or perhaps a small group of individuals, loosely organized, placing capital into risky business situations where the profit pay-off if successful is extremely attractive."[2] Most venture capitalists are likely to be found in law firms specializing in tax or corporate affairs, investment counseling services, and stockbroker houses. Little is really known about this group of investors since many prefer to remain inconspicuous. Writing about these professional "backers," Roland I. Robinson points out:

> The contractual terms on which professional "backers" offer funds to new small businesses are usually fairly harsh or demanding. When the degree of risk they assume is recognized, however, the terms the "backers" demand are reasonable.[3]

Commercial finance companies. Like the typical commercial bank, the commercial finance company is normally considered to be a supplier of short-term funds. However, to the extent that a minimun loan balance is kept with the commercial finance company and to the extent that it is not necessary to pay off loans over a period of less than a year, it does provide a rather constant source of long-term funds.

Finance companies can be divided into two general categories. The first group includes companies that loan funds secured by accounts receivable that have been "pledged." When the loan is repaid, title to the accounts receivable is returned to the borrower. While accounts-receivable financing can be a good source of working capital for the small firm, it can be expensive. The effective rate charged to a "preferred risk" company is about 10 percent per year, whereas a small firm may find that it is paying 17 to 20 percent because of its increased risk.

---

[2]R. Bruce Ricks, "The Capital Markets for Small Business." In *The Financing of Small Business,* edited by Irving Pfeffer (New York: Macmillan, 1967), p. 204.
[3]Roland I. Robinson, *Financing the Dynamic Small Firm* (Belmont, Calif.: Wadsworth, 1966), p. 21.

The second general category includes factors, which are finance companies that purchase accounts receivable. In practice, there is little difference between the company loaning money secured by receivables and the company purchasing the receivables with recourse (right to demand payment). The factor, however, does the credit investigation work, collects the accounts, and takes the risk. As a result, the small business firm needs no credit department. At the same time, this added service is reflected in a higher interest—it can run as high as 20 to 25 percent for small companies. It should also be noted that a finance company is likely to be the quickest way to obtain cash. Since the preceding is intended only as a survey of fund sources, the borrower who is contemplating a loan on accounts receivable is encouraged to consult one of the references listed at the end of this chapter for in-depth treatment of the topic.

Miscellaneous sources. Because of the difficulty in obtaining venture capital, the entrepreneur frequently will have to aggressively seek out less conventional sources of funds. For example, an increasing number of states and local communities are organizing development corporations, or industrial foundations, to promote the establishment of businesses in their areas. These organizations may be able to assist the entrepreneur by:

1. Providing funds through direct intermediate- or long-term loans or by purchase of stock in the business. In some cases, development companies will lend larger amounts (in proportion to the value of the security) for longer periods than banks.
2. Buying and building plants for lease or sale. For the small manufacturer, the purchase price may be lower or, if the plant is leased, the development corporation may require less investment in fixed assets.

Some entrepreneurs with limited funds have been able to get started by entering into a franchise agreement with an established franchisor. Today, many franchisors offer a "turn-key" operation, which requires a down payment with the balance financed by the franchisor. For example, a well-known chain franchises self-service drive-ins on the following basis: The franchisee must invest $25,000 and have available $5,000 to $7,000 in working capital. The balance of $22,000 is financed by the company over a period of several years. Of course, there are some disadvantages to purchasing a franchise as will be pointed out in Chapter 9.

Other sources of funds for the entrepreneur include savings and loan associations, which provide funds to small businesses through mortgage loans. These institutions are relatively unconcerned with the use of funds but look to the real-estate collateral as their source of security. Thus, these institutions are an unlikely source if the loan is on an unsecured basis or if real estate is a minor part of the collateral for the loan. Table 8–2 provides a comprehensive list of the kinds of financing available.

Table 8–2. Types of Financing.

1. *Accounts receivable financing:* The small businessman obtains funds on the strength of the assets represented by his accounts receivable.
2. *Bank credit cards:* BankAmericard allows a retail merchant to offer credit without using his own capital and with no credit risks, at a cost of 3% discount to the bank.
3. *Commercial loans:* The most widely used business loans; secured or unsecured. Meet seasonal or short-term money needs, usually 90 to 180 days.
4. *Commodity loans:* Loans made to manufacturers and wholesalers for the purchase of inventory consisting of readily marketable, nonperishable staples. (See Inventory Financing.)
5. *Convertible debentures:* Unsecured debts incurred by a corporation, convertible into the common stock of the corporation at agreed upon terms.
6. *Equipment financing:* Obtaining a loan using equipment as collateral. Can also mean obtaining financing to buy equipment.
7. *Equipment leasing:* Acquiring the use of equipment for negotiated periods of time and rental.
8. *Factoring:* Selling accounts receivable at a discount to a factor or factoring department of a bank which, in turn, takes care of collections.
9. *Flooring:* A line of credit to finance the inventory needs of a retailer of "large ticket" items such as autos or refrigerators. Retailer has possession of items although lender has legal ownership.
10. *Improvement loans:* A loan made to finance improvements to property, thereby increasing its value.
11. *Indirect collection financing:* Available to firms that generate a large volume of sales contracts and prefer to retain the control and collection function of these accounts.
12. *Installment loans (timeplan):* A consumer loan to be repaid in installments over the term of the loan.
13. *Inventory distribution financing:* Financing to allow a manufacturer to distribute inventories to his customers at a time and in quantities most favorable to his production capacity.
14. *Inventory financing:* Using inventory as collateral for a loan. Also financing to buy inventory.
15. *Passbook loans:* Loans made to individuals or companies using savings on deposit as security. Savings continue to earn interest, partly offsetting interest paid on loan.
16. *Professional term loans:* Equipment financing and capital loans available to dentists, physicians, and veterinarians.
17. *Real estate loans:* Loans secured by real estate for any reason including the acquisition of additional real estate, construction of buildings or other business purposes.
18. *Secured loans:* The lender's risk is reduced by the borrower pledging something of value (collateral) as security that the loan will be repaid.
19. *Term loans:* Secured or unsecured, with terms up to five years. Repayment made in periodic installments, often supported by a business loan agreement.

Table 8–2 (*continued*).

20. *Trade credit:* 30, 60, or 90 day terms for payment of merchandise. Sometimes there is a discount for prompt payment. No interest is charged if payment is made in the agreed time period.
21. *"Other" loans:* Loans made with no specific property pledged as security or collateral; borrower's honor and financial strength and business potential are security.
22. *Small Business Administration loans:*
    Bank Participation Loans: The Small Business Administration advances up to 75% of total funds required or $150,000 (whichever is less) with a bank putting up the remaining 25% of the loan.
    Direct Loans: When the Bureau of the Budget releases funds, the Small Business Administration can lend up to $100,000 directly to a small businessman.
    Displaced Business Loans: Loans to businesses displaced by federally funded programs such as urban renewal. Loans cannot be for more than 133% of the value of business displaced or $350,000 (whichever is less).
    Economic Opportunity Loans: Loans made available to handicapped and minority group businessmen for purposes of establishing a business.
    Guaranteed Loans: Provide guarantees for up to 90% or $350,000 (whichever is smaller) on all bank commercial loans at lenders' standard rates of interest.

From *Small Business Reporter* 8, No. 5 (1969), pp. 1–8. Reprinted with permission of the Bank of America National Trust and Savings Association.

Establishing Credit Relationships

Even the established businessman occasionally faces difficulty in getting funds because of a poor approach or because he fails to show how the money will be repaid. Entrepreneurs often consider a loan refusal a personal blow to their egos. It need not be so. In fact, if a request for a loan is turned down, it is important to accept the refusal gracefully and try to determine the real reason for the rejection. There are a number of things that the lender looks for, which we will discuss in the following section.

Dealing with the Lender

Since commercial banks provide more than 80 percent of the intermediate- and long-term funds borrowed by small firms for initiating or expanding a business, chances are good that the lender will be a banker. The loan officer for the bank will be looking for answers to questions such as: How much money do you need? Will it be enough? What kind of money do you need—equity funds, short-term credit, or long-term credit? Will your sales and profit margin be adequate? What is your plan for repayment?

Therefore, when applying for a loan, the owner–manager must be able to show that planned use of the funds is worthwhile and that he can repay the loan on time. The manager should prepare a projection of his cash needs to show how the funds will be used; he should be able to show how the borrowed funds will increase his firm's profitability; and he should prepare a cash flow showing his proposed schedule for repayment. Conservative estimates are best; if figures are forced, the owner–manager may fail to achieve his goals and thus weaken his future relations with his bank.

Part of the information the lender needs will be furnished by the entrepreneur and the rest will come from the lender's credit files and from outside sources. Basically, the banker will want to know about the "C's" of credit:[4]

Character. To the banker, "character" means two things in particular:

1. The borrower will do everything in his power to conserve his business assets and so ensure repayment of his loan. He will manage his business to the best of his ability. He will not squander his own or other funds.
2. The borrower is a man of his word. When he says that he will repay his borrowings promptly, he means it. If he does not keep his promise, he at least will have made every possible effort to do so.

Capacity. The management skill shown by the small businessman in using his investment and enlarging it is another important business asset. For those just embarking on a business career or entering a new field, however, past experience may carry little weight. For example, experience as a machinist, salesman, or bookkeeper alone—however successful—does not qualify a person to direct all the activities of a machine shop.

Capital. The small businessman's investment in his own business is evidence of his faith in its future. He himself must furnish the management and most of the capital until others have enough confidence in his business to be willing to invest in it.

Collateral. Businessmen who have a high credit standing do much of their borrowing on an unsecured basis. Others, especially new small businessmen, are often obliged to back up their credit standing with collateral. If the borrower owns a home or other improved real estate, life-insurance policies with a cash surrender value, or marketable securities, he may be able to use such assets as collateral for business loans.

---

[4]See Jack Zwick, *A Handbook of Small Business Finance,* Small Business Management Series, No. 15 (Washington, D. C.: Small Business Administration, 1965), pp. 54–55.

Before borrowing on these terms, however, the borrower should consider the consequences to himself and his family if he should be forced to withdraw from the business before it becomes firmly established. A small businessman who retires from business prematurely usually does so at a loss.

Circumstances. Some factors over which the small businessman has no control may have a bearing on the granting of a bank loan and its repayment. These include seasonal character of the business, long-run business changes, the level of community business activity, the competitive position of the firm, and the nature of the product.

Coverage. Proper insurance coverage is extremely important. Small businessmen are subject to possible losses from many causes, such as the death of an owner, partner, or principal stockholder; physical damage or interruption of operations as the result of fire, explosion, flood, tornado, or other violent causes; or theft, embezzlement, or other acts of dishonesty by owners, officers, employees, and others. While a new small businessman may not be able to insure his company as fully as the owner of an established business, he should recognize the need.

In addition, when applying for a loan, the entrepreneur should check in advance with the lender to see whether any special statement forms will be needed. The lender will probably want details about liabilities, contingent liabilities, property owned, insurance, other business connections, and so on. It is also recommended that the borrower prepare a cash budget and projected financial statements for the period to be covered by the loan. These statements should support his explanation of how the money is to be used and how the loan will be repaid.

Establishing a Borrowing Philosophy

It is common sense that an entrepreneur should borrow only the amount of money he needs. It is surprising, therefore, to see the number of businessmen holding to the philosophy that the more you can borrow, the better it is. Still others feel that all their business ills would be cured if they had access to more funds. In some cases, this may in fact be true. Too frequently, however, the borrower overlooks the fact that idle funds are a luxury that few firms can enjoy. Thus, if money is borrowed, the entrepreneur should plan carefully so that he can obtain enough funds to accomplish what he has planned, but at the same time avoid paying expensive interest charges for funds he does not need.

On the other hand, experience has demonstrated that some entrepreneurs are reluctant to borrow funds. They seem to maintain a philosophy that borrowing should be avoided except in very rare circumstances. To follow this line of thought is unfortunate in that the businessman misses out on the advantages of using leverage—that is, making money with someone else's money. Although it is important to avoid borrowing unnecessary money, at the same time the entrepreneur should be aware of the following benefits of borrowing:

1. Borrowed funds can earn more than they cost. The rate of interest that lenders charge is generally lower than the rate of return a borrower expects his investment to earn. As a result, borrowed funds, if they are used successfully, increase the return on an investment over what it would have been without the borrowing.
2. Interest payments on borrowed funds are tax deductible; dividend payments or other returns to investors are not.
3. Some credit is a matter of convenience. Buying merchandise on open account and services on an accrual basis are examples of using credit for convenience. Wages are another example, since even a very small businessman would find it difficult to make daily wage settlements.
4. Borrowing is more flexible than ownership. When a business owner supplies the entire investment, he may find that part of his capital is idle during off seasons. As a result, he may receive a lower average return than if he had invested some of his money elsewhere and used short-term borrowed funds during his own company's periods of peak needs. The small businessman can usually increase or decrease the amount of borrowed funds to correspond fairly well with his business capital requirements.
5. Loan funds are easier to find than equity funds. The prospects of profits are often too uncertain to satisfy a potential owner–investor. Since lenders, as creditors, have prior claims to income and assets, loan funds are usually more plentiful than equity capital.

Incident 8: Money Problems

Pete Smith wants to expand his business by taking on a line of antique auto parts. He figures that he can get a gross margin of 40 percent in this business, and through his experience in restoring old cars, he has a very good idea of the items in demand. Recently he has been advertising at relatively low cost in national antique car magazines, and his business has been increasing. Many owners want parts, too, so the two sides of the business will complement each other nicely.

Pete figures that if he could get an inventory of $30,000 of parts, he could begin to gross around $80,000 per year. He would have to hire one extra man to handle this business, or part of it—much of it he could handle himself. A good parts man is worth $10,000 per year. He would also have to build a small storage warehouse and shop counter next to his present building for $14,000.

The problem, as usual, is money. Pete does not have this kind of cash, and he is not sure how to get it. In examining his books (see Attachment 8–1), Pete felt that he was finally in good enough shape to start actively searching for a loan. But he knew from sad experience that finding $44,000 was not exactly the easiest job in the world. Still, others had managed, and he felt that he could do it too.

1. Take a close look at Pete's financial statement (Attachment 8–1). Is he in good enough shape to qualify easily for credit? Why or why not?
2. Pete's business is a proprietorship. His personal net assets are $17,455. Does this change your answer? Why or why not?
3. Pete has had his money problems, but he has never failed to pay his bills on time for 9 years. Does this influence your answer? Why or why not?
4. What sources of credit do you think Pete might tap? Why?
5. In the above incident, what possible costs might occur that Pete did not think of? Would anyone lending money think of them? Why?

Discussion Questions

1. What is the meaning of promotional capital? How does it differ from working capital?
2. What are two ways of estimating the capital requirements of a new business?
3. How does the estimated sales volume affect estimated capital requirements?
4. Discuss the major sources of funds for the entrepreneur. Which of these sources do you consider the most important?
5. Under what conditions are loans from the government available to the entrepreneur?
6. Explain the difference between factoring and accounts receivable financing.
7. List the major considerations in selecting a bank for a loan.
8. Briefly discuss the major criteria used by the bank when making a loan decision. Which of these do you consider the most important?
9. Comment on the following statement: "When it comes to borrowing money, take all you can get."
10. What are the possible benefits of borrowing for a new business?

Smith the Smith

Profit and Loss Statement — Most Recent Year

Gross Sales	57,445	
Less: Bad Debts	620	
Net Sales		56,825

Expenses:
Labor Cost		
Rent	3,900	
Utilities	1,112	
Materials, Supplies, Parts	14,337	
Insurance	377	
Depreciation	2,000	
State and Local Taxes	1,525	
Advertising	625	
Pickup Truck Expense	1,437	
Miscellaneous	557	
Total Expenses		45,506
Net Profit (including owner withdrawals of $9,400)		11,319

Balance Sheet

Assets:
Tools and Machinery (Net of Depreciation)	11,377
Accounts Receivable	15,375
Cash on hand and in Banks	1,320
Inventory — Paint, Supplies, etc.	8,326
Pickup Truck	2,116
Total Assets	38,514

Liabilities:
Accounts Payable	16,275
Loans Payable {Bank / Father-in-law}	3,500 / 1,000
Taxes Payable	857
	21,632
Net Worth	16,882

Attachment 8–1. Pete's Financial Statement.

Suggested Readings

Anthony, Edward L., and Comstock, A. Barr, eds., *Equity Capital and Small Business*, Small Business Research Series, No. 24. Washington, D. C.: Small Business Administration, 1960.

"Applying for Minority Business Loans," *Small Business Reporter*, Bank of America, 1969.

Becker, Benjamin M., and Becker, Samuel S., "Practical Suggestions for Financing a Business Enterprise," *Journal of Accountancy*, CXII (December 1961), 42–46.

Beckman, Theodore N., and Foster, Ronald S. *Credits and Collections: Management and Theory*, 8th ed. New York: McGraw-Hill, 1969. Pp. 160–164.

Broom, H. N. and Longenecker, J. G., *Small Business Management*, 3rd ed. Cincinnati: South-Western Publishing, 1971. Ch. 9.

Cashin, James A., "Building Strong Relations with Your Bank," *Small Marketers Aids*, No. 107. Washington, D. C.: Small Business Administration, 1964.

"Financing Small Business" (theme for entire issue), *Journal of Small Business Management* 9, (April 1971).

"Financing Small Business," *Small Business Reporter* 8, No. 5 (1969). Reprinted in *Managing the Dynamic Small Firm: Readings*, edited by Lawrence A. Klatt. Belmont, Calif.: Wadsworth, 1971. Pp. 188–201.

"Helping the Banker Help You," *Management Aids Annual No. 8*. Washington, D. C.: Small Business Administration, 1961. Pp. 41–46.

Kelley, Pearce C., Lawyer, Kenneth, and Baumback, Clifford W. *How to Organize and Operate a Small Business*, 4th ed. Englewood Cliffs, N. J.: Prentice-Hall, 1968. Ch. 10.

Konopa, Leonard S., "Using Security to Get a Bank Loan," *Small Marketers Aids*, No. 102. Washington, D. C.: Small Business Administration, 1964.

Krentzman, Harvey C., *Managing for Profits*. Washington, D. C.: Small Business Administration, 1968. Pp. 81–91.

Nason, Richard, "Borrowing and the Small Businessman," *Dun's Review and Modern Industry*, LXXXII (October 1963), 61–62, 117–18, 120.

Petrof, John V., Carusone, Peter S., and McDavid, John E. *Small Business Management: Concepts and Techniques for Improving Decisions*. New York: McGraw-Hill, 1972. Ch. 10.

Pugh, Olin S., "Small Business Investment Companies," *Business Topics*, XI (Autumn 1963), 64–78.

Ricks, Bruce R., "The Capital Markets for Small Business." In *The Financing of Small Business*, edited by Irving Pfeffer. Macmillan, Company, 1967. Pp. 197–210.

Robinson, Roland A., *Financing the Dynamic Small Firm*. Belmont, Calif.: Wadsworth, 1966.

Steinmetz, Lawrence L., Kline, John B., and Stegall, Donald P. *Managing the Small Business*. Homewood, Ill.: Richard D. Irwin, 1968. Ch. 12.

Zwick, Jack, *A Handbook of Small Business Finance*, 7th ed. Washington, D. C.: Small Business Administration, 1965.

How about a Franchise?

Chapter 9

Franchising is one of the most rapidly growing business arrangements because it offers an opportunity for an individual with limited capital and experience to own or operate his own business.

While there are no exact figures to measure the magnitude of franchising, there are a number of estimates that indicate both the significant size and rapid growth. Dr. Charles L. Vaughn, Executive Director of the Boston College Center for the Study of Franchise Distribution, has estimated that franchised business now accounts for over $120 billion in annual sales—equal to about 34 percent of retail sales and 13 percent of the Gross National Product.

The National Federation of Independent Businessmen estimates that 23 percent of the nation's 5.1 million independent enterprises now operate under some kind of franchise agreement. They suggest that more than 1,200 franchisors have licensed from 600,000 to 700,000 franchises. Surprisingly, automobile dealerships and service stations account for more than half the total retail sales of all franchises in the United States.

While the big franchising boom has occurred during the past two decades, franchising is not new to the marketplace. In fact, one of the first examples of franchising dates back to 1898 when independent dealers were licensed to sell and service electric and steam automobiles.

Today franchised businesses range from advertising specialties to mobile dog-grooming centers to water softeners. The number of franchise holders is currently growing at the phenomenal rate of 40,000 a year with every indication that this trend will continue for at least the next several years.

What Is a Franchise?

The term "franchise" is used to describe widely differing business agreements. Furthermore, the form of franchise agreements differ by industry and by company within an industry. In certain cases a franchise may merely be a contract to sell a product, method, or service within a geographic area with some nominal payment involved. The product, method, or service being marketed is identified by a brand name, and the franchisor maintains control over the marketing methods employed.

Most franchise agreements, however, emphasize continuing relationship between the parent company or franchisor and the individual owner or franchisee. For example, the International Franchise Association (the IFA is an organization that represents franchisors) explains franchising in the following manner: "A franchise is a continuing relationship between the franchisor and the franchisee in which the sum total of the franchisor's knowledge, image, success, manufacturing and marketing techniques are supplied to the franchisee for consideration."

According to this "continuing relationship" concept, the franchisee is an independent businessman who contracts for a "package" business. This package usually includes use of the franchisor's name, symbols, and designs along with some sort of financial assistance. In addition, the franchisor provides some type of professional training and guidance and offers supplies and merchandise at wholesale prices. In return, the franchisee is normally obligated to make a minimum investment of money, obtain and maintain a standardized inventory and/or equipment package, maintain specified levels of quality and performance, follow specified promotional and operating procedures, and pay royalty fees.

Advantages of Franchising

1. A purchaser of a franchise buys a "success" package, in which all the headaches of development work—preparing a consumer-accepted image, establishing goodwill, designing fixtures, and perfecting handling methods—have been done for him.
2. The franchisee receives assistance in finding a suitable location, designing the structure, setting up and operating inventory-control and accounting procedures, and planning advertising and promotion.
3. Many franchisors provide initial training and ongoing management assistance. For example, McDonald's franchisees spend three weeks at "Hamburger U" before starting their own business. Some franchisors have traveling representatives who visit each business from time to time.
4. With a well-established franchisor behind him, the franchisee's credit

standing is enhanced, increasing his chances of obtaining funds. Some franchisors will co-sign notes with a bank, thereby guaranteeing the franchisee's borrowing. In addition, many franchisors offer long-term financing to buy equipment.
5. Most importantly, the risk of failure in owning a franchise is less than starting a business from scratch. For example, it is widely accepted in the food-service field that one out of two restaurants fail during their first year of operation. At the same time, according to the International Franchise Association, the overall failure rate for the entire industry is less than 10 percent.

Disadvantages of Franchising

1. A major disadvantage is the cost. In addition to the initial charge, which may run from $1,000 to hundreds of thousands of dollars, the franchisee must pay a royalty fee. This fee is typically a percentage of gross sales — from 2 to 14 percent depending on the services provided. For example, a Holiday Inn franchise costs an initial fee of about $15,000, plus royalties and fees of 6 percent on the annual gross.
2. The franchisee may have to handle as part of his "total package" a product or products that are carried by all franchisees but may not be profitable in his marketing area. Similarly, he may be subject to policies and business practices that benefit others in the chain but are disagreeable to him, or even injurious to his particular business.
3. Most importantly, many businessmen who enter into a franchise agreement find that it is not the answer to the American Dream. Because of the strong controls exercised by the parent company, the individual discovers that in a sense he has become a "manager" rather than an "entrepreneur."

Finding Franchise Opportunities

Before locating specific franchises, the prospective franchisee should take the time to become very familiar with franchising in general. A number of excellent books and articles are listed in the "Suggested Readings" at the end of this chapter. Once the franchisee has done some reading on franchising, he can turn to a number of good sources to help him find the right franchise opportunity.

Annual directories. Two comprehensive directories of franchising companies are published annually. One is *The Franchise Annual*, prepared by

National Franchise Reports, 333 No. Michigan Avenue, Chicago, Illinois 60601. The other is *A Franchise Directory*, issued annually by International Franchise Opportunities, 421 Center Street, Lewiston, New York 14092.

Daily newspapers. The classified sections of most daily metropolitan newspapers carry franchise opportunities under the "Business Opportunities" heading. The classified ad section of the *Wall Street Journal*, known as "The Mart," is another excellent source.

Trade publications. Many companies seek franchisees through advertisements placed in trade publications that are related to the franchised business. Public libraries in most large cities subscribe to a variety of these trade magazines. The prospective franchisee should keep in mind, however, that because an ad appears in a reputable newspaper or directory does not guarantee that the franchisor is reputable. The publishers themselves do not usually investigate to insure that an offer is a good one.

Franchising publications. Publications devoted strictly to franchising are also excellent sources of information. "National Franchise Reports" is a monthly newsletter, sold by subscription, that is considered by many authorities to be the "bible" of franchising. This publication reports the details of new franchise offers in each issue, lists the current franchise shows, and contains general editorial comments by the publisher. *Modern Franchising*, 1033 First Avenue, Des Plaines, Illinois 60016, is a bimonthly news and information magazine aimed at prospective franchisees. Advertisements in the magazine are an excellent source of franchise offers. The Boston College Center for the Study of Franchise Distribution also has a collection of written materials on franchising.

Franchisor exhibitions. Franchisor exhibitions are held in major cities all over the nation and offer the prospective franchisee the opportunity to meet with franchisor representatives and evaluate a number of offers in one visit. The International Franchise Association is a good source of information for the schedule of these exhibitions. Some of the more popular franchisors, however, do not patronize the shows since they have large waiting lists of prospective franchisees. For example, Holiday Inn receives about 10,000 requests for franchises a year, but only 200 or so are granted.

Franchise marketing agencies. While relatively new to the industry, franchise marketing agencies and franchise consultants show prospects of being an important link between franchisors and franchisees. (A list of franchise consultants is available in *The Franchise Boom*, by Harry Kurch.) However, since many of these agencies and consultants earn their fees through commissions paid by the franchisors, they are not likely to make a very objective recommendation.

Factors to Consider about the Franchise

Once a franchise has been tentatively chosen, the offer should be investigated in detail. Some of the factors to investigate are:

The Company[1]

The company should have a solid financial position, satisfactory credit rating, and a good reputation. It should have been in business long enough to prove its ability and the competitiveness of its product or service. It should be willing to provide detailed histories on the background of its principals. It should provide information on how many other franchisees are actually in operation, not just on paper, and how many have been bought back and under what circumstances. The prospective franchisee should try to talk with some of the company's operating franchisees informally, rather than prearranged by the franchisor. The company should be one that is committed to franchising and will not buy out the franchisee as soon as they can afford to.

The Salesman or Company Representative

Any attempt to evade questions on the part of the franchise salesman is suspect. So also is attempting to pressure the prospective franchisee into signing up for the "last territory available" or any other pretext.

The Costs

The franchisee should be quite clear about what he is being charged for the franchise and what he is getting for his money; what is included in the

---

[1] From "Franchising," *Small Business Reporter* 9, No. 9 (San Francisco: Bank of America, Small Business Advisory Service, 1970), pp. 6–7. Reprinted with permission of the Bank of America National Trust and Savings Association.

franchise fee; what the down payment covers and what it does not; whether the equipment, if any, is reasonable in price and of good make; who pays for extensive delays in getting started; whether the continuing percentage on sales is a reasonable amount that he will be able to afford and what services the franchisor is providing in return. He should also make sure that any "hidden costs" are explained.

The Product or Service

The product or service is of prime importance. The company's ads may be excellent but if the product is mediocre or unsuited to the prospective franchisee's area the outlet will fail. Even if the franchisor is carrying out site evaluation or market surveys it is a good idea to do some double checking, particularly if the franchisee is more familiar with the locality than the franchisor. A few franchise companies have run into trouble by trying to transplant a successful idea, product, or format from one area to another—where it failed. If the product is patented, the franchisee should ensure the patents extend to him and know his obligations in the case of product guarantees.

The Legal Aspects

The legal framework of franchising is constantly changing. Even ethical franchisors may have overlooked something, which is why a prospective franchisee should learn all he can about franchising and talk the franchise offer over with a competent attorney. Also, there may be local or state laws affecting the operation of the franchisee that the franchisor may not be aware of: for example, local building and health codes or zoning regulations. More and more communities are showing concern over garish, outsized signs and unattractive, cheaply constructed buildings which are often associated, rightly or wrongly, with franchising.

The Contract

The franchisee should make sure that the territory he has been assigned is a reasonable size and that it will not be encroached on by other franchisees of the same company.
The franchisee should make sure he understands and is willing to accept the restrictions involved in the particular franchise: he may not be able to buy from other than franchisor-specified sources; he may not be able to choose his inventory mix, or add profit-making lines over and above those laid down by the franchisor.

Most important are the circumstances under which the contract can be terminated. The franchisor may have very arbitrary powers in this respect — for example, a 30-days notice with no prior warning.

The franchisee should be sure he understands the contract's other termination provisions with regard to transfers, goodwill, and restrictions on his opening another business after termination.

Checklist for Evaluating a Franchise

Dr. Wilford L. White, formerly Assistant Deputy Administrator of the Small Business Administration and currently Professional Lecturer, Howard University, has devised the following list of 24 questions to help potential franchisees evaluate a franchise opportunity.

The Franchise

1. Did your lawyer approve the franchise contract you are considering after he studied it paragraph by paragraph?
2. Does the franchise call upon you to take any steps which are, according to your lawyer, unwise or illegal in your state, county, or city?
3. Does the franchise give you an exclusive territory for the length of the franchise or can the franchisor sell a second or third franchise in your territory?
4. Is the franchisor connected in any way with any other franchise company handling similar merchandise or services?
5. If the answer to the last question is "yes," what is your protection against this second franchisor organization?
6. Under what circumstances can you terminate the franchise contract and at what cost to you, if you decide for any reason at all that you wish to cancel it?
7. If you sell your franchise, will you be compensated for your goodwill or will the goodwill you have built into the business be lost by you?

The Franchisor

8. For how many years has the firm offering you a franchise been in operation?
9. Has it a reputation for honesty and fair dealing among the local firms holding its franchise?
10. Has the franchisor shown you any certified figures indicating exact net

profits of one or more going firms which you personally checked yourself with the franchisee?
11. Will the firm assist you with:
    (a) A management training program?
    (b) An employee training program?
    (c) A public relations program?
    (d) Capital?
    (e) Credit?
    (f) Merchandising ideas?
12. Will the firm assist you in finding a good location for your new business?
13. Is the franchising firm adequately financed so that it can carry out its stated plan of financial assistance and expansion?
14. Is the franchisor a one-man company or a corporation with an experienced management trained in depth (so that there would always be an experienced man at its head)?
15. Exactly what can the franchisor do for you which you cannot do for yourself?
16. Has the franchisor investigated you carefully enough to assure itself that you can successfully operate one of their franchises at a profit both to them and to you?

You — The Franchisee

17. How much equity capital will you have to have to purchase the franchise and operate it until your income equals your expenses? Where are you going to get it?
18. Are you prepared to give up some independence of action to secure the advantages offered by the franchise?
19. Do YOU really believe you have the innate ability, training, and experience to work smoothly and profitably with the franchisor, your employees, and your customers?
20. Are you ready to spend much or all of the remainder of your business life with this franchisor, offering his product or service to your public?

Your Market

21. Have you made any study to determine whether the product or service which you propose to sell under franchise has a market in your territory at the prices you will have to charge?
22. Will the population in the territory given you increase, remain static, or decrease over the next 5 years?

23. Will the product or service you are considering be in greater demand, about the same, or less demand 5 years from now than today?
24. What competition exists in your territory already for the product or service you contemplate selling?
    (a) Nonfranchise firms?
    (b) Franchise firms?

Some Final Thoughts on Franchising

Franchising has become a very controversial topic today. To some it is "the last frontier" for the small businessman and the opportunity to fulfill the American Dream. To its opponents, it is a fraudulent gimmick to separate the small investor from his funds. In reality, both views have some validity. For example, franchising has enabled thousands of individuals to enter the business world who would otherwise have been unable to. A few franchisees have even become millionaires. At the same time, other franchisees have ended in bankruptcy or continued as disenchanted, marginal businessmen.

The majority of franchisees probably end up making a reasonable living but not getting the big return on their investment that the franchisor suggested they would. Thomas Hawder, staff attorney for the Federal Trade Commission, concluded after three weeks of hearings on the franchise industry that the most numerous complaints the FTC has received deal with misrepresentation of the profitability of franchises. He cited a University of Wisconsin study that showed that about 72 percent of the franchises earned less than the minimum income projections and about 98 percent earned less than the average expected earnings.[2]

As might be expected in any new and growing field, several fraudulent companies have emerged to damage the image of franchising. Consequently, the franchise industry has attempted self-control, and courts have undertaken an examination of the basic promises of the franchise relationship. There is every indication that the future will bring increased legislation and surveillance by all levels of government. At the same time, as franchising growth reaches a level of maturity, franchisors with little to offer will be forced out of business and those with experience and managerial competence will remain.

In the last analysis, the feasibility of franchising depends on each situation. As in any type of business undertaking, the return in franchising is related directly to the amount of time and money the franchisee invests. Franchising is not a "get rich quick" deal, and it does not guarantee success or high profits with little effort. However, it does significantly minimize chances of failure,

---

[2] "High-Blown Claims May Hide Pitfalls in Franchise Deals," *Detroit Free Press* (June 12, 1972), pp. 7–13.

and, for many with limited capital and experience, it provides the best business opportunity.

Incident 9: Franchise Potential

Pete Smith was recently visited by Mr. Allen Baxter, who identified himself as a representative of Antique Autos of America, Inc. (AAA). Mr. Baxter stated that his company had been established for 5 years and that it provides marketing and supply advice, along with national advertising, for selected firms involved in antique auto restoration.

AAA would provide Pete with names of owners of cars in need of restoration all over the country. These potential clients would be carefully selected for interest and financial responsibility. Most of them would be in Pete's general area, although for special jobs they could be anywhere in the country. Since Pete was rapidly acquiring a reputation as an outstanding craftsman, Mr. Baxter said that certain special jobs would be routed to him.

AAA would also provide replica parts unavailable anywhere in the country. AAA had secured supply sources from countries like India and Argentina, where old cars are plentiful and labor is cheap. Pete could buy these imported parts from AAA at low prices. Mr. Baxter assured Pete that the parts were of the highest quality. Gross margins would be 50 percent in most cases.

Mr. Baxter showed Pete an impressive catalog, and Pete had to admit that many items listed were totally unavailable anywhere else. In fact, he immediately ordered $165 worth of material, since one of his customers had been looking for these items for some time. Mr. Baxter noted that it would take about 5 months for delivery, since the material was now in India.

In return for these services, AAA would get 8 percent of Pete's gross sales on all items. Pete would get some national advertising coverage, since AAA advertised regularly in the car magazines. Pete knew this was true, since he had seen the ads.

AAA could also help Pete with his credit problems. As a registered franchisee, he could expect to get somewhat better terms at his local bank. AAA was willing to stand full credit investigation, and the fact that Pete was locked into such a reliable franchisor would help him greatly.

Pete promised to think it over and let Mr. Baxter know about his decision in a few weeks. He knew that AAA might do him some good, but that 8 percent bothered him, particularly on sales he was already making. Why should he give AAA a piece of this action? But it was very difficult to get new business, and it took a lot of his time. If they could handle some of the marketing problems for him, perhaps he could get other more important things done.

Pete also knew that much antique auto material made in Argentina was of very poor quality. Yet, when he needed a camshaft for a 1933 Hupmobile, what else could he do? He had never even seen an Indian part, but he suspected that there might be real quality control problems in importing parts.

1. How could Pete check out AAA?
2. What are the advantages of joining this group as a franchisee? What are the disadvantages?
3. Should Pete sign up with AAA? Why or why not?

Discussion Questions

1. How important is franchising as a way of doing business in the country today?
2. Explain what is meant by the term "franchise"?
3. List and briefly discuss the pros and cons of franchising.
4. How can you locate franchise opportunities?
5. What areas or topics should be considered by the prospective franchisee before buying a franchise?
6. What are some of the weaknesses in franchise contracts?
7. Explain in some detail the steps you would go through and the questions you would ask if you were evaluating a specific franchise.
8. Does franchising really provide the opportunity to be an "entrepreneur"? Why or why not?
9. What do you see as the future of franchising? Explain.

Suggested Readings

"A Close Look at Food Franchising." Fair Lawn, N. J.: The American Institute of Food Distribution, 1968.

Alexander, Sandy, *Franchising and You*. Long Beach, Calif.: The Franchise Journal, 1968.

Broom, H. N., and Longenecker, J. G., *Small Business Management*, 3rd. ed. Cincinnati: South-Western Publishing, 1971. Ch. 22.

Brown, Harold, *Franchising: Trap for the Trusting*, rev. ed. Boston: Little, Brown, 1970.

Buckley, Noel, "Fortunes in Franchising," *Dun's Review and Modern Industry* LXXXIII (April 1964), 36–37, 82–84.

Diaz, Robert M., and Gurnick, Stanley I., *Franchising: The Investor's Complete Handbook*. New York: Hastings House, 1969.

"Facts About Franchising," rev. ed. (free pamphlet). New York: National Better Business Bureau.

Franchise Company Data. Washington, D. C.: Department of Commerce, Business and Defense Services Administration, 1969.

Glickman, Gladys, *Franchising.* New York: Matthew Bender, 1968.

Journal of Retailing 44, No. 4 (Winter 1968–69). Special issue on franchising.

Klatt, Lawrence A., ed., *Managing the Dynamic Small Firm: Readings.* Belmont, Calif.: Wadsworth, 1971. See franchising section.

Kursh, Harry, *The Franchise Boom,* rev. ed. Englewood Cliffs, N. J.: Prentice-Hall, 1969.

Lewis, E. H., and Hancock, R. S., *The Franchise System of Distribution.* Minneapolis: University of Minnesota Press, 1973.

"McDonald's Makes Franchising Sizzle," *Business Week,* No. 2024 (June 15, 1968), pp. 102–107.

Metz, Robert, *Franchising: How to Select a Business of Your Own.* New York: Hawthorne Books, 1969.

Munsinger, Gary M., "Decision-Making and the Franchise Package," *Arizona Review* 17 (February 1968), 4–6.

Nagourney, Donald, "Franchising—Retailing's Stepchild," *The New York Retailer* 21 (May 1968), 3–8.

Partners for Profit. New York: American Management Association, 1966.

Selz, D. D., "How to 'Check Out' a Prospective Franchise," *Modern Franchising* 6, No. 3, (July–August 1964), 20–23.

Tunick, A. L., "Are You Ready for Franchising," *Small Marketers Aids,* No. 115. Washington, D. C.: Small Business Administration, 1970.

Vaughn, Charles L., *Franchising Today.* Long Island, N. Y.: Farnsworth Publishing, 1969.

"What It Takes to Succeed in a Franchise Business," *Changing Times,* The Kiplinger Magazine (May 1970), 25–28.

Part Four **Operating the Business**

Marketing Practices

Chapter 10

Although it is important that a small enterprise provide a *quality* good or service, it is not necessarily enough, for the product must be sold at a profit in order for the organization to survive. Thus, every businessman must be a marketer to some extent, particularly the small businessman since he is called upon to perform all managerial functions.

Emergence of Marketing Activity

The typical business enterprise is started by someone who is knowledgeable in the *physical* creation and provision of the particular good or service. For instance, most service station operators probably worked as mechanics before starting their own business. Similarly, most new dry-cleaning establishments are opened by entrepreneurs who know about the physical process of cleaning clothes. Further, most small manufacturing firms are started by engineers or technicians. Consequently, it is a fairly safe generalization to say that most new entrepreneurs are production-minded.

Later the wise small businessman realizes that he must be involved in another activity—the sales function. He must develop an effective selling program to guarantee that the good or service reaches the intended consumers. He comes to realize that production and sales must share equal status as they are key functions in any business organization. The failure to recognize the importance of personal selling is one of the primary explanations for numerous failures among enterprises.

Note: This chapter was written in collaboration with David L. Kurtz, Eastern Michigan University.

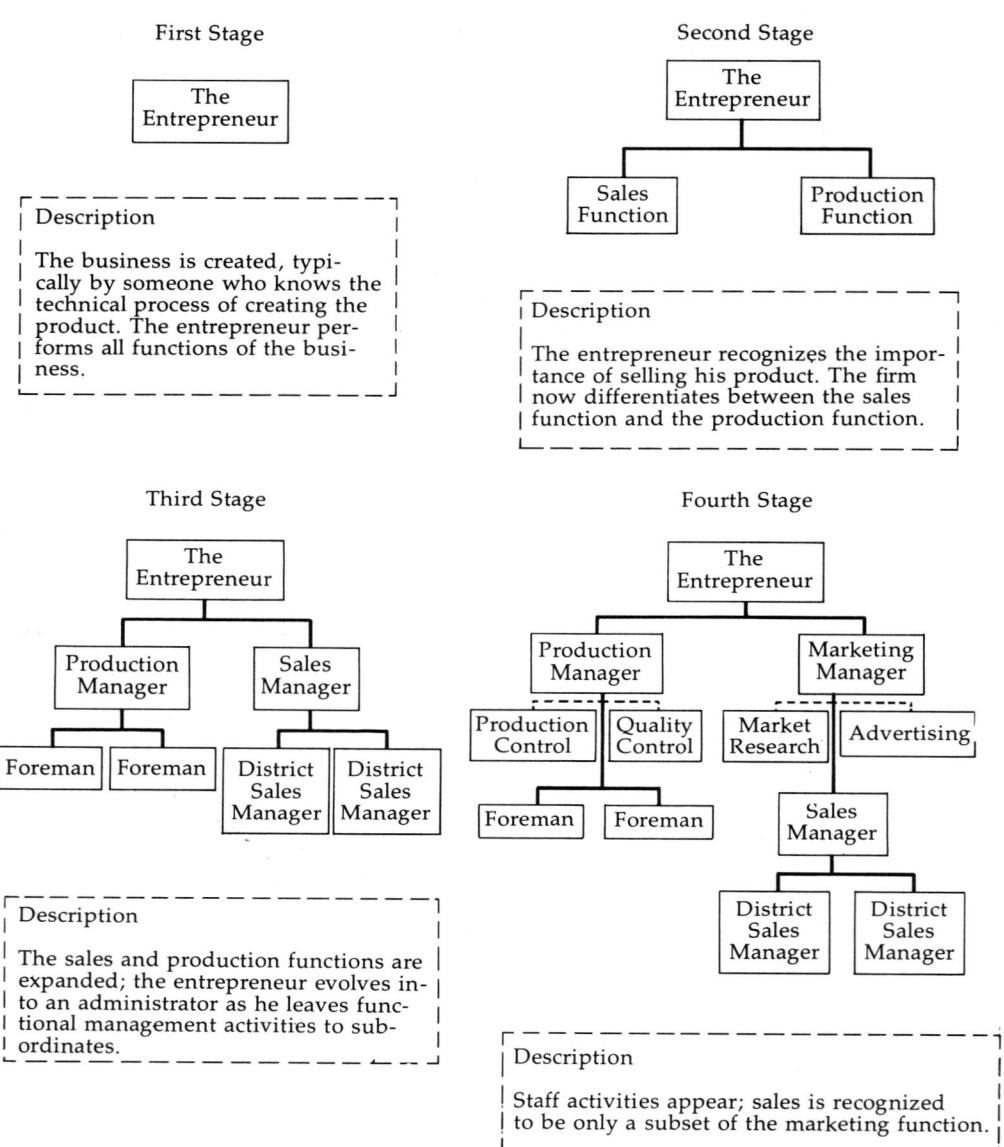

Figure 10–1. The Emergence of Marketing Activity.

Figure 10-1 represents the successive stages of marketing activity. The second stage of Figure 10-1 shows that sales is the second function to emerge in most fledgling organizations. Upon recognizing its importance, the entrepreneur usually hires a salesman, while he continues to run the production side of the firm. In a sense, then, the entrepreneur now performs two roles. First, he assumes production responsibilities, and second, he acts as a general administrator over both aspects of his organization.

The third stage in the emergence of marketing activity is the expansion of both the production and sales functions. As expansion becomes necessary, the entrepreneur delegates production responsibilities to someone else and becomes strictly an administrator. He now leaves functional management duties entirely to subordinates.

Finally, as the organization continues to grow, he needs to develop staff activities, such as advertising, marketing research, production control, and quality control. It is also important that sales now becomes only a subset of the total marketing process. Thus, this stage brings a tremendous expansion of staff or advisory functions.

This description of a growth pattern may not apply to all firms, but it is a good approximation of what occurs in most cases. Thus, the key for the small businessman is to develop a true appreciation of the marketing function as well as production know-how. One example of the fate of those who overlook marketing problems is the Pioneer Tool and Die Company, which attempted to follow Ralph Waldo Emerson's advice to "build a better mousetrap, and the world will beat a path to your door." In 1956, Pioneer constructed the "perfect" mousetrap since it was automatic, faultless, and odorless. However, they sold only 400 of the 5,600 traps produced—the result, a loss of $63,000. The firm failed to take into account the marketing implications of their $29.95 price tag.[1]

The Marketing Concept: A Better Way To Do Business

The marketing concept is by definition a company-wide consumer orientation with the objective of achieving long-run profit objectives. In short, customer satisfaction should be the cornerstone of effective management. This guideline is particularly important for the small businessman, since he has closer contact with the consumer.

Historically, wide acceptance of the marketing concept did not come about until after World War II. Until the war, our economy could be classified as a seller's market (one with a shortage of goods and services). There was little pressure to design an effective marketing program, since the very shortage of

---

[1] "Who Needs It?" *Wall Street Journal* (March 6, 1967), p. 1, for a discussion of this case.

products meant strong consumer demand. When the war ended, however, our factories stopped manufacturing military equipment and turned to the production of consumer durable goods again—an activity that had, for all practical purposes, ceased in early 1942. This renewed production was the beginning of the buyer's market (one with an abundance of goods and services) that characterizes our contemporary business environment. With the advent of a buyer's market, goods had to be sold, not just produced.

Perhaps the actual origin of the new managerial philosophy called the marketing concept was General Electric Company's Annual Report of 1952 in which the firm announced a new strategy toward business management.

> The concept . . . introduces the marketing man at the beginning rather than at the end of the production cycle and integrates marketing into each phase of the business. Thus marketing, through its studies and research, will establish for the engineer, the design and manufacturing man, what the customer wants in a given product, what price he is willing to pay, and where and when it will be wanted. Marketing will have authority in product planning, production scheduling, and inventory control, as well as in sales distribution and services of the product.[2]

The advent of the marketing concept meant that marketing would no longer be regarded as a supplemental activity to be performed after the production process. Thus, in most successful companies management is now "consumer oriented." In far too many cases, however, small businesses have failed to follow suit and adopt a philosophy of customer orientation. This no doubt is a partial explanation of the high failure rate for smaller companies.

Marketing Decision Making

The small businessman is essentially required to make three major types of business decisions: production decisions, marketing decisions, and financial decisions.

In attempting to achieve the goals and objectives of his firm, the entrepreneur has to develop a management strategy for each of these functional areas. As illustrated in Figure 10–2, the decision-making process in all three areas is influenced by the actions of competitors and the existing environmental factors.

---

[2] *1952 Annual Report* (Schenectady, N. Y.: General Electric Company, 1952), p. 21.

Figure 10-2. An Overview of the Decision-Making Process.

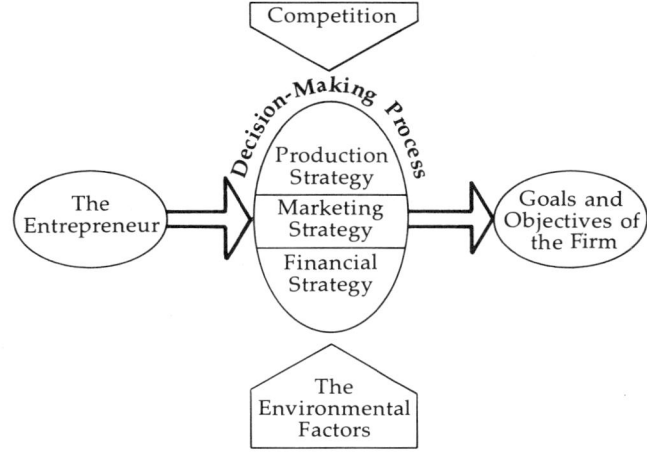

Environmental Factors

Although environmental factors must be considered in any marketing decision, they are beyond the entrepreneur's direct control. These factors can be divided into three categories: legal, economic, and social.

The *legal* variable consists primarily of pricing constraints and promotion constraints. The Sherman Act (1890) was the first piece of federal pricing legislation. This law, which was later supplemented by the Clayton Act (1914), prohibited "restraints of trade," including price collusion. The Fair Trade Laws, which were state legislative acts passed in the 1930s, permitted a manufacturer to stipulate a minimum retail price for his product. A more recent example of the "fair trade" philosophy is the proposed Quality Stabilization Act. The Unfair Trade Laws, on the other hand, set minimum prices for comparable merchandise. Most of these state laws set the retail price floor at "cost plus 6–8 percent." The Robinson-Patman Act of 1936 is another example of pricing legislation that has had a significant impact on small business in general, and retailing in particular. The Robinson-Patman Act prohibited price discrimination not justified by a cost differential.

Promotional constraints are laws controlling deceptive price advertising, labelling requirements, and false or inadequate product information. The most important legislation in this area is the Federal Trade Commission Act (1914). This bill, as amended by the Wheeler-Leo Act (1938), banned unfair methods of competition, including deceptive promotional practices.

The *economic* environment affects the marketing decisions made by the entrepreneur in many ways. For instance, inflation is probably the most important characteristic of our contemporary economy. Prolonged inflationary pressure has caused the typical consumer to become more conscious of prices than ever before. Various studies have indicated that customers are now more knowledgeable about average price levels. In the past, public resistance to price increases could be alleviated, or at least minimized, by an additional outlay for promotion. Now the marketing decision maker must adjust to increased price competition. The small businessman must particularly work to keep his firm's productivity at a level that will allow him to compete with larger companies. Other economic variables that can affect entrepreneurial decisions include the unemployment index, balance of trade (for those small businesses engaged in exporting), business productivity, and government economic policy. The entrepreneur, therefore, should be attuned to happenings in the economy and should question how they are likely to affect his marketing programs.

Social aspects of the business environment must also be considered when making marketing decisions. For example, the general public today is more aware of consumer issues as well as more attentive to the role of business in social problems and solutions. The current demand for ecological reform is an example of the type of societal influence that the small businessman must consider when marketing his product. Air pollution, water pollution, solid-waste disposal, and noise pollution are ecological issues receiving increased attention. Along with the increased attention have come federal and local regulations that directly affect marketing as well as the production of goods. For example, to combat the problem of solid-waste disposal, Oregon has banned the sale of no-deposit, no-return bottles.

Similarly, we have entered the age of consumerism, and consumers are becoming more vocal and more demanding in what they purchase. Duke Rose, director of marketing of Geneva, Inc., has pointed out that a successful manufacturer of consumer goods will have to concentrate more on product innovation and improvement. He notes that business will have to do a much better job of servicing the consumer and of getting to know him and his needs.

Elements of Marketing Strategy

Marketing decision making has four basic strategy elements: product strategy, channels strategy, promotional strategy, and pricing strategy. The combination of these elements forms what has been called the "marketing mix." The marketing decision maker must be certain that he has adequate marketing information before he begins to contemplate various strategy elements, however.

Marketing Information

Essentially, all marketing information can be classified into one of three categories: operating data, consumer data, or competitive data. These data provide the inputs for marketing decisions (see Figure 10–3). The outputs are the various strategy elements of the marketing program.

Operating information refers to the internal operation of the firm and includes sales analysis, marketing cost studies, and comparisons with industry statistics. For most small businesses, operating information probably constitutes 70–75 percent of all marketing information received by the entrepreneur: first, because it is easier to derive, and second, because it may be the most important information needed by a decision maker.

Consumer information is the most difficult type of information to secure since customers' tastes and preferences are in constant flux. Even the very largest firms with sophisticated marketing-research departments have problems pinning down consumer tastes. The best approach for the small businessman is to devote some time to reading published consumer research in his industry. Reading suggestions and advice can usually be obtained at the College of Business Administration of the nearest large university. It would be foolhardy for the entrepreneur to attempt his own consumer research unless he has been trained in marketing-research techniques, especially since much excellent research is already available in business publications.

Competitive information can be of immense value to the entrepreneur since it may allow him to alter one or more strategy elements in response to a competitor's action in the market. The small businessman must be constantly aware of what his competitors are doing in the marketplace. The key factor of gathering data on competitors is a good reporting system. Such data should be acquired continually rather than periodically as for operating and consumer information. The entrepreneur should allocate a reasonable amount of time to competitive investigation. His reporting system may be as simple as window-shopping in the neighborhood for one-half hour per week, or as complex as a computer-generated pricing report. In any case, the relatively limited investment in better marketing information will pay handsome dividends in the form of improved business decisions.

Marketing information is the foundation of a successful marketing program. The various aspects of marketing strategy are dependent on the entrepreneur's receiving the most complete business information available. The next section of this chapter will examine each of the four strategy elements and their relationship to the total marketing program.

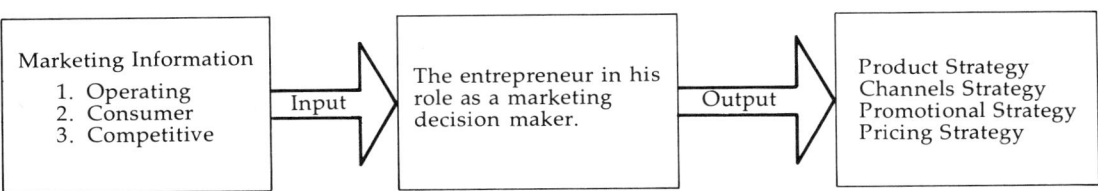

Figure 10–3. Implementation of the Marketing Information System.

Product Strategy

Marketers broadly define "product" as anything from which the consumer derives satisfaction. Therefore, basic product design should be consumer oriented rather than engineering or production oriented.

The first decision the entrepreneur must make in developing a product strategy is his marketing direction. And his marketing direction may take the form of product differentiation or market segmentation policies. *Product differentiation* is a strategy alternative that directs new consumer demand toward a firm's product. Sales promotion is therefore designed to convince the consumer that his product is better than those of competitors. A *market segmentation* policy recognizes the existence of many submarkets and then tries to direct the product toward those submarkets with the highest sales potential. For, in reality, while we often speak of the "market," all markets consist of many distinct market segments—that is, groupings of buyers with enough homogeneity to become the basis for market cultivation.

Another consideration is the company's total product line. Any new product should be consistent with an existing product policy. For example, branding is usually used to identify a firm's "family of products." A *brand* is any design, name, or symbol that is used to specify the goods of a particular marketer. The early guilds used them so that violaters of production quotas could be identified. Now branding is used primarily to develop customer loyalty through easy identification. The Lanham Act (1946) provides for federal registration of brands and trademarks.

The importance of effective packaging is often neglected by many businessmen. The basic rule is not to *over-* or *under-*package a product. Recognizing that the package is as much a sales tool as it is a container, under-packaging may mean reduced sales. "Over-packaging" occurs when a package adds more to marketing costs than it generates in additional revenues. Thus, although many products could be packaged more attractively, the additional cost of improving packaging may be disproportionate to the increased sales.

Products go through a life cycle similar to human beings: they are born, they mature, and they eventually die. Thus, an important consideration in formulating any product strategy is the stage of the product's life cycle. Many businessmen have suffered severe market reversals when they have failed to accept that an existing product has, in fact, died in the competitive marketplace.

The product life is usually visualized as consisting of four stages: introduction, growth, maturity, and decline (see Figure 10–4). In the "introduction" period, the innovator is rewarded with substantial sales increases because he has a temporary monopoly. Total market sales increase at an *increasing* rate. In the "growth" period, total market sales *increase* at a decreasing rate. Furthermore, the innovator has to share the market with several competitors that entered because of the rapid growth in the earlier period.

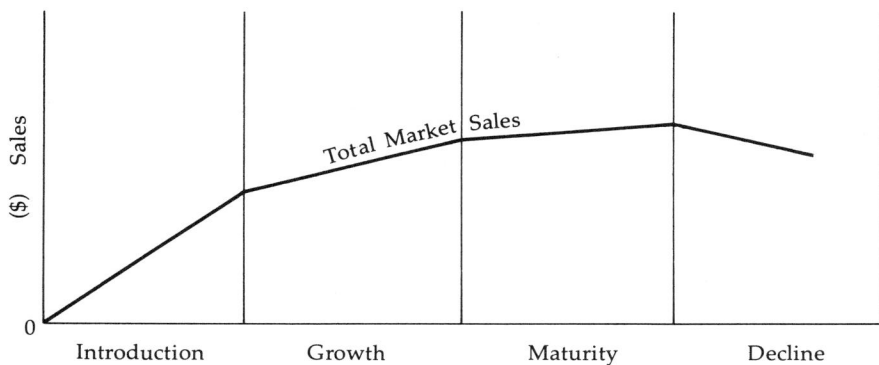

Figure 10–4. The Product Life Cycle.

Total market sales peak out in the "maturity" stage. Increased price competition also causes further decline. The final stage sees sales in a continual decline with the inevitable decision to discontinue the marketing of the product.

Product decisions clearly need to be related to the product's life cycle. For instance, the entrepreneur with a new product should seek brand recognition early in the cycle so as to help protect his product in the growth stages when competition will become extremely keen, as well as to prolong the later stages of the product's life. Conversely, product differentiation and market segmentation are viewed as alternative ways to enter the market for an established product. Once "in the market," the small firm must constantly examine and reexamine its product line. New or modified products will be required to replace products that reach the final stages of their life cycle.

Channel Strategy

The entrepreneur must also decide how he will distribute his product. A channel of distribution is the pathway a good follows from the manufacturer to the final consumer. The three basic types of distribution channels are illustrated in Figure 10–5. A direct channel of distribution is used when the manufacturer's sales force sells the product directly to the final consumer. Indirect channels involve institutional middlemen such as retailers and wholesalers. It is important to point out that these institutional middlemen come into existence only if there is a valid need for their services.

Marketing of goods and services includes eight basic functions that must be performed by someone, regardless of the distribution channel used: buying, selling, transporting, storing, grading, risk taking, financing, and marketing information. Historically, middlemen have performed all of these functions; particularly transporting, storing, risk taking, and financing. None of the eight

Figure 10–5.
Channels of
Distribution.

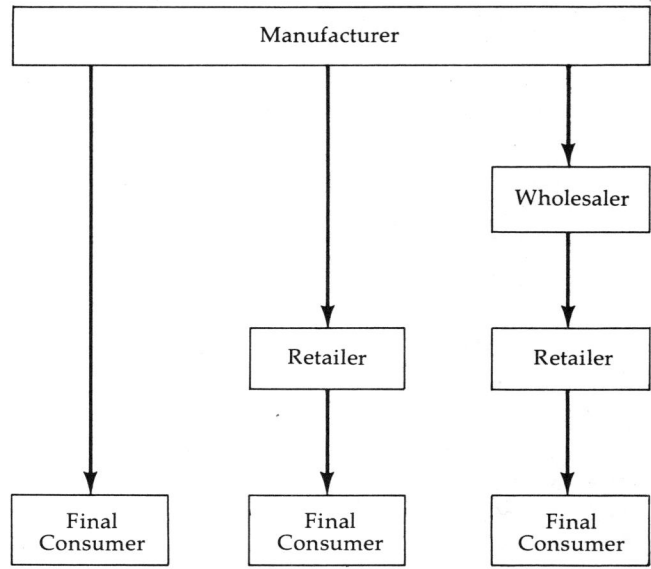

functions can be eliminated from the marketing strategy. The elimination of a middleman, for instance, does not eliminate the functions he has been performing. Some other channel member must absorb these functions.

The small businessman has two important decisions to make in developing his channel strategy: (1) He must decide which type of channel to employ, or to become part of in the case of an institutional middleman; and (2) he must decide how to effectively maintain the channel. This is often the most difficult part. An effective public relations program is an absolute necessity.

When deciding which type of channel to employ, the entrepreneur needs information about who buys the product as well as where, when, and how it is purchased. He also needs to know something about the selling methods of his outlets as well as their selling costs in order to determine what he can expect from them in return for a given margin.

In the early stage, a new product usually requires a different channel of distribution from that needed once the product is established and widely accepted. For example, the Whitefield Company initially distributed its new high-priced germicidal lotion through prestige department stores and drugstores. As consumer acceptance made the lotion more of a staple item, the firm moved it to food stores, which in time became the main outlets for the lotion.

Changes in market conditions and buyer attitudes necessitate the periodic checking of distribution channels to keep them in line with the changing marketplace. Some of the indicators that may reveal the need for channel changes include:

Consumers or Users

1. Shifting trends in buying habits:
    Types of sources from which they buy.
    How they buy—amounts, frequency, terms, and other products bought along with yours.
2. Development of new needs in relation to service, parts, or technical help.

Middlemen

1. Change in relative importance of outlet types applicable to your product.
2. Changes in the amount of profit distributors and dealers can make with your product.
3. Changes in policies and activities of each type of outlet in relation to your product on the following points:
    Priority of customer types and areas to which type of outlet sells.
    Inventory—what and how much will be stocked.
    Promotional effort devoted to product.

Your Own Organization

1. Change in financial strength.
2. Higher or lower sales volume of existing products.
3. Changes in marketing personnel or organization.
4. Revised marketing activities:
    New objectives in terms of the relative importance of different customer groups and areas to be sold.
    Addition of new products.
    More personal selling and advertising effort.
    Different order-filling procedures, physical distribution arrangements, and inventory policies.[3]

Competitors

If competitors change their distribution plans, the small businessman may have to adjust his plan. He may not want to copy their arrangements. What is

---

[3] Adapted from Richard M. Clewett, "Checking Your Marketing Channels." In *Management Aids for Small Manufacturers*, No. 120 (Washington, D. C.: Small Business Administration, 1963), pp. 43–44.

effective for his competitors may not be effective for him because of different policies, personnel, management experience, distribution points, and other differences. However, he should be alert to the possibility that his competitor may have started on a new course at the most opportune time. Poor timing may doom an otherwise useful plan.

Promotional Strategy

This strategy involves the nonprice selling activities of the business. Basically there are three components to promotion: advertising, personal selling, and sales promotion. *Advertising* includes all nonpersonalized methods of mass selling and is most effective for consumer goods that are widely distributed. *Personal selling* is the process of aiding and persuading someone to buy a product or service in a face-to-face situation. It is more useful for higher-priced items, such as industrial products. It is also of vital importance to the institutional middlemen—wholesalers and retailers. Personal selling has become increasingly expensive in recent years. Thus, many goods with low margins can no longer be sold profitably by any means other than mass advertising. *Sales promotion* is the third aspect of promotion. It includes:

1. Point-of-purchase advertising, such as store displays.
2. Specialty advertising—selective or limited advertising methods, such as calendars, matchbook covers, and holiday favors.
3. Dealer supports, such as institutional promotions.
4. Public relations, such as information releases concerning new products.

Of course, the small businessman cannot afford the luxury of employing specialists in each of these areas. Therefore, a few generalizations about advertising, personal selling, and sales promotion might be helpful.

Developing an Effective Promotional Strategy

To the small businessman, personal selling is probably the most important promotion variable. The traditional adage that "nothing happens until someone sells something" should be a part of every entrepreneur's operational philosophy. The entrepreneur—no matter how busy he is with other tasks—should always remain involved with the personal selling of his good or service. To do otherwise is to void the most crucial tenets of the marketing concept. But what constitutes good personal selling?

According to Donald F. Mulvihill, three elements are needed for good personal selling: a customer-centered attitude, an administrative climate that encourages improvement, and an appreciation of the importance of certain basic personal-selling skills. A salesperson with a customer-centered attitude accepts and tries to understand the customer's behavior in the selling situation. Accordingly, he centers his attention primarily on the customer rather than the product, the company, or himself. The proper administrative climate depends, of course, on the owner or manager. He must provide the environment in which the salesperson will want to improve and will be helped to do so. It is the third element, an appreciation of certain basic personal-selling skills, that seems to be lacking most frequently. Thus, the entrepreneur may want to consider the following points suggested by Mulvihill:[4]

To begin with, the salesperson's main function is not so much finding out whether a customer wants something, but rather finding out what is wanted. After that, it is a question of helping to fill that want and insuring satisfaction.

If you were to study a cross-section of men and women noted for success in personal selling, you would find several main functions which these experts all did well. These common skills are:

1. Putting customers in a good frame of mind.
2. Showing interest.
3. Using opinions as selling points.
4. Supplying facts.
5. Answering questions.
6. Meeting objections.
7. Agreeing with customers.
8. Suggesting additional merchandise.
9. Building repeat business.

Most able salespersons rely on ordinary acts of courtesy and friendliness to get customers in good frames of mind and keep them there: offering a seat or hanging up a coat are typical. They pay close attention, too, to customers' comments and reactions.

Crack sales personnel show interest by remembering names and past purchases of regular customers, by inviting new ones to put their names on a mailing list for announcements, and by offering such special services as gift wrapping or combining several bundles for easier carrying.

---

[4]Donald F. Mulvihill, "Improving Personal Selling in Small Business," *Small Marketers Aids*, No. 16 (Washington, D. C.: Small Business Administration), pp. 2–3.

On the use of opinions as selling points, astute selling employees note that customers are often more interested in what somebody thinks of an item than in specific facts about it. Many times the salesperson who reminds a customer that an article is "popular," "smart," "good-looking," or "right" will have better success than someone who outlines physical specifications.

In supplying facts, the best sellers stick to the merits of their own products and avoid discussion of a competing item's shortcomings. They are conversant with product features, but they don't burden customers with more information than is requested.

When answering customers' questions, expert salespeople are usually specific and candid. To a customer wondering whether an electrical appliance would need to be serviced, a good salesperson would reply, "Equipment of that kind will wear with use and sooner or later will need to be serviced." Prices are quoted promptly and accurately, without hedging.

Meeting objections takes tact and understanding. Valid ones must, of course, be admitted as fact. Competent salespeople usually answer them by pointing out the article's compensating virtues. If the customer simply indicates a preference for a competing brand the reply may be, "Perhaps you'd be wise to try our brand so as to make a comparison. It's a very fine product, and many people, once they've used it, like it better than anything else."

Even when a customer is entirely wrong, the expert salesman will not contradict or correct unless specifically asked for a confirmation of facts or an expression of opinion. Agreement helps to dissipate sales resistance, to avoid argument, and to establish an atmosphere conducive to making the purchase.

Proficient sellers seek opportunities to suggest additional merchandise after a customer has made an initial purchase. In some cases this means simply saying, "Why not take our larger $1.95 size? It contains three times as much as the regular $1 size, and the larger package is very handy." Subtler applications may involve proposing related articles; calling attention to special-sale items; suggesting seasonal merchandise; and promoting "new" goods which have just come in, or unusual goods being distributed exclusively.

Top-flight sales personnel try to have customers leave with goods which are suited to their wants and budgets and with the feeling that their patronage is welcomed and sought in the future. Frequently used are parting remarks like, "Many thanks, Mrs. Madison, I'm sure you'll be pleased with this item. It's always a pleasure to help you." Sometimes a friendly comment makes the difference between a repeat customer and one who buys somewhere else next time.

In order to use his advertising budget effectively, the small businessman must develop a concentrated, planned program. The shotgun approach with limited funds usually has very limited impact.

Advertising budgets should reflect the relative difficulty of the task advertising is to perform. Too often, businessmen allocate advertising expenditures based on some percentage of the preceding year's sales. A better approach is to first define the task to be accomplished—say, a 10 percent sales increase—and then allocate the advertising budget accordingly. This, of course, requires that the entrepreneur make some estimate of the productivity of his advertising dollars, which he can do by examining sales and expense records. He should pay as much attention to the effectiveness of his advertising dollar as to the results of his inventory or new machine expenditure. The small businessman can make his advertising successful by creating or supervising the creation of his ads with care; by zeroing in on his market; by using the best medium, or the combination of media, for his purpose; and finally, by selecting one product or sales claim and presenting it with force, clarity, and originality. (For a more detailed discussion of advertising see the appendix to this chapter.)[5]

Sales promotion can be very effective in improving a firm's sales performance, but the small businessman must recognize the dangers as well as the opportunities of such promotions. For example, special price deals can promote new products as "leaders" to sell an entire line. At the same time, it is easy to be trapped into using a low-profit sales deal as a continuous method of doing business. The effect of this approach, however, is to cause a long-run reduction in price and gross profit. Therefore, the entrepreneur must exercise some degree of caution when engaging in certain promotional activities. It is often wise to commit the terms of his promotions to writing, spelling out all the elements, such as the closing or ending date and the specific brands that will be reduced in price.

Pricing Strategy

Many entrepreneurs consider pricing strategy the critical part of their marketing program since prices are what determines the amount of revenue the firm is going to receive. The other strategy elements are supportive in that they make it possible for a particular good or service to be sold at a price that is profitable to the firm.

Pricing is also the most complex marketing variable. There is no one correct formula to use in determining a price. In fact, some marketers argue that pricing should be considered an "art" rather than a "science." All pricing methods have been subject to question, and none have proven acceptable to all segments of the business community.

However, most actual pricing techniques are versions of the "cost-plus" approach—that is, they start with some cost figure and then add an amount

---

[5] Also see D. Peter Bowles, "Advertising for Profit and Prestige," *Small Marketers Aids*, No. 5 (Washington, D. C.: Small Business Administration, 1963), pp. 31–38.

(often calculated by use of a standard percentage) to cover *all other costs plus profit*. While specific methods may vary, the basic format of most pricing formulas stays the same. For example, a local shoe store may determine its prices by adding a 40 percent markup to invoice cost. In this case, the "plus" factor (or markup) has to account for a considerable portion of total cost in addition to the profit margin. A manufacturer, on the other hand, may add a considerably smaller percentage to the basic cost figure. The plant cost accountant may have produced a far more comprehensive cost figure that included some overhead expenses, for example, that the retailer considered in his higher markup. In other words, variation in pricing formulas is often more a function of differing levels of accounting sophistication than of any real differences in pricing methodology.

All pricing techniques, however, have one basic fallacy: they tend to ignore the aspect of consumer demand. A pricing strategy can be effective only if the customer is willing to pay the prices so determined. A cost-oriented pricing procedure typically fails to respond to differences in consumer demand. The best way to handle this problem is to adjust the markup percentage in relation to the stock turn (or turnover). Since stock turn is in fact a type of sales ratio, it should be somewhat representative of consumer demand for the particular product.

Stock turn (or turnover) is the number of times the "average" inventory of a given product is sold annually. Stock turn can be calculated by the following equations:

If inventory is recorded at cost:

$$\text{Stock Turn} = \frac{\text{Cost of Goods Sold}}{\text{Average Inventory}}.$$

If inventory is recorded at retail:

$$\text{Stock Turn} = \frac{\text{Sales}}{\text{Average Inventory}}.$$

Items with high turnover, such as grocery products, should carry lower markups than items with a lower stock turn, such as consumer durables. Therefore, the entrepreneur would be well advised to consider turnover before he sets a product's price. This relationship (between stock turn and markup) is shown in Table 10–1.

Since pricing is fundamental to the entire marketing program, the small businessman must give considerable thought to his pricing strategy. He must know his costs and understand buyer motivation, timing, and his competitors. The following checklist is designed to assist the small businessman in evaluating his pricing policies and practices.[6]

---

[6]Checklist developed by Joseph D. O'Brien, *Small Marketers Aids*, No. 105 (Washington, D. C.: Small Business Administration, 1969).

Table 10–1. Relationship between Markup and Stock Turnover.

If stock turnover (relative to the industry average) is:	then the	markup (relative to the industry average) should be:
High		Low
Average		Average
Low		High

Source: Louis E. Boone and David L. Kurtz, *Contemporary Marketing* (New York,: Holt, Rinehart and Winston, forthcoming).

Examining Costs, Sales Volume, and Profits

The questions in this part should be helpful when you look at prices from the viewpoint of costs, sales volume, and profits.

Costs and prices. The small businessman who sets the price for an item by applying a standard markup may be overlooking certain cost factors which are connected with that item. The following questions are designed to help you gather information which should be helpful when you are determining prices on specific types of items.

1. Do you know which of your operating costs remain the same regardless of sales volume?
2. Do you know which of your operating costs decrease percentage-wise as your sales volume increases?
3. Have you ever figured out the break-even point for your items selling at varying price levels?
4. Do you look behind high gross margin percentages? (For example, a product with a high gross margin may also be a slow turnover item with high handling costs. Thus, it may be less profitable than lower margin items which turn over fast.)
5. When you select items for price reductions, do you project the effects on profits? (For example, if a good marketer considers whether to run canned ham or rump steak on sale, an important cost factor is labor. Practically none is involved in featuring canned ham; however, a rump steak sale requires the skill of a meat-cutter and this labor cost might mean little or no profits.)

Pricing and sales volume. An effective pricing program should also consider sales volume. For example, high prices might limit your sales volume while low prices might result in a large, but unprofitable volume. The following questions should be helpful in determining what is right for your situation.

6. Have you considered setting a sales volume goal and then studying to see if your prices will help you reach it?
7. Have you set a target of a certain number of new customers for next year? (If so, how can pricing help you to get them?)
8. Should you limit the quantities of low-margin items which any one customer can buy when they are on sale? (If so, will you advertise this policy?)
9. What is your policy when a sale item is sold out before the end of the advertised period? Do you allow disappointed customers to buy the item later at the sale price?

Pricing and profits. Prices should help bring in sales which are profitable over the long pull. The following questions are designed to help you think about pricing policies and their effect on your annual profits.

10. Do you have all facts on costs, sales, and competitive behavior?
11. Do you set prices with the hope of accomplishing definite objectives, such as a 1 percent profit increase over last year?
12. Have you set a given level of profits in dollars and in percent of sales?
13. Do you keep records which will give you the needed facts on profits, losses, and prices?
14. Do you review your pricing practices periodically to make sure that they are helping to achieve your profit goals?

Judging the Buyer, Timing, and Competitors

The questions in this part are designed to help you check your practices for judging the buyer (your customers), your timing, and your competitors.

The buyer and pricing strategy. After you have your facts on costs, the next point must be the *customer*—whether you are changing a price, putting in a new item, or checking out your present price practices. Knowledge of your customers helps you to determine how to vary prices in order to get the average gross margin you need for making a profit. (For example, to get an average gross margin of 35 percent, some retailers put a low markup—10 percent, for instance—on items which they promote as traffic builders and use high markup —sometimes as much as 60 percent—on slow-moving items.) The following questions should be helpful in checking your knowledge about your customers.

15. Do you know whether your customers shop around and for what items?
16. Do you know how your customers make their comparisons? By reading newspaper ads? Hearsay?
17. Are you trying to appeal to customers who buy on price alone? To those who buy on quality alone? To those who combine the two?
18. Do any of your customers tell you that your prices are in line with those of your competitors? Higher? Lower?
19. Do you know which item (or types of items) your customers call for even though you raise the price?
20. Do you know which items (or types of items) your customers leave on your shelves when you raise the price?
21. Do certain items seem to appeal to customers more than others when you run weekend, clearance, or special-days purchases?
22. Have you used your individual sales records to classify your present customers according to the volume of their purchases?
23. Will your customers buy more if you use multiple pricing? (For example, 3 for 39 cents for products with rapid turnover.)
24. Do your customers respond to odd prices more readily than even prices, for example, 99 cents rather than $1?
25. Have you decided on a pricing strategy to create a favorable price image with your customers? (For example, a retailer with 8,000 different items might decide to make a full margin on all medium or slow movers while featuring—at low price levels—the remaining fast movers.)
26. If you are trying to build a quality price image, do your individual customer records, such as charge account statements, show that you are selling a larger number of higher priced items than you were 12 months ago?
27. Do your records of individual customer accounts and your observations of customer behavior in the store show price as the important factor in their buying? Service? Assortment? Some other consideration?

Time and pricing. Effective merchandising means that you have the right product, at the right place, at the right price, and at the *right time*. All are important, but timing is the critical element for the small retailer. The following questions should be helpful in determining what is the right time for you to adjust prices.

28. Are you a "leader" or a "follower" in announcing your price reductions? (The follower, even though he matches his competitors, creates a negative impression on his customers.)
29. Have you studied your competitors to see whether they follow any sort of pattern when making price changes? (For example, do some of them run clearance sales earlier than others?)
30. Is there a pattern to the kinds of items which competitors promote at lower prices at certain times of the month or year?
31. Have you decided whether it is better to take early markdowns on seasonal or style goods or to run a clearance sale at the end of the season?
32. Have you made regular annual sales, such as Anniversary Sales, Fall Clearance, or Holiday Cleanup, so popular that many customers wait for them rather than buying in season?
33. When you change a price, do you make sure that *all* customers know about it through price tags and so on?
34. Do you try to time price reductions so they can be promoted in your advertising?

Competition and pricing. When you set prices, you have to consider how your competitors might react to your prices. The starting place is learning as much as you can about their price structures. The following questions are designed to help you check out this phase of pricing.

35. Do you use all the available channels of information to keep you up to date on your competitors' price policies? (Some useful sources of information are: things your customers tell you; the competitor's price list and catalogs, if he uses them; his advertising; reports from your suppliers; trade paper studies; and shoppers employed by you.)
36. Should your policy be to try always to sell above or below competition? Only to meet it?
37. Is there a pattern to the way your competitors respond to your price cuts?
38. Have you lost certain customers because competitors match your price cuts?
39. Is the leader pricing of your competitors affecting your sales volume to such an extent that you must alter your pricing policy on individual items (or types of items) of merchandise?
40. Do you realize that no two competitors have identical cost curves? (This difference in costs means that certain price levels may be profitable for you but unprofitable for your competitor or vice versa.)

Practices to Help Offset Price

Some small retailers take advantage of the fact that price is not always the determining factor in making a sale. They supply customer services and offer other inducements to offset the effect of competitors' lower prices. Delivery service is an example. Comfortable shopper's meeting place is another. The following questions are designed to help you take a look at some of these practices.

41. Do the items or services which you sell have advantages for which customers are willing to pay a little more?
42. From personal observation of customer behavior in your store can you tell about how much more customers will pay for such advantages?
43. Should you change your services so as to create an advantage for which your customers are willing to pay?
44. Does your advertising emphasize customer benefits rather than price?
45. Are you using the most common nonprice competitive tools? (For example, have you tried to alter your product or service to the existing market? Have you tried stamps, bonus purchase gifts, or other plans for building repeat business?
46. Should policies on returned goods be changed so as to impress your customers better?
47. If you sell repair services, have you checked out your guarantee policy?
48. Should you alter assortments of merchandise to increase sales?

Credit: The Other Dimension of Marketing

Credit is an important variable that affects all forms of marketing strategy. It must be considered in any marketing management decision regardless of whether it is in the area of product planning, channels of distribution, promotion, or pricing. Credit is simply inseparable from the marketing function.

One of the most serious problems that can face a small businessman is excessive, and/or doubtful, accounts receivable. However, this problem is a marketing dilemma as well as a financial problem. To a large extent, marketing is oriented toward what might be called "sales expansion." In other words, the marketing man's objective is to achieve a maximum increase in sales, and this desire for expanded sales volume leads to making "high risk" credit sales.

Two suggestions can be offered to the small businessman:

1. Be sure your salesmen are aware of their role as credit investigators. They should realize that "qualifying a customer" is as important as "closing the sale." The entrepreneur should then assume personal responsibility for much of the credit-granting function. Before deciding whether to accept bank credit cards, the small businessman should thoroughly investigate all alternatives (and their corresponding costs).
2. The entrepreneur should keep abreast of the numerous changes that are taking place in consumer and industrial credit. For instance, the recent "truth-in-lending" legislation requires firms to state the annual rates of interest charged on credit purchases, rather than monthly rates. Further modifications in credit regulations are being contemplated at all levels of government. The effective marketing decision maker needs to be aware of this changing environment.

Future Outlook

The small businessman who develops a good marketing program can be optimistic about the near future. Excluding a sudden shift in the economy, it seems reasonable to assume that the competitive environment will continue to provide a buyer's market. The result will be increased sophistication among buyers and the expansion of consumer-education projects in many communities.

Another factor will be increased competition. In the past, competition was viewed as an adversary relationship between two or more companies in the same industry. A more enlightened viewpoint is that modern competition is for the consumer dollar, rather than between firms or products. Thus, businesses that fail to acquire a consumer orientation will face almost certain failure. The small businessman has a definite advantage over larger firms in that he is closer to his customers. This allows him to personalize his business relationship to an extent that is not possible in a larger firm.

Finally, the entrepreneur should realize that future marketing strategy will be developed in a more socially aware environment. Hopefully, this public scrutiny will encourage improved business decisions rather than hinder our free-enterprise system.

Appendix: Effective Advertising[7]

Just as sales are the lifeblood of a business, advertising and sales promotion are the transfusions that keep sales alive and active and the business profitable.

---

[7] Adapted from *Effective Advertising*, Administrative Management Course Program, Topic 14. Washington, D. C.: Small Business Administration, 1965.

Advertising and sales promotion are, of course, parts of the same effort. This appendix, however, will deal specifically with advertising.

Never has advertising been a more vital tool to managers of small business than it is today. The finest product or service is useless until it is in the hands of a consumer or user. Inventories, as long as they remain on shelves or in stock bins, are not a profit but an expense.

Role of Advertising

Most people must be motivated to want something before they will buy it, and advertising is a mass motivator. Of course, when he greets his customer, an entrepreneur is advertising. When he displays an item in his showroom instead of storing it in his stockroom, he is advertising. And when Mrs. Smith tells Mrs. Jones about the wonderful service she received at a certain business, that's advertising of the most valuable kind.

Yet word-of-mouth advertising and point-of-sale advertising (such as a showroom display) are slow and, to a degree, unpredictable. Many times, the difference between point-of-sale and mass advertising is as great as the difference between creeping and running. Thus, whether a business organization should advertise is no longer the question. Now we ask "How much?" and "What kind?"

Strengths and Limitations of Advertising

But what about those businessmen who are satisfied with the status quo, the volume of business they're now doing? Fortunately, there aren't many because no business can stand still for long. It must do better or it will do worse. It must attract new customers because the market is in a constant state of flux. Consumer tastes and loyalties change, and people are continually moving into or away from a trade area. An older generation dies or retires and a younger one takes its place. In other words, in addition to having "drawing power," advertising has "holding power." Even if a businessman doesn't want more business, he must protect what he already has.

The National Retail Merchants Association estimates that the average store would have to go out of business in 3 or 4 years if it did no advertising, because the average store loses between 20 and 25 percent of its customers each year, and these customers must be replaced just to maintain the status quo. Thus, if a business man has 1,200 customers, he must add one customer a day to replace the one he loses.

Thus, we have two top objectives of advertising: to draw in new customers, and to help hold old ones. Advertising can also identify a business with the goods or service it offers in the public's mind. In addition, advertising can build confidence in a business; it can create goodwill; it can increase sales and speed turnover; and, it can reduce expenses by spreading them over a larger volume.

However, there are a number of things advertising cannot do.

1. It cannot make a business prosper if that business offers only a poor product or an inferior kind of service.
2. It cannot lead to sales if the prospects it brings in are ignored or poorly treated.
3. It cannot create traffic overnight, or increase sales with a single ad. (Unfortunately, many smaller businesses follow this kind of touch-and-go advertising policy.)
4. It will not build confidence in the business that sponsors it if the advertising is untruthful or misleading.

Advertising and Management Decisions

Most alert businessmen want to advertise. The problems are: What to advertise? Where to advertise? When to advertise? How to go about it?

No book—and no outsider—can provide the specific answers to these questions. Only the owner knows all of the factors that go into the decisions affecting his business. What we can point up, however, are the kinds of information he will need to make his decisions intelligently so that he will bring in more customers, more sales, and more profits.

Some of these decisions will center on these questions: Should I advertise goods or services? Should I always feature a price-cut come-on? Should I advertise myself and my employees?

The answers will, of course, depend on each business situation and where the business is going. Thus, each businessman should first think about his business in particular: In what ways is it unique or outstanding? What are its strengths? What do I have to offer that the competition can't or doesn't duplicate?

The answers to these questions are the starting points for making advertising decisions. The basic determination of what to advertise depends largely on the type and nature of your business. As a preliminary step in setting up an advertising program, the entrepreneur should analyze his marketing area, bearing in mind that: (1) The average independent store draws customers from not more than a quarter of a mile. (2) The average chain store draws customers from not more than three-quarters of a mile. (3) The average shopping center draws customers from as far away as 4 miles.

Any advertising outside of one's market wastes the advertising dollar. To maximize his advertising expenditure, the businessman should consider: Who are my customers or potential customers? What income groups are they in? Why do they buy? (Home or office, price or quality? On recommendation, or through advertising?) How do they buy? (Cash or charge; do they want discounts? How often do they buy; what quantities?) Where do they live? (In the neighborhood, or some distance from the store?) How do they like my facilities, products, service?

It is also important to analyze the best, next best, and poorest prospects in one's market area to be informed about sales possibilities, the buying habits and the ability to buy of people in the market area, and basic trends in the area.

Sell Price or Quality?

If low price is the basis of a business, then price should be the focus of the advertising. On the other hand, a business built on quality goods and services has two main types of advertising open to it. First, the small businessman may want to stress new quality products or improved designs; fresh, varied, and prestige stock or services; and occasional sales for anniversaries or other special occasions, discontinued lines or remnant stock, or a new business development.

Second, he may want to advertise himself and/or his business rather than its products. This is called institutional advertising. Institutional advertising can either be dull and waste a lot of money, or it can be some of the most interesting, effective, and customer-producing advertising that a business can command. Institutional advertising should emphasize your years in business in the community, important jobs you have done, and the prestige of your service.

However, in advertising, it is most effective to say only one thing at a time. Thus, the owner–manager must choose the major point he wants to make and then make it as effectively as he can. If he tries to feature everything in the same ad, he will end up by featuring nothing.

Name Brands and Product Advertising

A small businessman can give his advertising dollar a running start when he features nationally advertised products or services, materials, or equipment. Manufacturers spend millions of dollars annually to advertise their products. By using these brand names and symbols in his own promotion, the entrepreneur can associate his firm with this national advertising and reap the benefits of the drawing power of household names and the holding power of what the public regards as quality products or services.

National advertising helps to presell a product, but it doesn't tell where to buy it. When an entrepreneur ties in with national advertising, he tells his trade area, "We've Got It!"

The Consumer Buying Cycle

Long before they visit a store, most customers do preliminary shopping in their homes through newspaper and magazine advertising, television and radio commercials, and direct-mail literature or circulars delivered to the home.

When customers do go to a store, it is only natural that they go to the ones whose names, products, and services are familiar to them through advertising. In making purchases, customers almost always go through the following steps:

1. They develop an awareness of the product and service through advertising.
2. They are stimulated to know more about it by the advertising appeal.
3. They go to a store to investigate.
4. They analyze benefits and compare value.
5. They then make a decision, helped by point-of-sale promotion and intelligent selling.
6. They are satisfied and buy.

Advertising Appeals

To understand the job his advertising will have to do, the small businessman must look beyond the obvious and search out the intangible appeals that cause people to buy. People don't buy *things*—they buy goods that satisfy their wants. Every product or service that is marketable has some benefit that the potential customer must see and want before a business can make a sale. For example, a toothpaste maker uses these appeals:

It helps to remove dingy film.
It penetrates crevices.
It washes away food particles.
It cleans and beautifies the teeth.

And a motor-oil refiner uses these:

It gives a motor pep and power.
It provides a quicker get-away.
It dissolves sludge, carbon, and motor varnish.

It saves up to 15 percent in gas and oil.
It frees sticky valves and rings.

Peoples' wants are fairly standard. Most will react to one or another of the following appeals:

Convenience or comfort.
Love or friendship.
Security.
Social approval or status.
Life, health, and well-being.
Profit, savings, or economy.
Stylishness.

And these may be further simplified to the three basic appeals: thrift (bargain appeal), service (convenience appeal), and quality (snob appeal).

Therefore, a small business advertiser is wise to interpret his products or services in terms of these appeals. Some appeals will get better results than others. Naturally, the entrepreneur will learn to stick with these appeals and reject the weaker ones. In deciding on appeals, remember that women (1) generally read advertising more than men, (2) buy approximately 80 percent of all necessities, and (3) greatly influence all other purchases. Only at the lowest income levels do men assert greater influence than women.

Selecting Media

The time and place of advertising are as important as what the advertiser says. The object, of course, is to get the advertising message to good prospects, and to reach his prospects, the entrepreneur must determine his best media of communications. Should he use newspapers (city, neighborhood, shopping); direct mail (letters, bulletins, manufacturer's literature); radio-television spots (time? when? what?), programs (prestige? public service?); telephone and city directories (long-range, not immediate)?

For a business located in a small town, where most people normally come into town to buy, the town newspaper, television, or radio can give you good coverage without waste. On the other hand, for a business located in a section of a good-size city where it would be inconvenient for people from other sections of the city to shop, it would be foolish to advertise in the city paper or television or radio because the entrepreneur would be buying too many readers or listeners who could not conveniently shop at his business. In this instance, it's better to use a community paper or direct mail.

It is very important to select the media that will thoroughly cover the market and allow the businessman to tell his story the way he wants. For instance, the postman will deliver a direct-mail message right to the homes of the consumers a businessman wants to reach, in any form he desires, and as large or small as he wishes. This is one of the most effective advertising media, yet few businessmen use it properly.

Newspapers

Newspapers are the retailer's primary medium because, daily or weekly, they reach the greatest number of consumers. It is certain that a newspaper's readers are three or four times the announced circulation because almost every copy is seen by several readers.

Use of the local newspaper for advertising will depend on how much of the market area is covered by the newspaper's circulation. If the bulk of business is drawn from only a small portion of the area the paper covers, the businessman will be paying a premium for advertising that does no good. Very small neighborhood businesses might do well to look at the possibility of using limited-circulation neighborhood or shopping papers for advertising within a specified area. Here again, however, the entrepreneur must check the reader interest of such papers. In some areas, well-edited neighborhood papers are read with great interest, but in others they are thrown away or regarded as a nuisance. Also, contract rates make it possible to use only one newspaper and follow a prearranged advertising schedule.

If an entrepreneur does not have his own advertising staff, he can get a lot of help—particularly with copy preparation and layout—by working with his newspaper's advertising department staff. Chances are, it will have a stock of attractive standard cuts or can prepare custom cuts at minimum cost.

Classified Ads

Before we move on to discuss other types of advertising, let's consider classified as contrasted with display advertising.

1. Most people use the classified pages to look for specific items or services at featured prices.
2. Merchandise that is a special value and that makes for "consumer bargains" is readily sold through classified ads.

3. Closing out discontinued lines or old models of major and minor household appliances is readily handled through classified ads.
4. Used cars, antiques, scarce items, and distress merchandise are inexpensively advertised in classified sections.

Telephone yellow pages and classified sections in city directories are based on similar appeals, but they have somewhat greater prestige and give an impression of stability. They are particularly effective in service businesses for which there is little opportunity for bargain sales or seasonal promotions. Directory advertising stresses availability, reliability, permanence, prestige, and economy.

Radio-TV Advertising

Only recently have smaller businesses begun to use radio and TV advertising to any appreciable extent. For the most part, rates have been so high that only a big organization with high-volume sales could support such advertising. General radio and TV advertising is costly to the small operator, but by offering "time rates" and group advertising, the broadcasting stations are now making significant efforts to bring costs within the budget of the smaller advertiser. "Spot" announcements, if worded appropriately and timed correctly, get good results and are not too expensive for normal small advertising budgets.

Before buying radio or TV advertising, the small businessman should consider several factors. For example, it is possible to buy coverage that does his business no good. If he buys time from a broadcasting company that has an effective range of 100 miles in every direction, he is charged a rate calculated on the entire broadcast range — even though his own trade area may extend only 2 miles in any direction from his business location. But this is the premium he will pay to get his message to the people within a few miles of his business. This is neither good advertising nor good management.

Here are some broad guides to radio-TV advertising for the small businessman:

1. Small stations or stations in small towns are less expensive and often more efficient in reaching a target audience.
2. Where possible, choose the station projecting the strongest listener appeal. If several stations are available, the entrepreneur should test all of them over a period of time to determine if their usual programs are the kind his potential customers would find appealing. For instance, if he is directing his advertising to the teen-age crowd, it would be unwise to select a station that plays classical music a good part of the time.

3. Check the number of commercials that are broadcast. You don't want your radio-TV announcements crowded in with scores of others. Find out if announcements are run together or are separated by interesting program elements that should hold audience attention.
4. Study a station's programming schedule. Try to get time just before, just after, or during a program having significant listener appeal. Sports events — such as baseball or football games, for instance — are excellent time periods for advertising male-appeal merchandise, sports equipment, and cars.
5. Make your announcement short and interesting. Prices and values should be featured in spot announcements. If you decide to use prestige and institutional advertising, sponsored programming is better.

Handbills

The handbill was at one time the most commonly used medium in retail advertising. It is still an important tool for many small retail and service businesses and the most economical means of small-volume advertising, if well handled. Handbill advertising is more readily controlled than other forms of promotion because it is distributed directly by the business doing the advertising, and it is cheap to produce — by mimeograph, multilith, or silk-screen printing. (Whichever method is used must be neat, legible, and attractive or the advantage is lost.) The handbills can be distributed over the specific area that is expected to give the greatest return, and they can also be passed out in the store or laid out on counters for customers. Another technique is to insert them in packages and bills.

Handbills can be costly if not properly distributed. The people hired to distribute them must be trustworthy, or else the entrepreneur may find his message being thrown away, stuffed in empty mailboxes, or otherwise misdirected. Also to be considered is community reaction to handbills. Some people resent finding unsolicited materials on their porch or in their mailbox.

Direct-Mail Ads

Direct mail has many of the advantages of handbills, and it is also a bit more dignified and personal because it can be directed to an individual customer.

Direct mail is more selective than newspaper, radio-TV, or handbills. To insure adequate but controlled coverage, the advertiser should use a selective mailing list compiled from his own business records or from various sources in his community, such as telephone and city residence directories.

Direct mail is somewhat more expensive than handbill advertising, but it will give the businessman latitude because he can say more, he can try novel ideas on selected clients, and he has a chance to use a more personal approach and appeal and thus get across his business "personality."

In addition to promotional sales letters and postcards, direct-mail advertising includes stuffers to go into other mail (for example, bills). Using stuffers can reduce postage costs as well.

The Advertising Budget

Promotion is an operating expense and should be budgeted like other expenses. In order to avoid overspending or underspending, it is important to set up an advertising budget that can be used as an effective policy guide. For example:

1. Include the expense of advertising in markup calculations.
2. Put a definite amount into the operating budget to cover the cost of promotion.
   a. Find out the national averages of advertising percentages to sales ratios for the type of business.
   b. Adjust them to local situations or conditions.
3. Remember that the amount of money put into advertising should be based on the business objectives to be achieved, the type of business, and the medium that will be the most economical and effective. Make provisions in the budget for:
   a. The time or duration of the advertising program.
   b. The size, type, and layout of the ads to be used.
   c. The media to be used.
4. Check the budget periodically to be sure that the established policy is getting results and that the estimated expenses were realistic.

Gear Advertising to Sales Goal

The first step the small businessman must take in planning an effective advertising campaign is to decide what he wants advertising to do for him. Suppose, for example, that the owner of a dry-cleaning business with a sales volume of $50,000 a year wants to double it within the next 5 years. Next year, then, he would need a volume of $60,000. After carefully considering all the factors that might determine the amount of money he could spend on advertising, suppose he decides that $750 would be about right. By dividing $750 by the planned sales volume of $60,000, he will find that the proposed advertising budget is equal to 1.25 percent of sales.

Most successful dry cleaners of his size spend between 2 and 3 percent of sales for advertising; thus, the proposed $750 expenditure would appear to be far short of the amount needed for the growth he expects. He would have to spend about twice that much just to keep from falling behind competition, and perhaps even more to aid in any planned expansion. If he can't afford to spend about $2,000 for advertising, his hopes for doubling his sales in 5 years are probably too optimistic.

The size of the advertising budget should be determined by both long-range and immediate sales objectives and by comparison with the amount spent in other businesses. Although the proportion of income spent on advertising varies with the type of retail establishment, the average is roughly 1.5 percent.

Measuring the Quality of an Ad

Advertising, like any other part of the business operation, must be frequently checked to determine if the business is getting its money's worth from the advertising dollar. In advertising, there is no middle ground of indifference; an indifferent ad is a bad ad. The entrepreneur must always, therefore, judge each piece of advertising in terms of its qualities and effects as well as its cost. A good ad should:

1. Be simple but informative.
2. Be enthusiastic but truthful.
3. "Talk" to the reader about himself or his interests.
4. Tell a complete story without being tiring.
5. Emphasize important features that are not evident.
6. Provide essential answers about who, what, when, where, how, and why.

Sources for Advertising Assistance

A small businessman can get useful ideas for his ads from suppliers, trade associations, and trade publications. Newspapers and radio stations can also give some aid and counsel, or an entrepreneur may want to hire the services of a local advertising agency. (This may not always be easy: a good many such agencies are not set up to handle relatively small accounts. But it may be worthwhile nonetheless to talk to agencies.) Should there be one that will take on a small account (and that a small businessman can afford to hire), its personnel can take much of the detail work and most of the ad execution off the owner's hands. It is important, however, that the client and the agency agree from the beginning on the purposes of the campaign.

In summary, the right type of advertising, pursued with taste, vigor, and imagination, can bind close ties with customers, attract new trade, and establish a business firmly in the minds of the public. It can build a positive image of a business for the future while it builds current profits.

Incident 10: Marketing Problems

Like so many other small businessmen, Pete Smith went into business because he was a good technician. For a long time, his work quality had been enough to get the business, and now after three years, he could still count on a steady flow of customers, who came because they had seen his work on other cars.

But this body work side of the business did not seem likely to expand much in the future. To completely restore an antique car costs between $2,000 and $8,000, depending on the work to be done. Pete would generally price jobs at seven dollars an hour, plus supplies and parts. These items rarely ran over $500 per car—it was the hand labor and skill that made the difference between a good and a poor job. Since people who had this money demanded the best, only a few craft shops could do the work right all the time and keep getting business, and fortunately Pete's shop was one of them.

But, unfortunately, not only were affluent customers rare, but good craftsmen were hard to find and often could get better money in more conventional shops. Pete did have several first-rate men, but he felt that he couldn't get many more.

In view of this, Pete had actively explored other ways to expand his business. One of these was the sale of spare parts for antique cars. He knew that these parts are manufactured in a number of countries (the United States, Argentina, India, Brazil, Japan) for various American cars in small quantities and that prices are high for all but Model A and Model T Ford parts. He knew that because so many Model A and Model T cars were still around there was a steady demand for most parts and that the relatively high volume of production kept prices low. It also meant a great deal of competition—perhaps forty retailers around the country advertised in the various antique car magazines constantly.

But Pete felt that he could do well by handling odd parts for odd cars. Here, there would be less competition, and he had enough experience to know which parts of the 5,000 to 10,000 parts of a car might be salable. This market looked good; if someone needed one small part to get his old car going, he would likely pay the price if he could find it. It was not at all uncommon to find parts selling for five to twenty dollars per pound. If a dealer knew what to buy, and if he could sell his inventory, then he could count on markups of as much as 100 percent.

The catch was that if something was unsalable, the dealer could really be stuck. Quite a few dealers in antique parts had learned the hard way that some parts wouldn't sell at any price.

Since no one area has many old cars of the same make and model, there is a nationwide market for parts. Thus, mail-order advertising is the best selling approach. Pete already knew about many manufacturers and importers, and he felt that he could get whatever parts he needed if he was willing to spend some time traveling around.

Another messy factor in this market was that no one really knew how many old cars of one type were out there. If one worked with modern cars, they were registered, and one could figure out how many potential sales (by state) were possible by looking at trade-magazine statistics. But old cars often had not been registered for years, so there were no good data on them. A collector might find a 1926 Pierce Arrow sitting in an old barn or he might not. If he did, there would be a demand for parts for a while, then nothing. If you had the right things at the right time, selling parts could be a profitable business.

Pete had checked the trade magazines and discovered that all data from 15 years ago back were lumped into the same category. That is, he could discover in a given state that there were 18,255 Fords of pre-1957 vintage that were licensed, but no one could say which ones were which year. Thus, it was difficult to predict what parts might be needed.

One possible marketing technique was the swap meet. Whenever an antique-car club had a meeting (which was often, typically around once a week someplace in the United States), there would be a swap meet connected with it. Various dealers would sell new and used parts at stalls located in the fairgrounds, supermarket parking lots, or wherever. Some dealers participated in swap meets year round, stopping up north when it got too cold. Pete knew a number of such dealers, and he felt that if he lined up a good stock of special parts, he could get several of them to act as his agents. They would expect at least half of the gross margin as their share of profits. However, Pete was not sure whether he could get exclusive sales rights from various importers and manufacturers. If he could not, it would be easy for a vender to buy direct and bypass him completely.

Pete also learned that there are no patents involved, since anyone can make a part that fits an old car. From time to time, however, trade names do matter. For example, if you are making hub caps for Chevrolet with the name on them, you have to get permission from General Motors to use the name. Auto companies sometimes charge for this privilege, but they are generous in granting permission, since most of them feel that having some of their very old cars around is a cheap way to get advertising. For very small production runs (say, 200 or so), some small manufacturers don't even bother getting permission, but if sales were to be conducted on a continuing basis, this factor would have to be considered. For about 50 percent of Pete's proposed business, this point would be irrelevant, since the companies had been out of business for years.

Pete had looked at a number of other options to expand his business, but none seemed to offer the potential that selling parts did. He would need at least $30,000 in new capital to finance inventories if he did expand in this way, however.

There are six magazines that specialize in old cars and related matters, with circulations ranging from perhaps 5,000 up to 60,000. Advertising rates are around $200 per page in the big ones and down to $50 for the little ones. These little ones, however, are read by real fans, so the response rates are very high for good advertising. There are also about thirty other magazines that specialize in specific types of cars (Ford Model A's, Chrysler products, and so on), which are read by persons who own the proper type of car, and circulations range from 800 to 10,000. Ad rates scale from $50 per page up to $200. Pete is considering advertising his expansion in one or more of these magazines.

1. Assume that Pete does decide to get into the parts business in a serious way. Lay out for him a really effective marketing plan. Show how he should operate to get the maximum number of customers; what marketing channels he should use; what kinds of advertising he should try; and how he might best figure out how to get the right inventory, along with other relevant suggestions.
2. What are the critical points in the plan you laid out in question 1? That is, what could go wrong, and why? How should Pete try to avoid these critical errors?

Discussion Questions

1. Briefly summarize the typical growth pattern of marketing activity in a business firm.
2. Explain the "marketing concept."
3. Using current examples, show how environmental factors affect marketing decisions.
4. What is meant by the "marketing mix"? How does the marketing mix relate to the marketing information system?
5. Using the four basic elements of a marketing strategy, explain how a restaurant manager might draw up a marketing plan to guide the future of his business.
6. Show how a product strategy is likely to be influenced by the life cycle of a product.
7. What information would you need before deciding which type of market channel to use?
8. Is personal selling or advertising more important to the small business? Give concrete examples.
9. Briefly summarize how a small businessman can make his promotional strategy more effective.
10. What is meant by "cost-plus" pricing. Is it a sound approach to pricing? Why or why not?
11. Explain the relationship between markup and stock turnover.
12. Why is credit inseparable from the marketing function?
13. How does advertising fit into the management decision-making process?
14. What should the small businessman consider when selecting the appropriate advertising process?
15. Compare and contrast appropriate advertising for a small manufacturer and a service establishment.

Suggested Readings

"All About Credit," *Changing Times,* The Kiplinger Magazine (March 1963).

Backman, Jules, "Is Advertising Wasteful?" *Journal of Marketing* 32 (January 1968), 2–8.

Bell, Martin L., *Marketing: Concepts and Strategy,* 2nd ed. Boston: Houghton Mifflin, 1972.

Berry, Leonard L., "The Marketing Concept: Some Preach It, Others Practice It," *Arizona Business Bulletin* XVI (April 1969), 94–102.

Boone, Louis E., and Kurtz, David L., *Contemporary Marketing: Principles and Techniques.* New York: Holt, Rinehart and Winston, forthcoming.

Broom, H. N., and Longenecker, J. G., *Small Business Management,* 3rd ed. Cincinnati: South-Western Publishing, 1971. Ch. 18–21.

Buzzell, Robert D., Nourse, Robert E., Matthews, John B., and Levitt, Theodore, *Marketing: A Contemporary Analysis.* New York: McGraw-Hill, 1972.

Davidson, William R., "Changes in Distributive Institutions," *Journal of Marketing* 34 (January 1970), 7–10.

Duncan, Delbert J., Phillips, Charles F., and Hollander, Stanley C., *Modern Retailing Management,* 8th ed. Homewood, Ill.: Richard D. Irwin, 1972.

Duvel, W. A., "Bad Debts: Threat to Small Business," *Dun's Review and Modern Industry* LXXXV (April 1965), 60–61.

Effective Advertising, Administrative Management Course Program, Topic 14. Washington, D. C.: Small Business Administration, 1965.

Gist, Ronald R., *Marketing and Society.* New York: Holt, Rinehart and Winston, 1971.

Hartley, Robert F., "The Importance of Price in Small-Town Shopping Behavior," *Southern Journal of Business* 5 (April 1970), 24–32.

Hartley, Robert F., *Marketing: Management and Social Change.* Scranton, Pa.: Intext Educational Publishers, 1972.

Kelley, Pearce C., Lawyer, K., and Baumback, C. M., *How to Organize and Operate a Small Business,* 4th ed. Englewood Cliffs, N. J.: Prentice-Hall, 1968. Ch. 17–19.

Klatt, Lawrence A., ed., *Managing the Dynamic Small Firm: Readings.* Belmont, Calif.: Wadsworth, 1971. See "Marketing" section.

Kurtz, David L., *Marketing: Concepts, Issues, and Viewpoints.* Morristown, N. J.: General Learning Press, 1972.

Managing to Sell, Administrative Management Course Program, Topic 3. Washington, D. C.: Small Business Administration, 1964.

McCarthy, Jerome E., *Basic Marketing.* Homewood, Ill.: Richard D. Irwin, 1971.

Pessemier, Edgar A., "New Product Ventures," *Business Horizons* XI (August 1968), 5–7, 9–16, 18–19.

Peterson, Robin T., "Government Regulation of Pricing," *Arizona Business Bulletin*, XVI (April 1970), 12–16.

Stanton, William J., *Fundamentals of Marketing*. New York: McGraw-Hill, 1971.

Steinmetz, Lawrence L., Kline, J. B., and Stegall, D. P., *Managing the Small Business*. Homewood, Ill.: Richard D. Irwin, 1968. Ch. 22–25.

Strengthening Small Business Management (Selections from the papers of L. T. White), edited by Joseph C. Schabacher. Washington, D. C.: Small Business Administration, 1971. See section on "Sales and Distribution."

Financial Management

Chapter 11

Once the small businessman has established his business operation as a going concern, his management decisions must be aimed at the perpetuation and growth of his business. In order to accomplish this growth, he must seek to achieve the dual goals of profitable operations and solvency. Good financial management can improve the owner's control over the business, improve profits, and make it easier to obtain funds.

The financial management of all businesses depends on the accounting system and records. Thus, an accounting system should provide for the recording of every financial event, for the periodic summarization of these entries in the financial statements, and for the analysis of these statements. The analysis of the historical accounting statements provides valuable information on what has happened in the past. The value of this analysis, however, lies in its application to planning the future performance of the firm. Forward-looking plans based on historical data will include cash budgets, break-even models, capital budgets, and *pro forma* financial statements.

After a small business is started and has been operating for some time, its financial management presents many of the same problems faced by larger firms. The two basic problems of financial management are profit planning and liquidity management and control. Profits don't "just happen." Good profits require foresight. Such problems as cost control, pricing policy, tax planning, and ultimately capital expenditure decisions must be considered. A business that runs out of money unexpectedly is in for some

---

Note: This chapter was written in collaboration with Lawrence R. Trussell, Appalachian State University.

unpleasant moments no matter how well it may be doing in sales, production, or other aspects of its operation.

Basic Accounting Definitions

Since the accounting system is such a valuable source of information, it is essential that the manager of the small business be familiar with basic accounting terminology and financial statements. Accounting systems are composed of five broad categories of account classifications, which are briefly described in the following paragraphs.

Assets. Assets are economic resources of the firm that benefit future operations. They are classified as either current or fixed. *Current assets* are cash and other resources that are expected to be realized in cash, sold, or consumed during the normal operating cycle of the business, usually one year. Current assets include cash, inventories, accounts and notes receivable, marketable securities, and prepaid expenses. *Fixed assets* are productive resources that will last for a long period of time and are not intended for resale, such as land, buildings, furniture, fixtures, and equipment.

Liabilities. Liabilities are the debts of the firm. They are classified as either current or long-term. *Current liabilities* are obligations whose liquidation requires the use of existing current assets or the creation of other current liabilities.

Debts that must be paid within 1 year are usually included in this classification. Examples of current liabilities include accounts payable, notes payable, salaries payable, and federal taxes withheld from employees' salaries. *Long-term liabilities* are obligations requiring repayment far enough in the future that existing current assets will not be used. Generally they are obligations due more than 1 year in the future. The most common types of long-term liabilities are bank term loans, mortgage loans, and bond issues.

Owner's equity. The owner's equity group of accounts shows the investment made by the owners of the business. In a sole proprietorship, the owner's equity, or net worth, is the total assets of the firm less the total liabilities. In a corporation, the owner's equity includes both capital stock and surplus. The capital-stock account represents the paid-in value of the shares issued to the owners of the business. The surplus or retained-earnings account represents the earnings of the firm that are not withdrawn by the owners. An unincorporated business does not have a surplus or retained-earnings account.

Revenue. Revenue is the income from the sale of goods and the rendering of services. It is measured by the charge made to customers, clients, or tenants for goods and services furnished to them. It also includes gains from the sale or exchange of assets (other than stock in trade), interest and dividends earned on investments, and other increases in the owner's equity, except those arising from capital contributions and capital adjustments. Revenue should be classified according to descriptive accounts depicting the source of the revenue such as sales, fees, commissions, and so on.

Expenses. Expense accounts will include all expired costs (expenses or losses) that are deductible from revenues. In income statements, distinction is made among various types of expenditures, such as cost of goods or services sold, operating expenses, selling and administrative expenses, and loss on sale of property.

Fundamental Accounting Equation

Examination of the accounting definitions should indicate that when a firm acquires an asset it must provide settlement, either by giving another asset in exchange, by incurring a liability, or by requiring an additional contribution from the owner. The total assets of the firm and any change therein must come from an increase in one or both of the last two of these sources—liabilities and owner's equity. This relationship can be depicted by the basic accounting equation: *Assets = Liabilities + Owner's Equity*.

To examine this basic accounting relationship, consider a series of business transactions common to a new business.

1. The owner invests $20,000 cash to establish a real-estate office.

Assets		=	Liabilities	+	Owner's Equity	
Cash	$20,000	=	0	+	Capital	$20,000

2. The firm buys office equipment for $8,000, paying $4,000 down with the balance due in 3 months.

Assets		=	Liabilities		+	Owner's Equity	
Cash	$16,000	=	Notes Payable	$4,000	+	Capital	$20,000
Office Equipment	8,000						

Revenue was defined as any increase, and expense as any decrease, in owner's equity, except those increases or decreases resulting from capital contributions or distributions. For purposes of illustrating the relationship between the balance sheet and income statement, revenue and expense will be included in the owner's equity account.

3. The firm sells a house, earning a commission of $6,000.

	Assets		=	Liabilities		+	Owner's Equity	
Cash		$22,000	=	Notes Payable	$4,000	+	Capital	$20,000
Office Equipment		8,000					Revenue	6,000

4. Paid expenses: Salesman's salary $3,000; rent $1,000

	Assets		=	Liabilities		+	Owner's Equity	
Cash		$18,000	=	Notes Payable	$4,000	+	Capital	$20,000
Office Equipment		8,000					Revenue	6,000
							Expenses	(4,000)

The basic accounting equation, *Assets = Liabilities + Owner's Equity*, holds true regardless of what transaction takes place. The preceding example is, of course, simplified, for new balance sheets are not prepared after every transaction. Each transaction is recorded separately and the summary effects of a large number of transactions are periodically transmitted to the balance sheet. The type of transaction and the accounting records are likely to vary from one firm to another, but the basic accounting equation is universally applicable.

Financial Statements

Accounting involves an orderly process by which the business transactions of a firm are recorded, classified, and summarized to accurately depict the condition of the firm to a variety of interested parties. The most obvious user of the accounting data is the owner–manager, who must be able to evaluate the impact of business decisions on the profitability and solvency of the firm. There are many other important users of the financial statements. Banks and other creditors want to evaluate the credit of the firm; investors desire information on the status of their interests; and the government is interested in taxing the income of the firm.

The accounting process summarizes the business transactions recorded during the past accounting period in order to show the impact of these events on the position of the firm. This objective is accomplished by three basic statements—the balance sheet, the income statement, and the flow of funds statement. Typical examples of these statements are shown in Tables 11–1, 11–2, and 11–3.

The *balance sheet* (Table 11–1) reports the assets, liabilities, and owner's equity of a firm as of a specific date. It is often referred to as the statement of financial position. In simplest terms, the balance sheet is a formal expression of the basic accounting equation. The purpose of the *income statement* (Table 11–2) is to report the results of operations for a specified accounting period. It reports all of the revenue recognized during the period and all of the expenses incurred

Table 11-1. Red Star Stores Balance Sheet, December 31, 197_ (with comparative data for December 31, 197_).

Assets		December 31, 197_			December 31, 197_	
Current Assets						
Cash			41		28	
Accounts receivable			182		199	
Inventories			474		496	
Total current assets				697		723
Fixed Assets						
Store fixtures	235			226		
Less: Accumulated depreciation	63	172		54	172	
Delivery equipment	108			97		
Less: Accumulated depreciation	21	87		14	83	
Total fixed assets			259			255
Total assets			956			978

Liabilities and Owner's Equity

		December 31, 197_		December 31, 197_
Current Liabilities				
Accounts payable		143		125
Notes payable		83		119
Federal and state income taxes		104		122
Total current liabilities		330		366
Long-term promissory notes, 6%		108		112
Owner's Equity				
Common stock, 300 shares authorized, 248 shares outstanding, $1 par value		248		248
Retained earnings		270		252
Total owner's equity		518		500
Total liabilities and owner's equity		956		978

Table 11-2. Red Star Stores Income Statement for Year Ended December 31, 197_.

Net sales		$2,143
Less: Cost of goods sold		1,704
Gross profit on sales		$ 439
Selling and administrative expenses	$348	
Interest	7	
Depreciation	16	371
Net income before taxes		$ 68
Taxes on net income (assume 50%)		34
Net income after taxes		$ 34
Common stock dividends		$ 16
Net income reinvested		$ 18

in earning this revenue. Net income then represents the increase in owner's equity resulting from profitable operations.

It is often beneficial to present balance sheets and income statements for both the current and preceding accounting periods. This provides management with comparisons of the current position of the firm with prior periods. Changes in operations between the two dates are analyzed in the *statement of sources and application of funds* (Table 11–3). This statement shows where funds came from and for what they were used. When a firm requests a loan, one of the first questions asked by the loan officer is, "What has the firm done with the money it had?" This question is answered by the source-and-application-of-funds statement. Sources of funds are those that provide the enterprise with the power to purchase, such as decreases in assets, increases in liabilities, and increases in owner's equity. The uses of funds are increases in assets, decreases in liabilities, and decreases in owner's equity.

Table 11–3. Red Star Stores Source and Application of Funds for Year Ended December 31, 197_.

Sources of Funds		
Operations: Net income	34	
Depreciation (non-cash expenses)	16	
Decrease in current assets	26	
Total sources		76
Application of Funds		
Cash dividend to stockholders	16	
Decrease in current liabilities	36	
Decrease in long-term notes	4	
Increase in fixed assets	20	
Total applications		76

Financial-Statement Analysis

Financial-statement analysis relates balance sheet and income statement values to one another and contributes to a better evaluation of the current position of the firm. It also enables the financial manager to anticipate the reactions of investors and creditors, and thus, gives him better insight into how his future requests for funds are likely to be met. In order to carry out the financial analysis, a useful tool is available to the entrepreneur in the form of financial ratios showing the relationship between two items. A financial ratio, however, is not meaningful in and of itself—it must be compared with something before it becomes useful. The two basic techniques used in ratio

Table 11–4. Financial Ratios, Red Star Stores, 197_.

Name of Ratio	Formula	Computed Value
1. Liquidity ratios: Indicate firm's ability to meet financial obligations.		
Net working capital	Current Assets − Current Liabilities	$367
Current ratio	$\dfrac{\text{Current Assets}}{\text{Current Liabilities}}$	2.11 times*
Acid test ratio	$\dfrac{\text{Cash} + \text{Accounts Receivable} + \text{Marketable Securities}}{\text{Current Liabilities}}$	.68 times
Debt to equity	$\dfrac{\text{Total Debt}}{\text{Owner's Equity}}$	.85 times
Coverage of interest	$\dfrac{\text{Net Income} + \text{Interest}}{\text{Interest}}$	5.86 times
Current liabilities to equity	$\dfrac{\text{Current Liabilities}}{\text{Owner's Equity}}$	.64 times
Fixed assets to equity	$\dfrac{\text{Fixed Assets}}{\text{Owner's Equity}}$	.50 times
2. Profitability ratios: Indicates success in achieving and maintaining profits.		
Gross operating profits to sales	$\dfrac{\text{Gross Profit on Sales}}{\text{Net Sales}}$	20%
Net operating profit to sales	$\dfrac{\text{Net Income Before Taxes}}{\text{Net Sales}}$	3%
Return on total assets	$\dfrac{\text{Net Income}}{\text{Total Assets}}$	4%
Return on equity	$\dfrac{\text{Net Income}}{\text{Owner's Equity}}$	7%
3. Activity ratios: Indicate efficiency in the use of assets.		
Inventory turnover	$\dfrac{\text{Net Sales}}{\text{Inventory}}$	4.52 times
Net working capital turnover	$\dfrac{\text{Net Sales}}{\text{Net Working Capital}}$	5.84 times
Total asset turnover	$\dfrac{\text{Net Sales}}{\text{Total Assets}}$	2.24 times
Average collection period	$\dfrac{\text{Accounts Receivable}}{\text{Average Daily Charge Sales}}$	3 days

*This ratio was calculated by dividing the current assets of $697 by the current liabilities of $330. The resulting ratio should be read as follows: "The current assets of the firm are 2.11 times the current liabilities." A generally popular rule of thumb for the current ratio is 2 to 1, but whether a specific ratio is satisfactory depends on the nature of the business and the characteristics of its current assets and liabilities.

analysis are trend analysis and comparative analysis. *Trend analysis* involves computing the ratios of a firm for several years and comparing the ratios over time to see if the firm is improving or deteriorating.

Comparative analysis involves comparing the key ratios of the firm under study with those of a similar firm in the same industry or with an industry average. These industry averages are available from a variety of sources, such as trade associations and *Dun and Bradstreet*. A checklist of financial ratios, with illustrated computations from the preceding financial statements, is presented in Table 11-4.

Financial Planning

The starting point in planning is a careful study of the past. The ratios analysis provides a basis for this study of past business performance. Although the past never repeats itself, past trends are helpful in determining the future course of the firm.

The sales history of the firm takes on particular importance in planning for the future. Out of sales dollars must come sufficient profits and cash to enable the firm to achieve its goals. Many items on the income statement and balance sheet are related to the level of sales (such as cost of goods sold, selling expenses, inventory, accounts receivable, and accounts payable). By studying these relationships and then accurately projecting sales, one can obtain the projected levels of these income-statement and balance-sheet items. Because of its importance, sales projection is often referred to as the matrix point in planning the goals of the firm.

Break-Even Analysis and Pro Forma *Statements*

Break-even analysis considers the relationship between sales and various expense items. For purposes of constructing a break-even model, one must categorize expenses as being either fixed or variable. Fixed expenses are those whose level remains unchanged when sales are changed (depreciation of plant and equipment, rentals, interest charges on debt, executive salaries, and many general office expenses). Variable expenses are those which change in proportion to changes in sales, such as sales commissions, factory labor, cost of goods sold, and other selling expenses.

The break-even point is the level of sales that exactly covers total cost, $S = F + V$ (Sales = Fixed Expenses + Variable Expenses). If we assume that fixed costs are \$15,000 and variable costs are 70 percent of sales, then the break-even level of sales can be computed in the following manner:

$$S = F + V$$
$$S = \$15{,}000 + .70S$$
$$.30S = \$15{,}000$$
$$S = \$50{,}000$$

At the $50,000 level of sales, fixed costs equal $15,000 and variable costs equal $35,000, resulting in no profit or loss. At any level of sales below $50,000 the firm will suffer losses, while for sales in excess of $50,000 there will be a profit. If a certain dollar profit is desired, this amount can be added to the fixed costs to determine the level of sales needed to earn that profit.

The break-even point can also be computed using physical units. For example, if the selling price is $2 per unit and the total sales break-even point is computed to be $50,000, the break-even point in units is 25,000. This relationship is shown graphically in Figure 11–1. Dollar sales volume and costs are charted on the vertical axis, while physical units are charted on the horizontal axis. Total fixed costs (TFC) are represented by a straight horizontal line at the $15,000 level in keeping with the fact that fixed costs are constant at all levels of output. The total variable cost (TVC) line comes from the origin (zero point) and increases at a constant rate. If we again assume a selling price of $2 per unit and a variable cost percentage of 70 percent, the variable cost per unit is $1.40. Total variable costs will increase by $1.40 for every unit that is added. Total costs (TC) are the summation of fixed and variable costs at every level of output. Graphically, this summation is accomplished by sliding the variable-cost line up the vertical axis until it emerges from the point of total fixed costs ($15,000). At zero output, total costs are equal to total fixed costs, or $15,000.

Figure 11–1. Break-Even Chart.

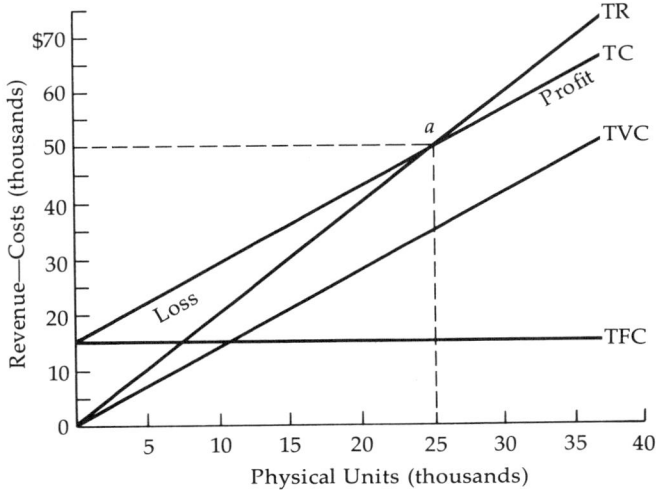

As output increases from zero, total costs are equal to total fixed costs ($15,000) plus total variable costs ($1.40 per unit).

To determine the break-even point, it is necessary to compare total costs to total revenue. With a selling price of $2 per unit, total revenue (TR) is determined by multiplying the quantity by $2. At zero quantity, total revenue is zero; at 10,000 units, total revenue is $20,000. The break-even point is the point at which total revenue equals total costs. This point is shown graphically as point *a*; and reading from the graph, we confirm that the break-even point in sales dollars is $50,000, and in units is 25,000.

Examination of the break-even chart for levels of production either above or below the break-even point can give an estimate of the profit or loss achieved at various levels of production. For levels of production above 25,000 units, total revenue exceeds total costs, meaning that this firm would earn a profit. For production below 25,000 units, the amount of the loss can be estimated.

This relation between sales and expense items used in break-even analysis can also be employed to prepare *pro forma* financial statements. These statements are projected or anticipated financial statements and are a formal reflection of the plans for the firm. The *pro forma* income statement indicates the goals of management in sales, expenses, and net profit. The *pro forma* balance sheet shows the total amount of assets needed, the composition of the assets, and the sources of funds.

Cash Budget

While the sources-and-uses-of-funds statement shows where cash came from and where it was used, the cash budget indicates expected sources and uses of cash in the future. A cash budget may be prepared on a weekly or monthly basis for up to a year in the future. The preparation of a cash budget involves five basic steps:

1. Estimate monthly cash receipts, assuming no additional financing. This step generally requires a forecast of sales and an estimate of when cash will be collected for them.
2. Estimate monthly expenditures. The two basic categories of expenditures are payments on purchases and other operating expenses.
3. Compare monthly receipts with monthly expenditures, assuming no additional financing. This will result in a determination of the months during which cash receipts exceed or fall short of disbursements.
4. Estimate the end-of-month cash balances, assuming no additional financing, by combining the beginning balance each month with the change in cash balances computed in step 3.

5. Forecast the amount of financing needed in various months to maintain a desired minimum cash balance. The cash budget will also show the months the firm will have excess cash to repay any short-term financing.

The cash budget has several uses for management. It helps determine the months in which there will be a cash shortage or surplus. It indicates whether the need for funds is temporary or permanent. It is looked upon by potential creditors as a good management tool, showing them when cash is expected to be available for repayment. Finally, it provides for control over cash since management can compare actual with anticipated performance.

Capital Budget

Capital budgeting involves planning expenditures whose returns are expected to extend beyond 1 year and predicting the impact of proposed expansion on the firm. A capital budget provides a standard to aid management in ranking capital expenditures in order of their relative desirability and in determining the amount by which total assets should expand. Since decisions about capital expenditures must be lived with for many years, it is particularly important that these decisions be carefully evaluated prior to the commitment of funds.

It must be emphasized that in the capital budgeting process nothing is of greater importance than a reliable estimate of the cost savings, or increases in net income, that will be achieved by the proposed capital expenditure. The starting point for making this estimate is the impact of expansion on sales and variable expenses. Examples of other items that may affect benefits are changes in the quality and quantity of direct labor, the amount and cost of scrap and rework time, maintenance expenses, down time, safety, flexibility, and so on. The fact that so many variables may be involved does not minimize the importance of an analysis of the benefits derived from the capital expenditure. The subsequent procedures for ranking projects are no better than the data input.

Two common procedures used to rank investment proposals are the *payback period* and the *net present value*. The payback period is defined as the number of years required for an investment to generate cash inflow (net income plus depreciation) equal to the original outlay required. A short payback period indicates profitability and a lower level of risk since the investment is recovered more quickly. Because it emphasizes recovery of investment funds, the payback test focuses on liquidity and may be used effectively if this is the main concern. However, it must be noted that the payback test has serious weaknesses in that it ignores that some cash inflow comes in periods beyond the payback period and that a dollar received today is worth more than a dollar received in the future.

The net-present-value method overcomes these two weaknesses. Accordingly, it considers all cash inflows over the life of the investment and adjusts this cash inflow for the cost of waiting. The application of the net-present-value test requires a basic knowledge of discounting—that is, determining the current value of a dollar to be received sometime in the future. Table 11–5 shows a partial example of a present value table. It tells us that if the market rate of interest is 4 percent, one dollar to be received one year from now is worth 96.2 cents today. In other words, at that interest rate one would just as soon have 96.2 cents today as one dollar one year from now. If you were to put 96.2 cents in the bank today at 4 percent interest, you would have one dollar at the end of one year (96.2 cents plus 3.8 cents interest). If the market rate of interest is 10 percent, a dollar to be received at the end of four years has a current value of 68.3 cents.

Table 11–5. Partial Present Value at $10

Year	Market Rate of Interest			
	4%	6%	8%	10%
1	.962	.943	.926	.909
2	.925	.890	.857	.826
3	.889	.840	.794	.751
4	.855	.792	.735	.683
5	.822	.747	.681	.621

To find the net present value of a proposed investment, one finds the present value of future cash inflows and subtracts the cost of the asset. If the resulting net present value is positive, the project will be profitable. All projects with a positive net present value should be accepted, but if funds are limited, the projects with the greatest net present value are preferred. These two methods of capital budgeting are illustrated in Table 11–6.

Cost of Capital

To find the present value of future cash inflows, it is necessary to arrive at an appropriate rate of interest. In practice, this discount rate is the firm's weighted average cost of capital. The first step in computing the weighted

Table 11–6. Capital Budgeting Illustration.

Net Cash Inflows (Profit after taxes plus depreciation):

Year	Project	A	B	C
1		600	250	100
2		400	250	100
3		200	250	300
4		100	250	500
5			250	600

Cash outlay required is $1,000 for each project.

Payback test: Project A = 2 years (preferred project)
              B = 4 years
              C = 4 years

Net Present Value (6 percent cost of capital):

	A		B		C	
	$600 × .943 =	$ 565.80	$250 × .943 =	$ 235.75	$100 × .943 =	$ 94.30
	400 × .890 =	356.00	250 × .890 =	222.50	100 × .890 =	89.00
	200 × .840 =	168.00	250 × .840 =	210.00	300 × .840 =	252.00
	100 × .792 =	79.20	250 × .792 =	198.00	500 × .792 =	396.00
			250 × .747 =	186.75	600 × .747 =	448.20
Present value of inflow		$1,169.00		$1,053.00		$1,279.50
Less: Cash outlay		1,000.00		1,000.00		1,000.00
Net present value		$ 169.00		$ 53.00		$ 279.50
Ranking of projects		2		3		1

average cost of capital is to compute the cost of the individual capital components. There are four basic components of the capital structure of most firms.

1. Debt. The cost of debt is equal to the percentage paid on proceeds adjusted for the tax deductibility of interest. Assuming that an 8 percent term loan can be obtained from the bank and the average tax rate is 33 percent, the cost of debt can be computed as follows:

$$C_d = \text{percentage paid on proceeds} \times (1 - \text{tax rate})$$
$$C_d = .08 \ (1 - .33)$$
$$C_d = .08 \times .67$$
$$C_d = .0536 \text{ or } 5.36\%$$

2. Preferred stock. The cost of preferred stock is equal to the dollar dividend rate divided by the net proceeds per share. Assuming one can sell $6 preferred stock for a net price of $90 per share, the cost is computed in the following manner:

$$C_p = \frac{\text{Dividends}}{\text{Net Price}}$$

$$C_p = \frac{\$6}{.90}$$

$$C_p = .0667 \text{ or } 6.67\%$$

3. *Retained earnings* (and depreciation-generated cash). The cost of capital for internal funds is the required rate of return by the owner. Since the owner is leaving funds in the business rather than withdrawing them for alternative investment, the cost is represented by the return on the alternative investment sacrificed. For purposes of illustration, one can assume that the minimum opportunity cost is the yield that could be obtained on high quality bonds (7 percent assumed).

4. *New common stock.* The cost of new common stock is equal to the required rate of return by the owner (cost of retained earnings) adjusted for the cost of floating the new stock issue. If one can sell new common stock to the public for $50 and receive $45 after the underwriter deducts his fee, the percentage cost of flotation is 10 percent. Assuming the required rate of return is 7 percent, the percentage cost of common stock is computed in the following manner:

$$C_s = \frac{\text{Required Rate of Return}}{1 - \text{Percentage Cost of Flotation}}$$

$$C_s = \frac{.07}{1 - .10}$$

$$C_s = \frac{.07}{.90}$$

$$C_s = .0778 \text{ or } 7.78\%$$

After computing the cost of each component, the next step in computing the weighted average cost of capital is to determine the proper weights to apply to each component. This weight is equal to the percentage composition of the capital structure represented by each source. Multiplying these weights by the component costs and adding the products gives the weighted average cost of capital that management can use when evaluating investment decisions. This computation is illustrated in Table 11–7.

Table 11–7. Computation of Weighted Average Cost of Capital.

	Capitalization	Percent Capital Structure	Component Cost	Weighted Average Cost
Debt	$120	.15	.0536	.00804
Preferred stock	80	.10	.0667	.00667
Common stock	240	.30	.0778	.02334
Retained earnings	360	.45	.0700	.02800
Total	$800	1.00		
Weighted average cost of capital				.06605
				6.605%

Current-Asset Management

A small firm can minimize its investment in fixed assets by renting or leasing these items, but there is no way of avoiding an investment in receivables and inventories. Current assets may constitute well over half of the total assets of a firm. Also, the small firm has relatively limited access to long-term capital markets and must therefore rely more heavily on trade credit and short-term bank loans.

Current asset management emphasizes the cash-flow problems of a firm. Cash can be seen as flowing in a circular fashion through the other major current assets—inventory and accounts receivable (see Figure 11–2). The problem of current asset management becomes one of speeding this circular flow and of minimizing the total investment in current assets, keeping both consistent with maximum sales and profits.

Deciding how much cash to have on hand is difficult. Obviously, there must be enough cash to conduct the ordinary business of the firm and to meet minor unexpected emergencies. However, cash is a nonearning asset, so holdings should be minimized. Many firms are characterized by seasonal cash

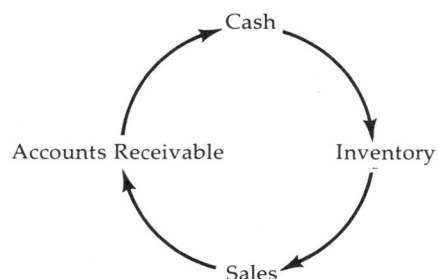

Figure 11–2. Cash Flow.

needs, such as requiring extra inventory for the Christmas season. If enough cash is kept available to meet these seasonal needs all year round, there are long periods when much of it is standing idle. Cash management, then, necessitates short-term investment of excess cash and short-term borrowing to meet extreme seasonal needs.

Many factors are important in determining the proper level of inventories. Among them are the perishability of the product, the assortment desired, the distance from the inventory source, the length of time needed to produce the product, and the cost of inventory storage. While past experience provides a good guide to controlling the level of inventories, elaborate methods for developing reorder points and economic ordering have been developed (see Chapter 13). It is important to keep in mind that an inventory can become obsolete, that excess inventory can lead to unnecessary expenses of storage, and that deficiencies in inventory can decrease sales and profit.

The major determinants of the level of receivables are the volume of credit sales, terms of sales, and credit and collection policies. A firm extends credit with the objective of increasing sales and profits. The more liberal the credit terms, the greater will be the firm's investment in accounts receivable. This additional investment in accounts receivable should be evaluated in the same manner as an investment in any other asset—that is, on the resulting increase in net income. Management should avoid extending credit simply because it is the popular thing to do without considering the resulting increased investment in accounts receivable. The growth in popularity of general credit cards has greatly helped the small businessman compete with the larger firms. By honoring a general credit card, the small business essentially passes the credit burden onto a larger financial institution. The cost of this service is a discount accepted by the merchant (usually 1 to 3 percent).

Financing Current Asset Needs

There are several means by which the small businessman can finance his current asset needs. It is important to emphasize that some of the current assets should be financed from permanent sources, such as contributions of owners. As a general rule, the regular working capital should be derived from long-term sources; fluctuating working capital should come from short-term debt.

Funds generated from operations are the most important source of working capital. For example, when funds are borrowed for investment in inventory, sales and cash collections can provide for repayment of the funds. Most short-term lenders will want to know the time needed for the loan to liquidate itself (time needed to complete one circuit from cash back to cash). The maturity of short-term financing should be fit to the length of time needed for this circular flow to be completed.

Trade credit. Trade credit is generally very convenient, for it allows one firm to extend credit to another when goods are purchased on account. Other advantages are that it provides for inspection of goods before payment and is easier to obtain than bank loans. The primary disadvantage of trade credit is that it is generally quite expensive. Typical credit terms provide for a cash discount if the account is paid within a certain number of days of purchase, with the net amount due at some future date. For example, the terms 2/10, n/30 (n = net) mean that the purchases may take a 2 percent cash discount if the bill is paid within 10 days but must pay the full amount at the end of 30 days. Note that if the discount is not taken, the purchaser has another 20 days to make payment, but the cost of obtaining credit for these 20 days is the sacrifice of the 2 percent discount. Interest of 2 percent for 20 days is equivalent to 36 percent on an annual basis—clearly an expensive loan. Other typical credit terms with the effective annual rate of interest are shown in Table 11–8.

Table 11–8. Effective Annual Interest for Various Credit Terms.

Terms	Effective Annual Interest	Terms	Effective Annual Interest
1/10, n/30	18.0%	3/10, n/30	54.0%
1/10, n/45	10.3%	3/10, n/45	30.9%
2/10, n/30	36.0%	4/10, n/45	41.2%
2/10, n/45	20.6%	4/10, n/60	28.8%
2/10, n/60	14.4%	5/10, n/60	36.0%

Short- and intermediate-term loans. A commercial bank is an important source for short- or intermediate-term loans for the small businessman. In obtaining a loan, it is imperative that the borrower show ability to repay. Short-term loans are usually obtained for temporary increases in working capital for such purposes as paying for merchandise in order to take advantage of a discount, building up inventories for seasonal increases in sale, and so on. It is expected that this type of loan will be paid out of ordinary operating income as the temporary need passes. Intermediate-term loans, also simply called term loans, enable the entrepreneur to increase his regular working capital or to meet temporary capital needs without having to yield business control. Of course, while a term loan is in force, the entrepreneur will be subject to certain restrictions on how he manages his business. The loan agreement is usually designed to protect the lender against drastic reductions in the value of collateral or in business income available for repayment of the loan.

Secured loans. Warehouse receipts are one way to use inventory as collateral for a loan. In this method of securing a loan, physical inventory is placed in the care of a bonded warehouseman who gives the firm a receipt setting forth the items he has in his possession. The receipt is then turned over to the bank as collateral for a loan. As the loan is repaid, the bank releases portions of the inventory. Other security might be offered by pledging accounts receivable on inventory to obtain a short-term loan.

Internal Control of Current Assets

To the small business manager, the physical protection of assets is often difficult. Most small businesses have limited bookkeeping and clerical staffs, thus limiting the opportunities for division of work and responsibilities. This condition promotes hesitation in taking definite steps toward achieving adequate internal control since the added costs may be considered to exceed any benefits. Furthermore, small businesses are often family-owned and the management desirous of having financial information known only to the family. These factors must be considered and overcome to the extent possible when designing a system of internal control for a small business.

Regardless of the size of the company, there are certain internal-control procedures that may be effectively and economically instituted. Assets can be protected by using safe-deposit vaults and adequate locks on storerooms, cash registers, office safes, and other protective devices. Forms such as requisitions, receipts, and sales orders, should be prenumbered and steps taken regularly to see that all numbers are properly accounted for and no forms are missing. Fidelity bonds offer particularly important protection for the small businessman, for they can insure him against employee fraud. All employees should be required to take annual vacations so that others can occasionally take their places and get an inside view of the job activities.

For small companies, one of the most effective substitutes for a formal program of internal control is the owner–manager's day-to-day observation of the business. By the nature of his position and the size of his company, the owner–manager is close to the significant details of the business. Thus, he is in a position to review the payroll records before payment is made and to periodically review the accounts-receivable ledger. Cash disbursements and the related records may be supervised and controlled by reviewing invoices and receiving records, passing on the reasonableness of the accounting classifications, and noting evidence that a check of prices and extensions was made. Finally, the owner–manager should ascertain if all invoices and supporting documents are immediately marked to indicate payment, thus reducing the possibilities of duplicate or fraudulent payments through a second submission of invoices or other supporting data.

Effective internal control demands effort that may seem excessive, unnecessary, and expensive at first glance. However, many failures of small businesses can be attributed to weaknesses that could have been exposed earlier if a simple system of internal control had been established. Generally, a regular audit by a certified public accountant will provide a good review of existing internal-control measures and recommendations for improvement.

Fixed-Asset Management

The capital budget is the starting point for managing fixed assets. This evaluation of proposed expansion provides management with information on how much total assets should be expanded and in what order projects should be undertaken. Decisions about fixed assets are particularly significant because of the magnitude of the expenditures involved and because of the length of time that management must live with the acquisitions resulting from these decisions.

Buying versus Leasing Assets

A firm need not own an asset in order to have the use of it; many needed items can be rented. When assets are leased, the owner permits a second party to have possession and exclusive use of the property for an agreed period of time. In many cases, the lessee is given an option to buy the asset at the end of the lease period and to apply a part of the lease payments to the purchase price. When the lease expires, in the absence of any agreement to the contrary, the landlord is entitled to all improvements made by the tenant.

Leasing and owning each offer certain advantages to the firm. Among the cited advantages to leasing are the following: less risk of obsolescence, more flexibility in moving or changing assets, less capital invested in fixed assets, ease of determining productivity of asset before purchase, and fewer bookkeeping and tax problems. On the other hand, owning the asset may offer the advantages of being cheaper, easier to adapt to the individual needs of the business, and not subject to return at a disadvantageous time. Either alternative may result in the most favorable profit situation depending on the facts of the case. The computation of the financial advantage of leasing or buying will involve consideration of depreciation, the implicit interest included in rental payments, and the tax deductibility of lease payments and maintenance expenses.

Financing Fixed Assets

Many businessmen make the common mistake of assuming that renting an asset will decrease the burden of financing fixed assets. Generally, a firm must have just as strong a credit rating to rent an asset as to borrow the funds to purchase the assets, for the rental payment represents a fixed charge as does a payment on an installment loan. When a firm rents an asset, it uses part of its borrowing power. Thus, it is all the more important to make a quantitative comparison of the impact of renting and borrowing to buy the asset.

Small firms generally find it difficult to obtain long-term financing from outside the business. Asset expansion is usually financed by internal cash flow (net income plus depreciation) or additional contribution by the owners. Intermediate-term loans (1 to 5 years) are often available from banks to help finance some asset acquisitions.

Many small businessmen overlook the possibility that other investors might be willing to supply funds for their firm. A well-managed, growing, and popular small firm is a desirable investment for many individuals. The small businessman may have to sacrifice some control when he sells capital stock to the public, but a financial advisor can often minimize this disadvantage. In short, a visit to an investment banker may reveal to the small businessman new ways to obtain additional permanent financing.

Retained earnings offer a major source of funds for financing fixed assets. As profits are earned, they can be plowed back into the business to be used for expanding permanent working capital and for investing in physical facilities or equipment. The entrepreneur might also consider visiting a small business investment company that is licensed by the Small Business Administration to provide equity capital and long-term loans to small businesses.

Managing Tax Obligations

The small businessman has two major tax responsibilities. First, he must act as an agent for the various levels of government in the withholding or collection and remission of funds. Second, he must pay his own taxes, many of which are a part of his business obligations.

The most significant taxes to be withheld from the salaries paid to employees are the federal and state income taxes and the social security (FICA) tax. The businessman's responsibility begins when a new employee joins the firm and he is asked to complete the W-4 form. This "Employees Withholding Exemption Certificate" authorizes the company to withhold income tax in accordance with the tables issued by the Internal Revenue Service (federal) and appropriate state agency. Periodically, the businessman will be required to remit the taxes withheld to the appropriate agency. At year end he must supply the employees with Form W-2, "Wage and Tax Statement," which is used in filing tax returns.

In paying the social security tax the businessman is both an agent and a payer. He deducts the tax from employees' wages and matches those deductions himself. Social security tax rates and the wages on which they are deducted seem to be constantly changing. The latest rates can be obtained from a local social security office.

State and local sales taxes are part of the businessman's responsibility as collecting agent. The amount he must collect is usually obtainable from a table, and the appropriate state or local agency can provide information on remitting the tax.

Other areas in which the businessman may be forced to act as either an agent or a payer of taxes include federal, state, and local excise taxes; federal or state unemployment taxes; and local real-estate, personal property, or franchise taxes. In all of these cases, local laws should be consulted to be certain that all obligations are being met.

The taxation of business earnings deserves special consideration as one area in which the businessman is a payer of taxes. The income from an unincorporated business is usually taxed as personal income to the owners and is, therefore, subject to personal income-tax rates. Both personal and corporate income-tax rates are progressive—the higher one's income, the higher his marginal tax rate (that rate at which additional income is taxed). Personal marginal tax rates start at 14 percent of taxable income (gross income less allowable deductions and exemptions) and rise to 70 percent of taxable income. The corporate tax rates are 22 percent on the first $25,000 and 48 percent of all taxable income above $25,000. The marginal tax rates for individuals start lower than for corporations but are more progressive so that at higher incomes the average tax rate (total tax divided by taxable income) becomes greater for individuals than for corporations. These relationships are presented in Table 11–10, in which the tax situation with the advantage is italicized for both the marginal and average rates.

The significance of comparing the corporate and personal tax rates is that under certain circumstances unincorporated businesses can elect to be taxed as corporations, and corporations can elect to be taxed as unincorporated businesses. For some business decisions—such as whether to set up a new venture as a proprietorship or corporation or what to do when an individual's income comes from many sources—a comparison of marginal tax rates will be the deciding factor. When the taxpayer's income will be derived mainly from the business he is forming, however, he is more likely to compare average tax rates.

The objective of tax planning should always be to minimize the firm's tax liability. Electing to be taxed under the least expensive form of business is one way of accomplishing this objective. Another way is to be certain that maximum deductions are taken. A tax consultant or certified public accountant can provide assistance about techniques for postponing taxes, such as accelerated depreciation, last-in-first-out inventory techniques, and the proper timing of purchases and sales of assets.

Table 11–10. Average and Marginal Tax Rates for Individuals Filing Joint Returns and Corporations.

Taxable Income		Marginal Rate		Average Rate	
		Individual	Corporation	Individual	Joint
$ 0–$	1,000	14.0%	22.0%	14.0%	22.0%
1,000–	2,000	15.0	22.0	14.5	22.0
2,000–	3,000	16.0	22.0	15.0	22.0
3,000–	4,000	17.0	22.0	15.5	22.0
4,000–	8,000	19.0	22.0	17.4	22.0
8,000–	12,000	22.0	22.0	18.8	22.0
12,000–	16,000	25.0	22.0	20.4	22.0
16,000–	20,000	28.0	22.0	21.9	22.0
20,000–	24,000	32.0	22.0	23.6	22.0
24,000–	28,000	36.0	48.0	25.4	24.8
28,000–	32,000	39.0	48.0	27.1	27.7
32,000–	36,000	42.0	48.0	28.7	29.9
36,000–	40,000	45.0	48.0	30.4	31.8
40,000–	44,000	48.0	48.0	32.0	33.2
44,000–	52,000	50.0	48.0	34.7	35.5
52,000–	64,000	53.0	48.0	38.2	37.8
64,000–	76,000	55.0	48.0	40.8	39.4
76,000–	88,000	58.0	48.0	43.2	40.6
88,000–	100,000	60.0	48.0	45.2	41.5
100,000–	120,000	62.0	48.0	48.0	42.6
120,000–	140,000	64.0	48.0	50.3	43.4
140,000–	160,000	66.0	48.0	52.2	43.9
160,000–	180,000	68.0	48.0	54.0	44.4
180,000–	200,000	69	48.0	55.5	44.8
200,000–	300,000	70	48.0	60.3	45.8
300,000–	400,000	70	48.0	62.7	46.4
400,000–	1,000,000	70	48.0	67.1	47.4
1,000,000–	10,000,000	70	48.0	69.7	47.9
10,000,000–	100,000,000	70	48.0	70.0	48.0

Incident 11: Financial Problems Revisited

Attachment 8–1 (p. 139) showed Pete Smith's financial statements for the latest year. Take another look at these statements, and then work up the following data:

1. Pete figures that sales next year are going to be $73,500. His rent will be the same; utilities will probably go up 10 percent; insurance will be 5 percent higher; advertising will double; depreciation will rise by $425; and other expense items should rise in proportion to sales. Make a budget for Pete for next year, using this information, plus the data given on his income statement for the latest year. What are forecasted profits?

2. Suppose that after this year is completed, your budget turns out to be absolutely accurate. Pete draws $12,000 from profits for his share as owner, leaving the rest of the profits in the business. If everything else on the balance sheet stays exactly the same as Attachment 8–1, what happens to net worth? Why? What asset item would change (or could change) to reflect this increment?
3. Work out all the financial ratios you can based on these statements. Do you think Pete is in good shape or not? Why?
4. If you were buying Pete's business, what would you pay for it, based on these statements? Why?

Discussion Questions

1. How does good financial management help the perpetuation and growth of a business?
2. "Accounting statements are historical; financial management is forward looking." Explain.
3. Define the terms *asset, liabilities, owner's equity, revenue,* and *expenses.*
4. Explain the fundamental accounting equation.
5. What purposes do accounting statements serve?
6. Differentiate between the balance sheet and the income statement.
7. Explain the statement of sources and application of funds.
8. What is the relationship between trend analysis and financial-statement analysis?
9. Discuss the relationship between forcasted sales and financial planning.
10. What is the difference between fixed and variable expenses? Give examples of each.
11. How was the break-even chart in the chapter constructed? How would you use such a chart?
12. What is the value of break-even analysis to an entrepreneur in the process of starting a new venture?
13. List and discuss the steps involved in preparing a cash budget.
14. What basic uses does the cash budget have?
15. What is meant by capital budgeting? What is the starting point for a good capital budget?
16. Discuss the payback-period and the net-present-value approaches to ranking investment proposals.
17. What is meant by the "weighted average cost of capital"?
18. How would you go about determining a firm's cost of capital?
19. Relate the "cash flow" concept to current-asset management.

20. Briefly list and discuss some of the factors determining the proper level to maintain of the following current assets: cash, inventories, and accounts receivable.
21. Discuss several ways by which the small businessman can finance his current-asset needs.
22. What are some internal-control procedures that can be instituted in the smaller firm to reduce current-asset losses?
23. Should the small businessman buy or lease his fixed assets? Discuss.
24. Outline the major sources of funds for financing fixed assets.
25. In what respect is the businessman both a taxpayer and a tax collector? Give examples.
26. How might tax rates influence the entrepreneur's decisions whether to set up a new venture as a proprietorship or corporation?

Suggested Readings

Berke, Samuel, "Break-Even Point Studies for Small Marketers," *Small Marketers Aids,* No. 5, Washington, D. C.: Small Business Administration, 1963.

Bradley, Joseph F., *Administrative Financial Management,* 2nd ed. New York: Holt, Rinehart and Winston, 1969.

Broom, H. N., and Longenecker, J. G., *Small Business Management,* 3rd ed. Cincinnati: South-Western Publishing, 1971. Ch. 13–15.

"Getting the Facts for Income Tax Reporting," *Small Marketers Aids,* No. 144, Washington, D. C.: Small Business Administration, 1970.

Holmes, Arthur W., *Auditing Principles and Procedures,* 6th ed. Homewood, Ill.: Richard D. Irwin, 1964.

Johnson, Glenn L., and Gentry, James A., *Principles of Accounting,* 7th ed. Englewood Cliffs, N. J.: Prentice-Hall, 1970.

Kelley, Pearce C., Lawyer, Kenneth, and Baumback, Clifford M., *How to Organize and Operate a Small Business,* 4th ed. Englewood Cliffs, N. J.: Prentice-Hall, 1968. Ch. 19–22.

Klatt, Lawrence A., *Managing the Dynamic Small Firm: Readings.* Belmont, Calif.: Wadsworth, 1971. Pp. 187–236.

Krentzman, Harvey C., *Managing for Profits.* Washington, D. C.: Small Business Administration, 1968.

Meigs, Walter B., and Larsen, E. John, *Principles of Auditing,* 4th ed. Homewood, Ill.: Richard D. Irwin, 1969.

Pyle, William W., and White, John Arch, *Fundamental Accounting Principles,* 5th ed. Homewood, Ill.: Richard D. Irwin, 1969.

Robinson, Roland I., *Financing the Dynamic Small Firm.* Belmont, Calif.: Wadsworth, 1966.

Sanzo, Richard, *Ratio Analysis for Small Business.* Washington, D. C.: Small Business Administration, 1970.

Schultz, Raymond G., *Readings in Financial Management,* 2nd ed. Scranton, Pa.: International Textbook Company, 1970.

Steinmetz, Lawrence L., Kline, J. B., and Stegall, D. P., *Managing the Small Business.* Homewood, Ill.: Richard D. Irwin, 1968. Ch. 13–15.

"Steps in Meeting Your Tax Obligations," *Small Marketers Aids,* No. 142, Washington, D. C.: Small Business Administration, 1970.

The Why and What of Bookkeeping, Administrative Management Course Program, Topic 4. Washington, D. C.: Small Business Administration, 1965.

Weston, J. Fred, and Brigham, Eugene F., *Essentials of Managerial Finance.* New York: Holt, Rinehart and Winston, 1968.

Zwick, Jack, *A Handbook of Small Business Finance.* Washington, D. C.: Small Business Administration, 1965.

Managing the Human Resource

Chapter 12

Perhaps the most important asset of a business is the men and women who work in it. Without a staff of qualified, motivated employees a business is at a competitive disadvantage. Furthermore, the profitable operation of a business depends on the ability and desire of the personnel to do their jobs effectively and economically.

A business organization, like every organization, is people, and its management involves people. For management is *attempting to reach certain goals through the effective use of manpower.* While managing personnel may appear to be a simple and straightforward task, it is not. In fact, manpower management is perhaps the most complex function anyone can undertake.

Complexities develop the moment a management–employee relationship develops. Every individual has a set of "needs" that must somehow be met. In addition, when more than one individual attempts to satisfy his own "needs" in an organization, the situation becomes even more complex. It then becomes the goal of management to satisfy the needs of the worker while meeting the goals or needs of the organization. Reaching this objective can even be made more difficult by government regulations, union work values, existing customs or rules of conduct, and local labor markets.

The job of managing manpower in the small firm is further complicated by the close interpersonal relationship between the entrepreneur and his employees. Frequently, employees are close friends or even relatives of the owner, which can make professional dealings particularly sensitive. An entrepreneur may avoid adopting modern personnel policies and practices for fear that such policies might be too impersonal or might alienate the workers. At the same time, the small firm, because of better internal communication between management and employees, has a distinct advantage over the larger firm. Thus, the entrepreneur should do all he can to learn about modern manpower management in order to maintain this advantage of closeness as well as to prepare for the time when company growth necessitates a more formalized approach to recruiting and maintaining a work force. This chapter examines a number of concepts and practices of manpower management that are of importance to the smaller firm.

Hiring New Employees

When developing a manpower program, the manager should first determine his short- and long-term manpower needs, giving consideration to normal employee turnover. In this planning phase, it is helpful to prepare a description and a specification for every job in the firm. A *job description* is an attempt to describe every task involved in a job, including the types of equipment used, the working environment (if it varies much from job to job), and how the job relates to other jobs in the organization. A *job specification* describes the type of person best suited to fill the position in terms of education, skills, experience, and other personal characteristics. In other words, the job description sets forth duties; the job specification translates these duties into qualifications necessary to perform the duties. Figure 12-1 is a sample job description for an office and credit manager.

A great deal of time and effort should be devoted to the formulation of job descriptions and specifications since they become the bases for decisions about recruitment, placement, training, promotions, and compensation. It is especially important that the entrepreneur be realistic in his job specifications. While he may feel every job in the organization requires a "superman," if he fills a low-level job with an overqualified person it will be a waste of talent and money, for the employee is very likely to become dissatisfied and finally quit. Thus, educational and experience requirements should be carefully matched to the job.

Recruitment

The small firm is frequently at a disadvantage when it comes to recruiting qualified personnel, for it is often limited geographically to the local labor market. Also, it is frequently handicapped by the fact that the most qualified people may prefer the glamour and security of a large firm. To overcome these disadvantages, and to compete with other firms, the small business must develop an aggressive recruitment program rather than rely solely on recom-

Managing the Human Resource

SAMPLE JOB DESCRIPTION

Job title: Office and credit manager
Supervisor: Store manager

Job Summary

Responsible for all office and credit functions of the store. Has control of store's assets and expenditures. Helps manager administer store's policies and methods. Exercises mature judgement and initiative in carrying out duties.

Duties

1. Inspects sales tickets for accuracy and completeness of price, stock classifications, and delivery information. (Daily)

2. Prepares bank deposit, listing checks and cash, and takes deposit to bank. (Daily)

3. Keeps sales and expenses record sheets, posting sales and expenses, and accumulating them for the month. (Daily)

4. Processes credit applications: analyzes financial status and paying record of customers; checks references and credit bureau to determine credit responsibility. (Daily)

5. Sends collection notices to past-due accounts, using mails, telephone calls, and personal visits, if necessary, to collect. (Daily)

6. Sells merchandise during rush hours of the store. (Daily)

7. Checks invoices of outstanding purchases to verify receipt, quantity, price, etc. Gets store manager's approval. (Weekly)

8. Does all bookkeeping and prepares financial and profit and loss statements of store. (Monthly)

Figure 12-1. Sample Job Description.

mendations and "drop-ins" to supply the necessary manpower. Of course, the recruitment program should be adapted to the characteristics of the firm, the job to be filled, the local labor market, and economic conditions. For example, during a business boom in the economy when labor is scarce, more aggressive recruiting techniques may be required than those used during periods of high unemployment when "walk-in" applicants are likely to satisfy the firm's manpower needs.

Effective hiring requires having a large enough number of recruits from which to select the most suitable applicant. Depending on the job, the number of applicants might range from three or four for routine office and factory jobs to fifteen or more for management positions. In organizing a recruitment campaign, all necessary materials should be gathered in advance — brochures and photographs describing the company, an annual report suggesting the potential of the business, application blanks, and any appropriate tests.

Among the sources for recruiting manpower are:

1. *Present employees.* Whenever possible, present employees should hear about vacancies first. If they are good workers, their recommendations may provide excellent applicants. This is probably the most fruitful source of job applicants for small firms.
2. *Former employees.* Often, past employees may be acceptable if they left for good reason and under good circumstances. Also, they may be able to refer the manager to qualified friends.
3. *"Walk-in" applicants.* In a loose labor market there may be a substantial number of qualified applicants in this category.
4. *State employment agencies.* Branch offices of state agencies, which are affiliated with the United States Employment Service, are located throughout each state. Without cost, these agencies attempt to place applicants on the basis of education, experience, and extensive testing.
5. *Private employment agencies.* A reliable agency, when used properly, can be quite useful in locating applicants. Since most agencies will do initial screening, it is important to supply them with details about the job(s).
6. *Schools.* Trade schools, business schools, and universities often maintain a placement service for their students and alumni. Even if the institution lacks such a service, teachers often are interested in helping their graduating students get good jobs.
7. *Trade and professional associations.* These and other local organizations often have a placement service. For example, the local sales executive association might be able to help find a qualified sales manager.
8. *Other sources.* Customers and suppliers are in a position to recommend specialized personnel. In some industries, such as the building trades, the hiring hall of the local union has taken over the responsibility of supplying the employer with certain personnel. Advertising in local newspapers and trade magazines is perhaps the most common method of recruitment. In addition, the small businessman should carefully consider the employment of handicapped and older workers. If properly matched to a job, they can be more reliable and superior in performance.

Selection

Attracting job applicants is only the first step in the process of obtaining qualified manpower. Next, the entrepreneur must select from among these applicants. The selection tools available to the small business manager fall into four categories: (1) application forms, (2) interviewing, (3) testing, and (4) reference checks.

Application forms. Applications are a widely accepted means of recording information on biographical items such as age and number of dependents; work experience, including nature of duties, salary, length of time on the job, and reasons for leaving; education and training; and personal information, such as membership in associations and police records, if any. While the application form need not be elaborate or lengthy, it should be designed to fit the employer's particular needs. See the sample application in Figure 12–2. It is important that the information requested is not in violation of federal and state fair-employment-practices legislation. In general, applications should not contain any questions dealing with race, nationality, or religion.

The entrepreneur should consider the information on the form in light of the job for which the individual is being considered. If the job applicant is being hired to fill a "dead-end" job, it may be enough to hire only with that job in mind. But, if the entrepreneur is intending to grow and expand, he may want to look for potential supervisors in those he hires.

Interviewing. An interview is necessary to evaluate the applicant's appearance, poise, speech, and other characteristics. The interviewer's objective is to measure the applicant against the specific job requirements in order to decide how well the applicant will "fit." It also affords the applicant an opportunity to find out about the job and organization. To achieve this objective, the interviewer should study the completed application form, job description, and specifications prior to the interview.

It is a good practice to make a few notes of important points to look for or to ask the applicant about. A checklist of questions to ask each prospect will help gather important information and will enable more consistent evaluation for all applicants. Any interviewer can improve the quality of his interviewing by observing certain principles of interviewing:

1. Formulate the objective of the interview and the questions to be asked before seeing the applicant.
2. Conduct the interview in private and put the applicant at ease with a few general remarks about the business and the job.
3. Encourage the applicant to talk by asking pertinent questions and listening attentively to his answers.

Figure 12–2. Sample Application.

4. Retain control of the interview. That is, don't be dominant but keep the interview headed toward the objective.
5. Allow plenty of time but don't waste it.

Except when interviewing for the lowest-level jobs, it is a good practice, whenever possible, to have the applicant interviewed by at least one other person, preferably on a different day. The applicant's prospective supervisor should definitely be one of the other interviewers.

Testing. Testing programs have proved satisfactory for some small firms, especially for low-level jobs. If tests are used, two things must be kept in mind: (a) they should measure what the hirer really wants to measure; and (b) they should not be the sole tool for selecting applicants.

Tests have been developed to provide objective means of measuring the qualifications of job applicants. The primary benefit of employment tests is the discovery of incompetence rather than the prediction of degrees of job success. For the small firm, it is more appropriate to use performance or trade tests applied to specific jobs to be performed. For example, a typist may be requested to type a given number of words within a specified time period, or a machine operator may be asked to operate a machine that is going to be part of his regular job. There are also numerous psychological tests designed to measure intelligence, ability to learn, attitudes, and particular personality traits. When used, they should not be administered or interpreted without expert guidance. Such assistance is available from most universities, practicing psychologists, or consulting firms.

Finally, while some occupations require physical examinations by law, it is a good practice to discover physical limitations and possible contagious diseases of all new employees. Arrangements can be made with a local physician to administer the examination.

Reference checks. The applicant's references can be checked when he has met the preliminary requirements. In addition to verifying the truth of what the applicant has said on his application form and in his interviews, it is a way of getting additional information about the applicant.

Rather than rely solely on the statements of past employers or personal friends of the applicant, some firms obtain financial and personal data for a small fee from a local credit bureau. When considering someone for a very important position, it may be worthwhile to make a personal visit to previous employers.

When conducting a reference check, it is wise to watch out for incorrect dates of employment, claims of higher level of responsibility, inflated salary figures, and falsified information about experience or education. Of course, the potential employer must evaluate the information he receives from former employers and avoid accepting a past employer's severe criticism or undue praise blindly without also evaluating the person making the statements.

Training and Developing Employees

Although a small businessman may spend a lot of time and money in recruiting and selecting employees, his effort will be wasted unless it is backed up by an effective training program. Unfortunately, entrepreneurs frequently feel that they have no time or cannot afford to train employees. This thinking is unfortunate since employees who receive training are growing in their jobs and helping the business grow. Furthermore, depending on one's employees to "pick up" the knowledge and skill needed is inadequate and costly. The development of the ability to carry on the work of an organization is too important to leave to mere chance. An effective training program must include careful consideration of training needs and goals and the most practical training methods.

Establishing Training Needs and Goals

The small businessman should consider several questions: What vacancies are expected? Who needs to be trained? What type of training does each need? No matter how specialized or generalized the knowledge an individual has, he will require further training in the specific techniques and activities of the firm that hires him.

A training program may be geared toward a number of different goals, depending on the particular needs of the firm. One goal may be to orient new employees to the organization. Proper induction of a new employee is an integral part of the training program. Another goal may be to maximize the job performance of nonsupervisory employees. Still another goal may be the long-range development of current and potential supervisors and managers.

Selecting the Training Method

The type of employee training best suited to a specific firm depends on the skills required in jobs, the qualifications of employees, and kinds of operating problems. Thus, a training program should be developed to meet the specific need of the business. Several methods of training suitable for small businesses are discussed below.

On-the-job training. This method, which is the most commonly used, allows for two different approaches. One is to simply turn the man loose on the job and let him ask questions when he runs into problems. The other approach, which is much more desirable, recognizes that it is possible to assist a man in learning a job by giving him a well-planned program. This may be accomplished by following the four-step approach known as Job Instruction Training:

1. *Prepare* the trainee by explaining to him the nature and importance of the job, as well as how it fits into the overall process.
2. *Present* the operation to the trainee, being careful to patiently explain and demonstrate each task involved in the job. Be sure to stress key points and welcome the trainee's questions.
3. *Try out* the operation to see whether the trainee understands key points of the job. Have him explain key steps as he goes along and, if necessary, criticize diplomatically.
4. *Follow-up*, review, and evaluate the performance to see how effectively the instructions have succeeded and what improvements are desirable.

In small firms, the initial training may vary from a few hours to several days, depending on the complexity of the job and the previous training and experience of the employee. When many identical machines are used or when one operation is common to several jobs, *vestibule training* is useful. In this method the worker is trained in a simulated situation using mock-up equipment. Vestibule training allows the training of a large number of people while minimizing the cost of possible errors. On the other hand, it typically requires an investment in equipment, with no return in finished products that can be sold. As a general rule, it should be used only if the business plans to hire a large number of new employees on similar jobs over a long period of time.

Group training. Conferences, lectures, role playing, and informal discussions are especially useful for introducing a new process or machine to a group of workers or foremen; for developing future foremen or managers; for teaching certain techniques, such as "how to make a sale"; and for providing general information or solving common problems.

Group training can be conducted by the owner or one of the key employees depending on the nature of the session. Experts from outside the company, such as professors from local universities or representatives from trade associations or suppliers and distributors, might be used for certain subjects. For example, manufacturers of plant and office equipment often provide instructors on proper use, care, and maintenance of their equipment. Training films are also available from trade associations, government agencies, audiovisual centers of major universities, and film-renting agencies.

The advantages of properly planned and conducted group training for developing supervisors and managers cannot be overstated. For example, supervisory conferences in analyzing sales, production, financial, and manpower problems will foster empathy for one another's problems and will communicate to the participants the policies they will need for effectively solving these problems in the future. The conference approach may also help to satisfy the individual's need for participation while increasing his skill in effective decision making.

Specialized training. Federal- and state-sponsored vocational training, covering a wide range of jobs, is available at little or no cost in most every community. Adult training is available under programs administered by the U.S. Department of Labor and the U.S. Office of Education. Also, in nearly every state, local school systems employ coordinators who conduct programs for small businesses. One such program is a cooperative program for high school seniors in which the students spend part of the school day working in the business and part of the day in regular class work related to the particular firm. Another program allows for the coordinators to organize adult courses on a cost-sharing basis upon request from local businesses.

Following the example of larger corporations, some small firms have found it beneficial to provide special training for employees by enrolling them in courses at local community colleges and universities. For example, one successful small firm, following a rotation system, periodically sends its supervisory and managerial personnel to a 6-week management-training program conducted by the extension division of the local state university. As a final note, the entrepreneur should recognize that training need not be limited to employees, for he will also need to increase his managerial skills through ongoing training and development if he wants to avoid personal stagnation and obsolescence. Training and development, like other elements of successful management, are continuous.

Compensating Employees

Compensation policies have a direct bearing on a manager's ability to recruit qualified applicants, to hold them in the business, and to motivate them to maximum performance. It is very important, therefore, that the entrepreneur know how to compensate his workers, not only in "cash," but also in comparative salaries and pay scales—that is, how much one employee makes compared to another of greater or lesser competence. An additional consideration is how one "mixes" the monetary remuneration paid employees and the "fringe" benefits paid instead of cash. Table 12–1 provides a summary of legal obligations of employers toward their employees.

In determining the general level of wages or salaries to pay, the small businessman will find that many factors must be considered, several of which are beyond his control. For example, if the employees in a firm are represented

Table 12–1. Basic Obligations of Employers.

The following table summarizes the employer's basic legal obligations. Some businesses, such as those employing family members, may be exempt; others may have to meet requirements not discussed here and businessmen should check with state and local authorities or consult with their attorney or accountant.

Statute and Agency	Employers Affected	Basic Requirements
Federal Income Taxes. Internal Revenue Service. (For complete information, see the I.R.S. "Employer's Guide" and "Mr. Businessman's Kit.")	Those who pay taxable wages to employees or have employees who report tips. (This includes employees who are family members.)	Withhold from each paycheck according to employee's exemptions and applicable withholding rate. Deposit withheld amounts and employer contributions in bank or recognized depository semi-monthly or quarterly, depending on the amount involved.
Federal Unemployment Taxes (F.U.T.A.). I.R.S. as above.	Those who employ four or more people during 20 or more weeks annually.	Contribute required percentage of employee's wage. On or before Jan. 31, Form 940 must be filed.
Social Security Taxes (F.I.C.A.). Social Security Administration. (Information also in I.R.S. "Employer's Guide.")	Those who pay over $50 a quarter in wages.	Get employee Social Security number. At year end or within 30 days of termination, furnish employee with required number of copies of W-2 Wage and Earnings statements. Withhold required percentage of employee's salary from his paycheck and contribute a comparable amount. Deposit as above.
Federal Wage and Hour Laws. U.S. Dept. of Labor, Wage and Hour Div. (Some states have similar codes.)	Those who engage in interstate trade, hold government contracts or do a specified volume of business.	Pay the minimum hourly wage required and time-and-a-half for hours over 40 worked per week. Give "equal pay for equal work" and comply with regulations on child labor and employee health and safety. Retain basic payroll records for required length of time.
Civil Rights Act, Title VII. Equal Employment Opportunity Commission. (Some states have similar codes.)	Those employers who are covered by Wage and Hour laws.	Treat job applicants and employees fairly and equally regardless of race, color, religion, sex, age, or national origin.

Table 12–1 (*continued*)

Workmen's Compensation Insurance. The State Div. of Industrial Accidents or, in some states, the Workmen's Compensation Board.	Those who employ regular employees.	Cover all employees for possible injury on the job either through the state or a private plan approved by the state. Post notices indicating compliance with the law. Rates of insurance are based on the number of on-the-job injuries for all firms in state.
State Unemployment Insurance. (Pays benefits to people who are jobless but able and available for work.) The State Dept. of Human Resources Development, or, in some states, the Dept. of Labor.	Those who meet the particular state's eligibility standards. (In California, those who pay $100 or more in quarterly wages; in New York, those who pay $300 or more in quarterly wages.)	Obtain an Employer Identification number soon after becoming eligible. (This is sometimes given automatically to employers who file for a sales tax license.) Remit quarterly reports and contributions required. Contributions are based on employer's "experience rating." Retain required information for the stipulated time—usually 3 to 4 years.

From "Personnel for the Small Business," *Small Business Reporter* 9, No. 8 (1970), 8. Reprinted with permission of the Bank of America National Trust and Savings Association.

by a strong union, the employer may simply have to pay the "union scale" for those jobs in his area or locality. But even in the absence of a union or of strong union control, the small businessman has less control over wages than is commonly believed. For example, there are state and federal laws that establish minimum wages to be paid employees and the hours for which overtime must be paid. The small businessman must also consider the wages and salaries paid for comparable work by other firms within his industry as well as within his geographic area. If compensation is less than the going rate, the job is likely to attract only inferior or marginal workers. On the other hand, an employer who decides to pay more than the going rate will be in a poor competitive position unless his higher wage bill is offset by greater productivity.

Another consideration is the cost of living in the area in which the employees work. If it is unusually high, the small businessman will be expected to pay more than if he were in a low cost area. Thus a business located in a large city in the East is likely to have a higher wage bill than if it were located in a small rural area in the South. Similarly, some consideration must be given to the supply and demand for employees in the area; the small businessman may have to pay a higher wage to attract employees in an area in which the demand is greater than the supply.

Relative Worth of Jobs

Studies have shown that most dissatisfactions with wages arise not from the absolute amount so much as from the relative amounts—that is, the amount

I get relative to the amount that Joe (who works with me) gets. Thus, the employer has the dual problem of "equal pay for equal work" and "equity" in paying jobs at different levels within the organization.

A common method of determining the relative worth of each job *within* the organization is known as "job evaluation." While job evaluation does not determine the *absolute* pay level for employees, it does determine the value of one job as *compared* to other jobs performed by employees. Job evaluation in some firms becomes quite complex, since the evaluator must take into account such factors as skill, responsibility, education, effort, working conditions, and several subdivisions of these factors. For the smaller firm, a simpler approach may be followed, using the job descriptions and specifications formulated for the recruitment and selection program. Once general job classifications are set up for individual jobs of similar nature and content, the employer can establish an "average" salary for each classification and provide for an upward schedule within it, based on varying degrees of responsibility, productivity, or other yardsticks he feels are important. It is common practice in wage administration to establish a *range* for each job within the job classification, and to determine an individual employee's wage rate within that range on the basis of his merit and/or seniority.

Wage Supplements

Since World War II, there has been a tremendous increase in the supplements to wages given to employees. These supplements include any benefits to employees involving a cost to the company other than the employee's regular wages. While they are frequently referred to as fringe benefits, they are so costly that the term is misleading.

Typically, wage supplements average about 25 percent of the payroll and include items such as paid vacations, holidays, group insurances, pensions, bonuses, sick leaves, profit-sharing plans, and severance pay. Some of these supplements, like bonuses and profit-sharing plans, are used as a means of motivating employees to higher levels of performance. Bonuses may be based on individual or group performance and frequently are influenced by length of employment. Profit sharing, which seems well-suited for a smaller firm, usually provides for an annuity (based on profits earned) to all employees who have been with the company for a specified time. A disadvantage to bonuses and profit sharing is that employees may eventually take the "supplement" for granted. Then, not only does it lose its motivating appeal, but as workers adjust their standards of living to include the supplement, a great deal of dissatisfaction develops when there is no profit to share during lean business periods.

While many wage supplements are introduced by larger firms, the small business, if it is to compete for labor, must eventually offer the same. Since these supplements are expensive, and since employees tend to take them for granted, it is important that the entrepreneur communicate to his employees the cost and nature of the "benefits" provided.

Human Relations

The difficulty in motivating workers to achieve higher levels of productivity and to accept the goals of the firm in which they work has attracted much research and resulted in numerous management theories. With the growth of strong unions, tighter labor markets, and a general social concern with carrying out democratic practices in all areas of life, negative sanctions (fear and punishment) and systems of reward (economic incentives) have given way to more concern with human factors. This human-relations movement has challenged many assumptions of traditional management theories and has directed attention to the individual differences of human beings and their social interactions in quest of fulfilling certain needs.

"Human relations" has come to mean many different things to different people. Keith Davis defines *human relations* as the "integration of people into a work situation that motivates them to work together productively, cooperatively, and with economic, psychological, and social satisfaction."[1] According to this concept, human relations in business is more than "getting along with people." It is also the development of a sense of teamwork that will effectively fulfill individual needs while achieving organizational objectives. At the same time, it is important for the entrepreneur to note that human relations is not simply a set of techniques for handling people. Rather it is an analytical approach to understanding people. As Fred J. Carvell points out:

> ... a danger associated with ... human relations is the assumption that there are prepared solutions for human problems and conflicts. There are no prepared answers to the human problems of management; there are only the answers that evolve through the struggle to be mature, responsible, and open in dealing with other people whether they are peers, superiors, or subordinates.[2]

An effective human-relations program, therefore, requires an understanding of the varied needs, wants, and perceptions of employees. Thus, the effective manager takes a personal interest in individual employees but avoids

---

[1] Keith Davis, *Human Relations at Work*, 3rd ed. (New York: McGraw-Hill, 1967), p. 5.
[2] Fred J. Carvell, *Human Relations in Business* (New York: Macmillan, 1970), p. 8.

paternalism, pampering, or neglecting necessary discipline. A manager's problem is to fit together the logical operations of his business, the social structure of teamwork, and the individual characteristics of employees. The extent to which a manager's philosophy of human relations is translated into practice will be reflected in the manpower policies and programs of his firm. All such policies and programs should be formulated only after considering both the implications they will have on the working relationship of organizational members and their impact on operating efficiency.

Furthermore, as pointed out by Fred J. Carvell "...the implementation of human relations is closely related to the way company policies are administered as well as the way they are formulated."[3] Thus, effective management assures that organizational communications will operate in a spirit of mutual trust and consideration, that employee attitudes will be respected, that conflict and differences will be handled constructively, and that managers and supervisors will be influenced by the owner–manager's attitudes and practices when dealing with peers and subordinates.

It is beyond the scope of this book to discuss in depth the recent behavioral science findings and their impact on management techniques. (Chapter 5 discussed some findings dealing with motivation.) The reader is advised to consult the suggested readings at the end of this chapter for more complete coverage. Some mention must be made, nevertheless, of the often misused concept of morale. What is "morale"? Essentially, morale refers to the attitudes of either a person or a group. While recent studies have shown that high morale does not necessarily cause high productivity, it does make for a potentially more manageable work force and one which is more susceptible to change and to accepting the directions of management. There is also some relationship between high morale and low absenteeism and turnover. According to studies conducted by Renis Likert, the long-run costs of running an organization with a high morale work force will be less.

Union Relations

Small firms are less likely to be unionized than large firms, mainly because the cost of organizing a small firm is relatively high. On the other hand, small firms in certain industries, such as printing, manufacturing, trucking, and construction, are likely to be the object of a union drive the first day of business. Similarly, small businesses located in heavily industrialized areas are likely to be unionized. Not infrequently, a union that is attempting to make inroads into an industry will also seek to add new firms to their membership rolls, regardless of size. Thus, there is no guarantee that the businessman will not

---

[3] Carvell, *op. cit.*, p. 9

face a union organization drive. Even if the small firm is overlooked by the union organizer, the impetus for organization may come from the employees within the firm.

The typical entrepreneur seems to have strong feelings against unionization. Being a "self-made man," he tends to view workers' attempts to band together in a union as something fundamentally and philosophically wrong. When his own workers unionize, he perceives this as either a personal insult to him or as the result of outside agitators or radicals who created dissatisfaction among his workers. This attitude is unfortunate because there are many legitimate reasons why workers join unions. Strauss and Sayles summarized these reasons as "desire for better economic and working conditions, desire for control over benefits, and desire for self-expression and communication with higher management."[4] Some firms make a conscious effort to meet these desires by maintaining wages, hours, and conditions of employment that are equal to or better than union firms and by providing grievance procedures and devices to improve communication. But even here there is no guarantee that unionization will not take place. Workers may organize simply because they feel that labor and management cannot be combined and that their interests must be protected by an outside organization. In addition, in any particular company at a specific time, there may be some precipitating event to change the workers' attitude. Strauss and Sayles cite a number of such motivating events:

1. A change in the top management of the plant. Employees fear that the new management will be less friendly and will not preserve the favorable conditions they are used to.
2. Specific problems arising from incentive-payment systems, particularly new standards or new work assignments.
3. The cutting off of promotional ladders—for example, requiring that all new supervisors have college degrees.
4. Sudden cutbacks and layoffs.[5]

Of course, the presence of a union need not be regarded as a tragedy. Many successful small firms enjoy cooperative, friendly relationships with unions. Indeed, many experts regard the presence of a union as a strong impetus to more effective management. For example, in a study of small union and non-union firms, it was found that the single overriding difference between union

---

[4] George Strauss and Leonard Sayles, *The Human Problems of Management*, 2nd ed. (Englewood Cliffs, N. J.: Prentice-Hall, 1967), pp. 106–107. Reprinted with permission.
[5] *Ibid.*, p. 107

and non-union firms was the small non-union firm's reliance upon informal administration of the personnel function. The researchers concluded that the union firm's concern for a well-defined, formal approach had certain advantages over the informal practices within the non-union firm. In their words,

> Such an approach has certain advantages over the informal relationships that exist within the non-union firm. Written, standardized personnel policies encourage consistent interpretation and administration of personnel functions. Consistency increases the worker's confidence in management by equal and fair treatment if disagreements or disputes arise.[6]

Finally, it should be noted that when it comes to union–management relations, the entrepreneur is greatly outclassed. As pointed out by Donald J. Grabowski,

> Our small employer has little or no knowledge of federal or state labor law. He doesn't have the time to acquire this knowledge. He has little or no knowledge of the source of information regarding these laws. He has no trained staff man to rely upon, and labor attorneys and consultants are too expensive. Most of all, the small employer "doesn't want any trouble."[7]

Perhaps the situation is not quite so bleak as indicated by this statement, but it does suggest the need for employers to become familiar with labor laws that directly affect them. Labor legislation provides the boundaries within which a manpower program operates. While these laws are numerous and complex, several publishers, including Prentice-Hall, Commerce Clearing House, and the Bureau of National Affairs (available at the local university or public library) publish comprehensive information on contract clauses, grievance procedures, and so on that can be helpful in negotiating an agreement and in day-to-day relations with the union. Several practical books on labor relations are included in the bibliography at the end of the chapter. Also

---

[6] Max S. Wortman, Jr., and William E. Reif, "An Analysis of the Industrial Relations Function in Small Manufacturing Firms," *Journal of Small Business Management* 3, No. 4 (October 1965), p. 15.

[7] Donald J. Grabowski, "Labor Relations and the Small Employer," *Personnel Journal* 41, No. 3 (March 1962), p. 127.

see the appendix to this chapter for some practical information on the union contract. At times legal advice may be required. However, it is important to remember that management of manpower cannot be delegated to an attorney, nor can any amount of legal knowledge be an effective substitute for a well-planned manpower program.

Appendix: The Union Contract[8]

The signing of a union contract is an important occasion. It signifies that all the stresses and strains of the bargaining sessions are over and that the two parties have finally reached an agreement. The signing ceremony is an important symbol to many workers and it is a good idea to publicize it accordingly. Whether or not each worker gets a copy of the contract, the entrepreneur would do well to call a management meeting after the signing to make sure his employees understand each clause thoroughly. The managers can then clarify any point for employees under their supervision.

Smooth union–management relations are greatly enhanced if the contract is clear and concise on every point. In drawing up an agreement, it is therefore well worthwhile to include all of the following points:

Preamble. Since the union contract is in part a public-relations tool, it is not out of place to begin by briefly mentioning its purpose and the desire of management and union to reach a harmonious working agreement.

Conditions of recognition. Controversy sometimes develops because contracts were left vague on this point. Thus, it pays the manager to mention the kind of union security his company is offering: for example, union shop, maintenance-of-membership, sole bargaining, and/or check-off (in which union dues are deducted before paying union employees).

Management clause. Immediately following the union-recognition clause, there should be a statement of management's rights, responsibilities, and the areas of action in which it remains free from questioning by the union. This clause can be quite controversial. Thus, the employer needs as much contract protection as he can get. He should also make sure that he gets this clause in

---

[8] From Ernest L. Loen, *Personnel Management Guides for Small Business* (Washington, D. C.: Small Business Administration, 1961).

where it belongs, rather than tucked away somewhere at the end. The smaller employer cannot afford to have his rights merely implied.

Working conditions. Because this area of collective bargaining affects employees directly, the union contract should cover all these points and any others that may apply to the company because of environmental circumstances: right to hire and fire; hours of work, including clauses to explain when overtime begins, when Sunday begins and ends, and when holidays begin and end; seniority, including provision for all situations—plant-wide, departmental, job, ability, and family status.

Wages. It is wiser to cover wages in a supplementary agreement, or in an appendix, because the contract may provide for annual or semiannual review that will result in changes in wage rates.

Health and welfare clauses. The contract may provide that the employer make a deduction from the employee's salary for the union health and welfare fund. However, according to the Taft-Hartley Act, sums so deducted may be used only for deaths, sickness, accident, retirement, medical, and unemployment benefits. Employees are permitted to contribute only if the fund is established under a written agreement and is administered jointly by employer and employees. These points should be mentioned in the contract.

Grievance-handling procedure. No union contract should be without a clause specifying what a grievance is (wages usually are not included) and how to file a grievance, step by step. The employee should know exactly to whom he should present his grievance, what to expect after that, and what his next steps are if the first one brings no results.

Continuation clause. Every contract should provide an expiration clause. In the case of a blanket contract with several craft unions involved, it is wise to state the wages separately but use the same basic contract with identical expiration dates.

Incident 12: Finding the Right Man

Pete Smith has decided to hire a new mechanic, if he can find one, to take care of some of the mechanical work on the old cars he restores. Pete knows a few mechanics personally, but none of them meet his qualifications, for he is looking for special characteristics. The man should be a top-flight auto mechanic; he should know something about auto machine shop practice, so that he can do jobs such as truing brake drums and line boring older engine main bearings; he should be willing to work extra time to get the job right; and he should have a feel for old cars and enjoy working on them.

Pete feels that the typical modern auto mechanic won't necessarily be the right man — indeed, some modern skills, such as alternator and power-steering work, are irrelevant to his business. The kind of employee he wants must exist — the problem for Pete is to find one as quickly as possible. Since Pete can charge customers good prices for good work, he is willing to pay as much as a dollar an hour over going rates to get exactly the right man.

1. Suppose Pete's shop is in your area. Do some research about the job market for such people. Where could he find such a man? List all possible sources.
2. Of the sources you found in question 1, which is likely to be the best and easiest for Pete to use? Why?
3. Write a brief job description for this position. (Use any material you can find in the previous eleven incidents for clues to what is really required).
4. Do you think it would be a good deal for a top-flight mechanic to work in a small shop with two other technicians rather than in a very large shop with dozens of men? Why?

Discussion Questions

1. In what way is every manager a personnel manager?
2. How does the close personal relationship between the small-business manager and his employee complicate the job of manpower management?
3. Distinguish between a job description and a job specification? How does each affect personnel decisions?
4. Discuss some ways in which the entrepreneur might be aggressive in recruiting personnel.
5. How can the owner or manager of a small firm improve the quality of his interviewing?
6. Do you think a small firm should have a testing program as part of its selection procedure? Why or why not?
7. Briefly discuss how you would go about setting up a training program for a retail store employing fifty-five people.
8. What are the essential steps in the on-the-job training method?
9. Describe the various approaches the small businessman might take to training rank-and-file applicants; management personnel.

10. What factors affect the general *level* of wages or salaries the small businessman must pay?
11. What is the objective of job evaluation?
12. What is the major disadvantage to bonuses and profit-sharing plans?
13. "The human relations approach is no more than 'getting along with people.'" Comment.
14. What is morale? What is the relationship between morale and productivity?
15. Does the owner of a small business need to worry about a union organizational drive? Why or why not?
16. How do you explain the fact that even well-paid workers may join a union?
17. Do you agree that the entrepreneur is greatly outclassed when it comes to union–management relations? Why or why not?

Suggested Readings

Beach, Dale S., *Managing People at Work*. New York: Macmillan, 1971.

Beaumont, John A., "How to Write a Job Description," *Management Aide*, (February 1965). Washington, D. C.: Small Business Administration.

Blum, Albert A., *Industrial Relations and the Small Firm*, Bulletin No. 34 (July 1960). Ithaca, N. Y.: New York State School of Industrial and Labor Relations.

Brown, H. M., and Longenecker, J. G., *Small Business Management*, 3rd ed. Cincinnati: South-Western Publishing, 1971. Ch. 25.

Carvell, Fred J., *Human Relations in Business*. New York: Macmillan, 1970.

Davis, Keith, *Human Relations at Work*, 3rd ed. New York: McGraw-Hill, 1967.

Dawling, William M., Jr., and Sayles, Leonard R., *How Managers Motivate: The Imperatives of Supervision*. New York: McGraw-Hill, 1971.

Dunnette, Marvin D., *Personnel Selection and Placement*. Belmont, Calif.: Wadsworth, 1966.

Gellerman, Saul W., *The Management of Human Relations*. New York: Holt, Rinehart and Winston, 1966.

Klatt, Lawrence A., ed., *Managing the Dynamic Small Firm: Readings*. Belmont, Calif.: Wadsworth, 1971. Pp. 236–270.

Loen, Ernest L., *Personnel Management Guides for Small Business*. Washington, D. C.: Small Business Administration, 1961.

Muerst, Jean S., and Wiggins, John S., "How a Small Company Attracts and Keeps Above-Average Employees," *Personnel* XLI (January–February 1964), 40–41.

Odiorne, George S., *Personnel Administration by Objectives*. Homewood, Ill.: Richard D. Irwin, 1971.

"Personnel for the Small Business," *Small Business Reporter* 9, No. 8 (1970), Bank of America National Trust & Savings Association.

Rigors, Paul, and Myers, Charles A., *Personnel Administration*, 6th ed. New York: McGraw-Hill, 1969.

Sloane, Arthur A., and Witney, Fred, *Labor Relations*. Englewood Cliffs, N. J.: Prentice-Hall, 1967.

Strauss, George, and Sayles, Leonard, *The Human Problems of Management*, 2nd ed. Englewood Cliffs, N. J.: Prentice-Hall, 1967.

Chapter 13

The Production Process

The production process consists of converting inputs of labor, materials, capital (machinery, buildings, and so on), and management into outputs, such as products or services for sale. One of the major objectives in designing a production process is to minimize long-run production costs. To a large extent, the minimum production cost, whether it be for a service or a product, is determined by the "designer"—that is, the person who explicitly determines the product or service to be produced or offered. Given a description or specifications for a product or service, the entrepreneur's task becomes one of minimizing costs within the constraints or requirements of the design. Hence, he should examine his product or service to ascertain whether the design recognizes the customers' needs as well as the need for economical production. Thus, his goal is to satisfy his customers' needs at a price they are willing to pay and, at the same time, ensure himself a reasonable return on investment.

Discussion of the production process in this chapter will be organized around a number of topics of prime interest to the entrepreneur. More specifically, it will survey the major concepts involved in product design, production planning and control, plant layout, maintenance, work improvement, production standards, inventory control, quality control, and quantitative decision-making techniques.

Note: This chapter was written in collaboration with Donald Del Mar, University of Idaho.

Product Design

The minimum fabrication costs for a part or product are determined when a design is accepted for production. For products in which manufacturing is the major cost, the design stage is the period of greatest concern. Generally, once the functional requirements of design have been specified, the designer must determine alternative means and methods to achieve these requirements — the major concern must be the achievement of functional requirements (that is, why the product is purchased) and other *necessary* consumer requirements at the lowest manufacturing cost. This analytical approach to design is referred to as engineering analysis or value analysis depending on whether the designer is concerned with the initial design of a product or the modification of the design of an existing product to bring about lower costs or greater value for a particular product function.

If they are to achieve low manufacturing costs through the proper selection of fabrication or assembly processes, product designers must think in terms of alternative designs. However, many small companies limit the market for their products by leaving product design entirely in the hands of designers who may only see one or a few alternatives and who know little about manufacturing costs. Similarly, many entrepreneurs make the mistake of trying to compete in fields requiring large capital investments for machinery and equipment, in-depth technical organization, or a large national distribution organization.

Production Planning and Control

Production planning and control calls for the scheduling and routing of work through the firm; it includes the control of production times, processes, and methods of work. The control system of a plant consists of five functions — the first three are essentially planning functions while the last two are control functions.

1. *Planning*. In addition to determining material and parts requirements, the production planner must distribute work to different departments or work areas, determine the number of workers, decide on type and number of machines, and assign a completion time for each stage.
2. *Routing*. Routing takes into account the operations to be performed, their sequence, and the flow of materials through production. Usually, a route sheet or operations sheet, which describes what is to be done and how it is to be done, travels along with the materials or parts through the various stages of production.
3. *Scheduling*. The scheduling function is to set up the production timetable.

Master schedules show the dates on which delivery is promised to the customer, and detailed schedules for each of the semifinished parts ensure that all components will arrive at the proper place in time for the next operation.
4. *Dispatching.* Work orders for each job ensure that planning will be carried out, that routing will be arranged, and that the schedules will be adhered to. This issuance of work orders, along with regular reports on work progress, is known as dispatching.
5. *Expediting.* Expediting is the follow-up activity that determines whether plans are actually being executed and attempts to eliminate bottlenecks that develop.

Numerous kinds of charts are available to help the small businessman with the planning and control of the production process. Three commonly used charts are:

1. *Operation process charts.* Graphic representation of the various operations, time allowances, and materials used in the production process.
2. *Flow process charts.* Graphic representation of all operations, transportations, inspections, delays, and storages relating to a process. It is more detailed than the operation process chart, and one flow chart is often used for only one part of an assembly.
3. *Machine load chart.* Often referred to as a Gantt Chart, it is a bar chart with time on the horizontal axis and the factor to be scheduled on the vertical axis. The bars show the time schedules for several machines on the same chart.

Plant Layout

Given a product or products to manufacture and a suitable plant location, the next crucial step is to decide on a plant layout. Since the small businessman is concerned with producing a quality product at a low unit cost, he must make careful, detailed plans for eliminating, as far as possible, waste motion of men and materials. To keep unit costs down, the layout must permit the free flow of work, a minimum investment of capital, and desirable employee working conditions.

A good layout for machines and work stations will be arranged so that production operations are carried through to completion with efficiency — that is, with the lowest possible use of resources. Layouts that require employees to walk, carry, or convey materials from one location to another, when such movements can be avoided or minimized, produce higher than necessary labor costs.

The two basic layouts for physical facilities are product or line layout and process or functional layout. Most small manufacturing facilities are a combination of these two types. The *product* or *line layout* can most easily be understood by visualizing a series of machines that perform a sequence of transformation steps on material inputs in order to produce a desired product. These machines may be special purpose machines that perform one or more modifications on the inputs—for example, a line of machines that perform a sequence of operations such as milling, boring, drilling, and tapping on a rough casting, which produce a finished engine block ready for the installation of pistons, connecting rods, bearings, and so on.

To be successful in achieving the objective of low conversion cost using a line or product layout, the following conditions must be met:

1. An adequate volume for reasonable equipment utilization.
2. A reasonably stable demand for the product.
3. A standardized product.
4. Interchangeable parts.

The line or product layout is usually the most efficient method, and it tends to result in lowest unit cost (if volume allows high machine and labor efficiency) and lowest scrap (if quality control is strategically located along the line). On the other hand, this layout has a built-in tendency to incur excessive investment in tools and equipment, as well as requiring a very good maintenance program. This shortcoming can be costly if a product is subject to frequent changes or obsolescence that requires a new layout and/or new machine or tools.

In a *process* or *functional layout,* similar or identical machines or equipment are grouped together, and inputs are routed to the various areas as required. The typical job shop is likely to use the process layout in which the product is routed from one work station to another to have a specified process performed on it. This type of layout is also used when the same facilities must be used to fabricate a number of different parts or products.

Process layout is preferable to a product layout when the volume of any one product is low, when product designs are not stable, and when no one sequence of fabrication or assembly steps will accommodate many parts or products. Since machine process efficiency does not depend on the location of the machines, the primary concern in process layout is minimizing material-handling costs. Thus, consider that:

$$\text{Material-Handling Effort} = (\text{Loads Per Unit Time}) \times (\text{Distance between Process Areas}) = \text{To Be Minimized}$$

A "load" in the above formula may consist of any number of units that must be transported from one location to another. Since material-handling costs are a function of material-handling effort, the above formula is also a measure of these costs.

Learning to minimize material-handling effort is a process of trial and error. First, a plant layout is made, then a measure of the total material-handling effort for the various products is computed. When changes in the layout are made, a calculation of the required material-handling effort is computed for each new layout. These steps are continued until no further improvement is obtained. There is presently no means available except trial and error for determining when an "optimum" layout is achieved. However, computer programs have been written to do the tedious trial-and-error work. One such program is called CRAFT (available from IBM).

Plant Maintenance

The objective of a plant-maintenance program is to keep the firm's physical assets in repair so that the cost over their economic life is minimized. Maintenance includes such diverse tasks as lubrication of equipment, repair of broken equipment, replacement of worn parts, adjustments to equipment, and janitorial and routine building-maintenance activities.

The plant-maintenance task is generally divided into two categories: "breakdown" and "preventive." Most, if not all, smaller plants have programs incorporating aspects of both categories. Preventive maintenance involves routine tasks, such as lubrication and minor adjustments, that are intended to prevent a major breakdown. Breakdown maintenance, of course, involves repairing machines that have broken down. The proper balance between the two types of maintenance programs is primarily economic. To maintain any equipment requires that the owner either have spare parts and supplies on hand or wait until they can be delivered once a breakdown has occurred.

Preventive-maintenance programs require records on what was found, what was done, and other pertinent data that may be important to know for future maintenance tasks. Thus, record keeping is essential if maintenance costs are to be analyzed. Record keeping costs money, however, and to be of greatest value, they must be kept accurately over a long period of time. Therefore, decisions about what records are to be kept and for what purpose must be made in light of the costs involved and the probable gains from collecting and analyzing such data. Every maintenance program should produce information that will enable the manager to develop a more efficient maintenance system and to make better decisions about the purchase of new equipment in the future.

Given the necessary information, then, it is essential that the manager periodically examine his information in order to control his costs. For example, he should periodically examine his cost records and inspection reports for indication of excessive maintenance costs or frequent breakdowns. With heavy investment in equipment and the high per-hour cost of labor, the small plant cannot afford to tie up man or machine because of faulty equipment resulting from poor maintenance.

Work Improvement

The essential aim of work improvement is to eliminate the waste of time, materials, and machinery that occurs in most jobs. The intent is *not* to increase production through harder work on the part of the operator, but rather through better tooling or ways of doing the job, so that the operator can produce more with less effort.

For the manager, the key to effective work improvement is his awareness of precisely what is involved in an operation and the details of what must be done, as well as an inquiring attitude that searches for "the best way." The usual approach to work improvement consists of the following steps: (1) Select the job; (2) break down the job into its elements; (3) question every element of the job; (4) develop a new method; and (5) install the new method. While the entrepreneur will probably need to delegate the responsibility of methods study as the manufacturing process increases in size, he must still help to create a climate among employees to encourage new and better ways of doing jobs.

Rapid technological developments have led to the use of equipment and material factors well adapted to engineering requirements but often difficult for human operation. In recent years an area of study known as *human engineering* has been developed, in which researchers focus attention on the human factors of equipment and methods design. The findings of human-engineering research are numerous. For example, it is known that people need to change their position from time to time to work effectively and comfortably. For example, equipment that allows the operator to either sit or stand while working can reduce fatigue and increase productivity.

Work simplification is also a vital part of work improvement. Basically, the manager should investigate time, space, weight, distance, and other factors related to the manufacturing process in order to determine the movement sequence demanding the least physical effort and the shortest completion time. In order to be an effective observer, the small manufacturer should be familiar with the principles of motion economy involving the layout of the work area, the design and use of tools, and the use of hand and body. Some of

Table 13–1. Principles of Motion Economy— A Check Sheet for Motion Economy and Fatigue Reduction

These twenty-two rules or principles of motion economy may be profitably applied to shop and office work alike. Although not all are applicable to every operation, they do form a basis or a code for improving efficiency and reducing fatigue in manual work.

Use of the Human Body

1. The two hands should begin as well as complete their motions at the same time.
2. The two hands should not be idle at the same time except during rest periods.
3. Motions of the arms should be made in opposite and symmetrical directions and should be made simultaneously.
4. Hand motions should be confined to the lowest classification with which it is possible to perform the work satisfactorily.
5. Momentum should be employed to assist the worker wherever possible, and it should be reduced to a minimum if it must be overcome by muscular effort.
6. Smooth continuous motions of the hands are preferable to zigzag motions or straight-line motions involving sudden and sharp changes in direction.
7. Ballistic movements are faster, easier, and more accurate than restricted (fixation) or "controlled" movements.
8. Rhythm is essential to the smooth and automatic performance of an operation, and the work should be arranged to permit easy and natural rhythm wherever possible.

Arrangement of the Work Place

9. There should be a definite and fixed place for all tools and materials.
10. Tools, materials, and controls should be located close in and directly in front of the operator.
11. Gravity feedbins and containers should be used to deliver materials close to the point of use.
12. Drop deliveries should be used wherever possible.
13. Materials and tools should be located to permit the best sequence of motions.
14. Provisions should be made for adequate conditions for seeing. Good illumination is the first requirement for satisfactory visual perception.
15. The height of the workplace and the chair should preferably be arranged so that alternate sitting and standing at work are easily possible.
16. A chair of the type and height to permit good posture should be provided for every worker.

Design of Tools and Equipment

17. The hands should be relieved of all work that can be done more advantageously by a jig, a fixture, or a foot-operated device.
18. Two or more tools should be combined whenever possible.
19. Tools and materials should be prepositioned whenever possible.
20. Where each finger performs some specific movement such as in typewriting, the load should be distributed in accordance with the inherent capacities of the fingers.
21. Handles, such as those used on cranks and large screwdrivers, should be designed to permit as much of the surface of the hand to come in contact with the handle as possible. This is particularly true when considerable force is exerted in using the handle. For light assembly work the screwdriver handle should be so shaped that it is smaller at the bottom than at the top.
22. Levers, crossbars, and handwheels should be located in such positions that the operator can manipulate them with the least change in body position and with the greatest mechanical advantage.

From R. M. Barnes, *Motion and Time Study: Design and Measurement of Work*. 6th ed. (New York: John Wiley, 1968). p. 220. Reprinted with permission.

the most widely used principles are summarized in Table 13–1. Once the improved or "best" method is determined, it should be standardized so that all workers can be trained in the improved method.

Production Standards

Once the entrepreneur determines the most effective job method acceptable to the workers, he must then establish production standards. Properly developed standards serve several important functions:

1. They provide basic data for the operation of the plant and for scheduling production.
2. They provide the basis for labor cost control, such as incentive wage systems.
3. They provide the basis for investment and pricing decisions through outlining how much output can be expected per unit of time when bidding on jobs or selecting certain manufacturing processes.

Time study is the most widely used method of developing production standards in small firms, and in many cases it is the best available method. The only equipment necessary is a stopwatch and a time-study form. However, the success of this method depends primarily upon the ability and experience of the man conducting the study. Many small plants, especially those with repetitive and short-cycle operations, employ a time-study engineer to conduct the study. There are five basic steps in time study:

1. Select and describe the exact task to be studied.
2. Break down the task into smaller tasks or job elements. These "elements" should be a significant part of the total task and should have a well-defined beginning and end.
3. Observe the task (a number of times) and record the time for each element on the observation sheet. At the same time, rate the performance of the worker.
4. Compute the "normal time" — that is, the minimally acceptable (not average) time required to perform the task, or the time in which roughly 95 percent of all workers can perform the task if they have the ability and the training and have followed the prescribed method.
5. Compute the "standard time" by providing allowances for such things as unavoidable machine delay, personal time, and fatigue.

Standard time data systems is an alternative method to ordinary time study. This approach uses catalogs of motions with a table of time values for each motion. The time data in such time systems as Methods-Time Measurement (MTM) have been predetermined for the analyst. He then describes the motions required to perform an operation (reach, move, turn, grasp, and so on), checks the proper table in the catalog to determine the time for each motion, and totals the times of all the motions found in the operation.

This method provides a quick and low-cost approach to setting standards in many types of small plants, such as job-order shops, in which time study would be costly or difficult. The major shortcoming of this method is that it does not take into account any unique conditions in the plant.

Work sampling is another means of setting standards without using a stopwatch. A simple example of work sampling would be to determine what proportion of the time a maintenance crew is productive. If productive work is defined as actual maintenance work, and nonproductive work is defined as all other activities, the sampler can form two columns on a sheet of paper captioned "P" and "NP" and then make instantaneous, random observations and enter a tally mark after each observation in the appropriate column. Since the number of observations for any particular activity is statistically proportional to the amount of time spent on that activity, one can arrive at an estimate of the amount or proportion of productive and nonproductive time for the maintenance crew. The accuracy of the estimate is determined by the number of observations—the greater the number of observations, the greater the accuracy. Tables and charts have been developed for determining the number of observations needed to maintain a specified precision.

Material standards, or standards for material inputs into the production process, is an often neglected area. Briefly, the objective is to minimize production costs by evaluating the quality of inputs. Low-cost inputs do not necessarily reduce overall costs, since cheap inputs may be of low quality and may require additional labor and process effort that is not offset by the lower cost of procurement. Thus, the type and quality of production inputs must be considered in terms of the expected profits. Further, if a standard is set hastily or haphazardly, it will be difficult to instill employee confidence in that standard as well as in the entire standards program. And last, any standard, whether for materials or worker output, must be periodically reviewed, for setting standards is not a one-time activity.

Inventory Control

Proper control of inventories can help save money and increase the return on investments. Inventory control involves the procurement, care, and disposition of materials. There are three types of inventory that are of concern to managers: raw materials, in-process or semifinished goods, and finished goods.

If a manager effectively controls these three types of inventory, he can release capital that may be tied up in unnecessary inventory, improve production control, protect against obsolescence, deterioration, and theft, and gather useful information for planning ahead.

Consider the example of an entrepreneur who uses a purchased good in production. He must first place an order for the goods, wait for the delivery of the order to the supplier, wait for the supplier to process and fill the order, wait for the order to be transported to his plant, and finally, wait for the order to be checked for quantity and quality and delivered to the location where it will be used. Assume that (a) his production system will use the material at a rate of 200/week; (b) average delivery time (from the initiation of an order to delivery) averages 3 weeks; and (c) every time he receives a truckload of 200 items he immediately places another order for 200 items. The fluctuations in his inventory level can readily be seen in Figure 13–1. Note that the inventory level goes from a maximum of 600 units to zero—just at the time the next shipment arrives. Average inventory is 300 units. Of course, no recognition has been given to the fact that there will be times when delivery is not made in 3 weeks, thus interrupting the production process. He can provide protection against this occurrence at a cost of holding, say, an extra week's requirements on hand. However, now his inventory is 33 percent higher in cost and space requirements:

$$\frac{\text{Average}}{\text{Inventory}} = \frac{600 + 200}{2} = 400 \text{ units}$$

Although not explicitly recognized in this example, the quantity of goods ordered at one time is an important factor in inventory management. Recognition should also be given to two types of inventory costs: those that vary proportionally to quantity and those that are essentially fixed. The cost per unit purchased and the carrying cost are considered proportional to the quantity of inventory, whereas the cost of placing an order for one unit or 1000 units is

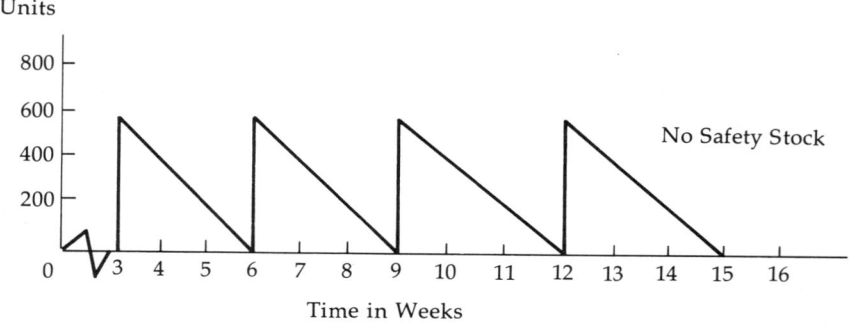

Figure 13–1. Three-Week Inventory Cycle.

essentially the same and can be considered fixed. The economic-order-quantity formula, or *EOQ*, recognizes the various costs in ordering and holding inventory:

$$EOQ = \sqrt{\frac{2RS}{KC}}$$

where
- R = annual rate of usage
- S = cost of placing an order
- K = inventory carrying cost
- C = cost per unit of item ordered

In this formula, the inventory carrying cost (K) includes such items as interest, depreciation, transportation, taxes, insurance, and storage. This formula runs into a major limitation when demand for the product is not regular or cannot be well predicted, in which case there are formulas for determining reorder points that recognize variation in demand. (One technique for determining inventory under conditions of uncertainty is discussed later in this chapter in the section on quantitative methods.)

If an entrepreneur intends to make items for production himself, he must consider how many should be made at one time. The economic production quantity formula, or *EPQ*, is commonly used for this calculation:

$$EPQ = \sqrt{\frac{2RC}{K\left(1 - \frac{r}{p}\right)}}$$

where
- R = annual requirements
- C = set-up cost of machine
- K = inventory carry cost
- r = usage rate (units per time period)
- p = production rate (units per time period)

It is important that the entrepreneur give considerable time to developing a system tailored to his needs. However, he should focus on items whose costs justify such control, for in some cases control efforts may cost more than the items are worth. At the same time, he will want to protect himself on low-cost items that are critical to the production process.

Quality Control

The small businessman must consistently produce a product that meets certain standards in order to compete, for poor quality control results in lost customers, rejected merchandise, and high costs.

Quality is not an absolute. It can best be viewed as a specified standard against which something is measured or compared. Thus, it can be defined in terms of dimension, strength, shape, color, finish, and workmanship. For any particular characteristic, quality can be measured by particular standards, and any deviation from these standards can be considered a variation in quality. Tolerance limits vary according to the product. For example, a customer may accept a shipment of certain products as long as the proportion of faulty items does not exceed a small percentage. The entrepreneur should find out how quality control is handled within his industry and then adopt the appropriate tolerances and controls. Good quality control is an excellent selling point and a necessity for building customer confidence. At the same time, the entrepreneur must keep in mind that unnecessarily high quality (that is, more than the customer needs or is willing to pay for) will cost him money and could put him at a cost disadvantage relative to his competition.

Inspection

Through inspection, the manager can determine whether and to what extent quality standards are being met. He may make no more than a cursory visual check to see that the product is painted or has a hole in a particular place. Or he may decide that a painstaking examination of every detail of every part of the product is necessary. Or his inspection may include each and every input or output of the manufacturing process. However, inspection is usually limited to the evaluation of statistical samples. The manager is able to make inferences from the sample results about general characteristics or attributes of the population from which the sample was taken. Sampling is sometimes the only feasible way of obtaining information—for example, in the testing of explosives or when the output is so large that inspection of every unit is impractical.

No two items are exactly the same; thus, variation is the common denominator in quality control. The manager's task is to set acceptable quality limits, to determine when an input, process, or output falls outside those limits, and to correct any significant deviations at the lowest possible cost. Inspection in itself costs money even before improving the quality of the individual product. Therefore, the small manufacturer should perform the minimum inspection necessary to provide the desired quality.

Statistical Quality Control

Statistical quality control has become a common part of the manufacturing process. Two important methods are available: sampling acceptance plans and quality control charts.

Sampling acceptance plans can be divided into two types: attributes plans and variable plans. *Acceptance sampling by attributes* involves separating the produced items into two groups—"good" ones and "bad" ones. A typical application would be to inspect wooden screws to determine whether they have slots in the heads. The inspector takes a random sample of size "n," and on the basis of the proportion of "bad" ones, accepts or rejects the whole lot. He uses an operating-characteristics curve (*OC* curve), which relates the true but unknown number of defectives in the lot to the probability of acceptance on the basis of a sample of size "n."

In *acceptance sampling by variables,* the inspector measures the degree to which sample items conform to output specifications. The advantage of this approach is that each item in the sample yields more information, so that the same degree of assurance can be obtained with a much smaller sample. The primary disadvantage is the number of computations required. Typical examples of how sampling by variable might be used are the evaluation of a shipment of parts from a vendor or the output from a screw machine making dowel pins. In either case, the inspector would typically take a sample of size "n," measure one or more dimensions (for example, the length of each part), and then compute one or more statistics, such as the mean length or length variance. On the basis of the statistical evidence, the inspector can then accept or reject the entire lot or shipment.

Control charts provide a ready and simple means of determining whether a process is actually operating within the limits of prescribed tolerance. Control charts are statistical charts and require an evaluation of samples taken in a prescribed manner. The samples will yield information which can be attributed to the population from which the samples came.

Control charts, like acceptance sampling plans, are decision-making devices. Their use presupposes that the process being controlled is stable—that is, it does not produce an output varying widely from what is desired. A process that is absolutely stable does not require monitoring, and monitoring an unstable process is a waste of time. If the process is unstable, it is better to spend time seeking causes than trying to control it. The cause may be due to the unsuitability of the equipment, material, labor, or machine deterioration.

Although there are numerous types of control charts employed in process control, this discussion will be limited to the two most commonly used: mean ($\overline{X}$) charts and range (R) charts.[1] The $\overline{X}$ chart controls the process average measurement for the given quality variable; the R chart controls the process variation among individual measurements.

The $\overline{X}$ chart (see Figure 13-2) prescribes the upper and lower limits within which the computed sample means must fall if the process is to be considered stable. To construct an $\overline{X}$ chart, first compute and draw a horizontal line that represents $\overline{X}$ (the estimated mean of the population) for the process or activity

---

[1] The reader with no knowledge of basic statistics may wish to skip the remainder of this section on control charts.

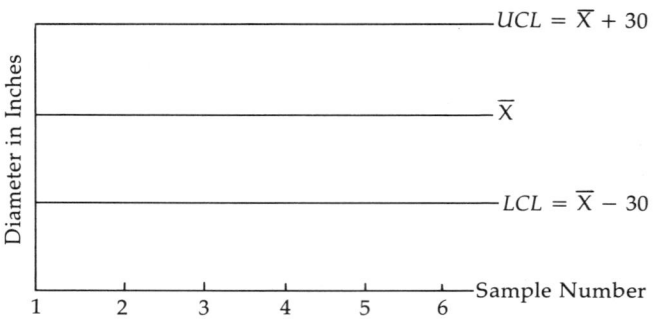

Figure 13–2.   A Typical $\overline{X}$ Chart.

being controlled. Parallel to this line, mark off an upper and lower control limit. These limit lines are often placed $\pm 2\sigma$ or $\pm 3\sigma$ from the estimated population mean value. Using limits of $\pm 2\sigma$ you will find, assuming variations are due to chance factors and are normally distributed, that 5 percent, or 50 sample means in 1000, will fall outside those limits and will require remedial action *even though the process remains stable.* For limits set at $\pm 3\sigma$, approximately 2.7 percent, or approximately 3 out of 1000 sample mean values, will fall outside these limits, even if the process has not changed and has remained stable. The lower axis of an $\overline{X}$ chart is designated in time units or sample numbers taken at stated intervals. Sometimes there is a warning limit line drawn inside the upper and lower control limits to draw attention to the drift of sample results toward the upper and lower control limits. If minor remedial action can be taken at this time, it may avoid more serious consequences later. Note that the upper and lower control limits do not have to be an equal distance from the mean or average value. For example, it may be more desirable to have a bearing fit tightly rather than loosely. Therefore, a control chart may be constructed with a $\pm 2\sigma$ upper limit and a $\pm 3\sigma$ lower limit.

Samples for an $\overline{X}$ chart are taken in a prescribed manner[2] and an $\overline{X}$ (estimate of the population mean value) is computed. Since the means of samples, according to the central limit theorem, tend to be normally distributed, the probability of a value falling outside the designated limits is predictable within a narrow range. Plot the $\overline{X}$ value on the chart and if it falls within the prescribed

---

[2] Appropriate formulas for determining the statistical values for constructing and maintaining an $\overline{X}$ chart are:

(1) $\overline{X} = \dfrac{\epsilon X_i}{n}$

X_i = individual measurements from samples
$\overline{X}$ = sample mean value
N_s = number of samples taken
n = size of sample (items)

(2) $\sigma \overline{X} \sqrt{\dfrac{\epsilon(X_i - X)2}{N_s (n-1)}}$

Used to set control limits. This is an estimate of the population standard deviation.

upper and lower control limits, consider the process stable and not requiring remedial action. If it falls outside of the prescribed limits, remedial action should be taken.

Sometimes a process remains stable as measured by its mean value, but the dispersion between sample means either increases or decreases. The $\overline{X}$ chart will indicate shifts in the process mean value and shifts in the distribution of these values. However, an $\overline{X}$ chart is not very sensitive to signaling changes in variance. An R chart is commonly used to control processes that produce outputs whose mean measurement tends to be stable, but whose variance on dispersion between sample item values varies considerably.

The R *chart* has an upper and lower control limit within which sample variances must fall if the process is to be considered stable. The construction of an R chart closely parallels that of an $\overline{X}$ chart except that the limits on the R chart represent maximum and minimum *variance* values rather than *mean* values. The distribution of sample variances has a Chi-square distribution rather than a normal distribution. The computation of sample variances requires considerably more effort than that for sample means and provides a greater chance for error. Consequently, the range of sample values rather than their variance is used. The range is simply the largest measurement from a sample minus the smallest measurement. An additional advantage of using the sample range values instead of the variance is that the range is more sensitive to change. If the process is stable, the range is a satisfactory substitute for the variance.

The R chart is constructed using an average R value and the variance of R in order to determine the values for the upper and lower control limits. Tables are available that approximate the variance of R from the R values. In fact, the small manufacturer should consult a book on statistical quality control for further clarification of the basic concepts presented in this section.

As with the $\overline{X}$ chart, random samples are taken and plotted on the R chart. When upper or lower limits are exceeded, or when a downward trend is evident, processing should stop pending examination of the assignable cause, and corrective action should be taken before processing is resumed.

Quantitative Analysis

Quantitative analysis is frequently considered something new and difficult to comprehend. In fact, however, quantitative analysis has been around for a long time and, with a little effort, can be employed by the entrepreneur.

The language of quantitative analysis is mathematics. Therefore, any analysis must begin with an expression of the relationships and interrelationships of all factors in terms of symbols and numbers. This analysis obviously requires a pervasive and explicit knowledge of the factors involved, as well as the ability to measure these factors more precisely than a strictly qualitative approach would require. Unlike the qualitative approach, quantitative analysis requires that the entrepreneur think out and state his problem in a concise and explicit form. If a manager does not intend to become a practitioner of the art of quantitative analysis, he should at least be aware of the opportunities and limitations of such techniques when applied to practical business problems.

A note of caution is in order at the outset: the results of quantitative analysis, although expressed in numbers, should be looked upon as estimates rather than *the* answer. Mathematical models are nothing more than abbreviated mathematical expressions of real-life situations and thus have definite limitations. Most importantly, the output is no better than the degree to which the model depicts reality. Of course, a business model will never completely describe the real world. Its purpose, however, is to help direct attention to the most important variables facing the businessman. In addition, qualitative judgment will still have to be employed when applying the results of quantitative analysis.

For the reader wanting to know more about quantitative analysis, three techniques of quantitative analysis that seem to be of greatest value to the small businessman—linear programming, network analysis, and decision making under uncertainty—will be introduced in the appendix to this chapter.

Appendix: Quantitative Analysis Techniques

Linear Programming

Linear-programming methods can be successfully applied to the small business in allocating scarce resources most effectively in problems of scheduling, product mix, and so on. These scarce resources include capital, materials, equipment, and personnel. The products or services produced by the firm represent the alternative ends for these resources. The criterion employed to judge the decision of resource allocation is generally profit maximization, although other criteria may be selected. Some areas of successful applications of linear programming include:

1. *Blending problems.* The blending of various ingredients to make such products as cattle food, petroleum products, paint, and a minimum cost diet that meets specific requirements of nutrition.
2. *Product-mix problems.* The types and quantities of products to produce during a period, recognizing limited equipment availability and the differences in profitability of various products.

3. *Inventory problems.* The recognition of limited production facilities and the need to meet the expected demand at a minimum inventory cost.
4. *Shipping problems.* Determining minimum production and distribution costs if products are made in various locations and used in others.

The successful application of linear programming requires that two assumptions be met. First, all variables, such as profits, costs, and volume, must be linearly related — that is, all functional relationships must be able to be expressed mathematically as straight lines. Second, costs are known or assumed to be known.

For purposes of illustration, let us consider the following example. A Montana rancher has decided to go into the pet business. Having made a market analysis, he concludes that he can sell a great number of aardvarks and/or zebras. He is knowledgeable about raising both animals, and he is faced with a limited amount of resources; he would like to determine whether he should raise all of one kind or some of each in order to maximize his income. An inventory of his resources and analysis of the requirements for raising these animals reveals the following:

1. Space to raise the animals is limited to 10,000 square feet. Each aardvark requires 100 square feet while each zebra requires 150.
2. A secret animal food he has developed and which both animals thrive on is limited by his processing machinery to 25,000 pounds for the period in which both animals reach marketable age. Each aardvark eats 250 pounds per period while zebras eat 500.
3. He must advertise in the newspapers to sell these animals. Statistics on the subject show that $350 of advertising is required to sell the relatively unknown aardvark, while only $70 is required to sell a zebra. His advertising budget is $1750.

Expressed mathematically, these three relationships are:

1. $100A + 100Z \leq 10{,}000$ sq. ft. (space)
2. $250A + 500Z \leq 25{,}000$ pounds (foods)
3. $350A + 70Z \leq 1{,}750$ dollars (advertising)

The rancher's problem is to determine which animal or combination of animals to raise in order to maximize his profits. Since this is a simple problem in which scarce resources are to be allocated between two possible uses, we can solve it graphically (see Figure 13–3). (More complex problems would be solved by a procedure called the simplex method, perhaps with the aid of a computer.)

Given our scarce resources, let us consider the range of alternatives open to the decision maker. Considering the space constraint, for example, he can accommodate 100 aardvarks and no zebras or 100 zebras and no aardvarks, or any combination of the two as long as the total does not exceed 100. If he "gives up" one zebra, he can accommodate one more aardvark, and the rate of substitution of aardvarks for zebras is said to be one. A similar computation and analysis can be carried out for the other two scarce resources as linear equations. Looking only at the "space" line in Figure 13–3, note that for every point on

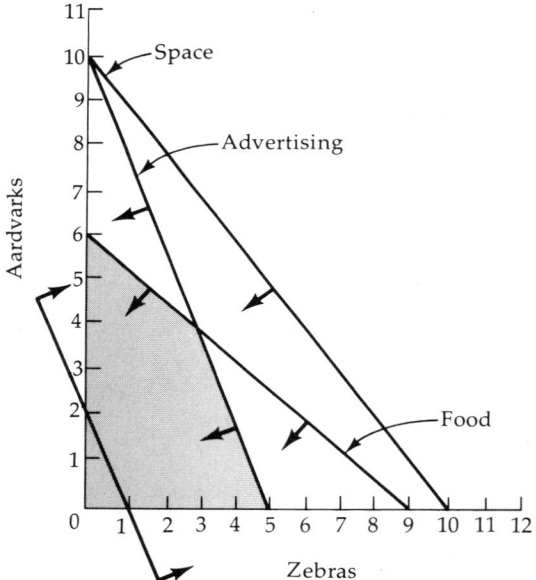

Figure 13–3.
Aardvark–Zebra Problem Graphic Solution.

the line the combination of aardvarks and zebras times 100 square feet equals the amount available. Any point in the space bounded by the line and the two axes represents a combination that requires less than that available.

The combinations of aardvarks and zebras represented by the "space" line and the area bounded by the line and the two axes are attainable with the given resources—thus, the area including the line is referred to as the area of feasible solutions. Taking into consideration the other constraints due to limits on food and space, we can see that by piling constraint upon constraint, the area of feasible solutions is getting more restricted.

In order to maximize profits, one must consider how to determine the optimum combination of aardvarks and zebras. This combination will not be found in the bounded area but on one of the boundary lines, since the solutions in the bounded area, although technically feasible, do not employ all of one scarce resource. There are two means of arriving at the solution: (1) compute the profits for the many combinations represented by the restriction lines and select the largest; or (2) take the profit relationship line between aardvarks and zebras and move it out from the origin to the farthest point. To do the latter, take an arbitrary profit figure such as \$20,000 and express the profit equation thus: $100A + 200Z = \$20,000$. The end points of this line can be obtained as was done for the restriction equations by alternately setting $A = 0$ and $Z = 0$, which will give the slope of the profit function. By using a line with this slope one can sweep the area of feasible solutions from the origin out (that is, move the line *away* from the origin keeping it parallel to the original line), and the last point (5) exposed in the sweep will be the optimum combination of aardvarks and zebras. Thus, the most profitable decision the Montana rancher could make is to raise 400 aardvarks and 300 zebras. Using these figures, he can enter the values into each of the four equations and find out the amount of unused resources and the expected profit. Observe that the resource of "space" was *not* a limiting factor.

Network Analysis

Another useful technique has been developed to aid in the planning, coordinating, scheduling, and control of complex systems of production and contracting operations. The technique known as network analysis has found wide application in activities such as the building of plants, the installation of new processes, and the maintenance of complex equipment. The specific technique to be illustrated here is the *Critical Path Method*.

The sequence of steps required to perform this type of network analysis is as follows:

1. List every job or activity that has to be done to complete the project.
2. Assign each job a letter or number code.
3. Make a diagram of the project by using circles to represent individual jobs or tasks and arrows between the jobs to indicate sequence. Before drawing arrows between jobs, ask the following questions:
   a. What job(s) must immediately precede this job?
   b. What job(s) immediately follows this job?

c. What other jobs can be done at the same time as this one?
Only consider those jobs immediately related to the job at hand. The length of the arrow is unimportant, but the direction indicates job sequence. By constructing such a diagram you have a means of assigning responsibility and avoiding overlooking jobs.
4. Insert the time required to complete each job in the job circles. These times are important since if they are not reasonably accurate, the exercise is futile. These times should be standard times or most likely time estimates.
5. Add up the times for all the jobs on each possible path through the network as noted by the arrow sequence. The path with the longest time is the critical path, since any delay in this path will delay the whole project. Other paths have some "float" — that is, you have some leeway in the time to complete that particular sequence of jobs.

To illustrate this approach, consider the following project, which can be building an addition to a plant, opening a new store, or renovating some facility.

Activity	Letter Code	Code of Predecessor	Normal Time (Days)	Normal Cost	Crash Time (Days)	Crash Cost	Max. Time Saved	Cost per Day Saved
Start	A	—	0	—	—	—	—	—
———	B	A	3	$ 50	2	$100	1	$ 50
———	C	A	6	140	4	340	2	100
———	D	A	2	25	1	50	1	25
———	E	B	5	100	3	180	2	40
———	F	D	2	80	2	80	0	—
———	G	B,C,F	7	115	5	175	2	30
———	H	E,G	0	—	—	—	—	—
				$510				

The network diagram would look as follows:

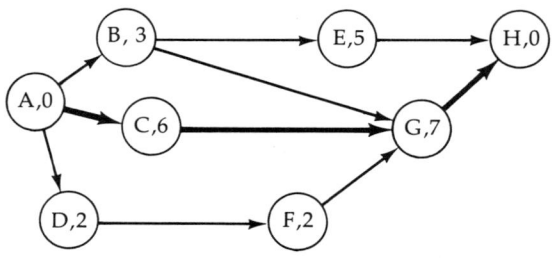

The possible paths are:

    A,B,E,H   = 8 days
    A,B,G,H   = 10 days
    A,C,G,H   = 13 days — this is the critical path
    A,D,F,G,H = 11 days

To reduce the time to complete the project, one or more of the jobs on the critical path must be expedited. It should be noted that sometimes there is more than one critical path and that due to performance problems and poor time estimates the critical path may shift. If each shortening of the project by one day is considered as an alternative decision, the possible alternatives can be listed as follows:

    Alternative 1   Normal time — 13 days
      Project Cost = $510

    Alternative 2   12 days — expedite job G by one day
      Project Cost = 510 + 30 = $540

    Alternative 3   11 days — expedite job G by one more day
      Project Cost = 510 + 30 + 30 = $570

    Alternative 4   10 days — expedite job C by one day
      Project Cost = 510 + 30 + 30 + 100 = $670

    Alternative 5   9 days — expedite C by one more day
      Project Cost = 510 + 30 + 30 + 100 + 100 = $770

If one considers the profit to be realized by completing the project early, or the cost of not completing the project on time, one can arrive at a rational decision among the five possible alternatives. For example, if the loss of profits for each day the facility is not operating is $80 (outage cost), one could analyze the five alternatives as follows:

Alternative	1	2	3	4	5
Days	13	12	11	10	9
Project Cost	510	540	570	670	770
Outage Cost	1040	960	880	800	720
Total Cost	1550	1500	1450	1470	1490

From a financial point of view, alternative number 3 is best. It would be necessary to go to great lengths if we were to explain other methods of network analysis. However, the foregoing discussion should be adequate to illustrate the basic nature of all network analysis and to suggest its usefulness to a small manufacturer or contractor.

Decision Making under Uncertainty

A third useful technique of quantitative analysis is to employ probabilistic models or probability distributions. This approach offers both a conceptual framework for decisions and a numerical result to evaluate the alternatives. The following simple illustration will demonstrate the use of a probabilistic technique to decision making under conditions of uncertainty.

Assume you are in a business in which you ordered your stock today to be delivered tomorrow morning. Assume further that any merchandise left over at the end of the day is a complete loss; your sales have no cyclical trend; you purchase the merchandise at $8 per case and sell it for $10 per case.

Your records for the last 250 selling days provide the following data:

Demand for Cases	Days Sold	Relative Frequency of Sales
24	0	.00
25	25	.10
26	75	.30
27	125	.50
28	25	.10
29	0	.00
	250	1.00

Observe that you never sold fewer than 25 cases and never more than 28. If you now compute a table showing the profit realized for every possible level of demand for every possible level of cases you would rationally stock, you obtain a conditional profit table—the profit realized for stocking X cases if demand was for Y cases (see Table 13–2).

Table 13–2. Conditional Profit Table.

Demand	Cases Stocked			
	25	26	27	28
25	$50.	42.	34.	26.
26	50.	52.	44.	36.
27	50.	52.	64.	46.
28	50.	52.	54.	56.

Having determined the conditional profits for all the possible combinations of demand and cases stocked, consider the profits expected if only 25 cases are stocked (see Table 13–3).

Table 13–3. Expected Profits if You Stock 25 Cases.

Possible Demand	Probability of Demand	Conditional Profit (25)	Expected Profit
25	.10	$50.	$ 5.00
26	.30	50.	15.00
27	.50	50.	25.00
28	.10	50.	5.00
	1.00		$50.00

Note that the conditional profit column is taken from the previous figure, the probability of demand is taken from the company's records, and the expected profit is the product of the probability of demand and the conditional profit. The answer should not be a surprise, since you always sell a minimum of 25 cases. Consider now the merits of stocking 26 or 27 cases (see Table 13–4). Thus, profits will be maximized in the *long run* if 26 cases are stocked each day. Of course, this does not take into consideration the long-run cost of

Table 13–4. Expected Profits if You Stock 26/27 Cases.

Possible Demand	Probability of Demand	Conditional Profit	Expected Profit
Stock 26 Cases			
25	.10	$42.	$ 4.20
26	.30	52.	15.60
27	.50	52.	26.00
28	.10	52.	5.20
	1.00		$51.00
Stock 27 Cases			
25	.10	$34.	$ 3.40
26	.30	44.	13.20
27	.50	54.	27.00
28	.10	54.	5.40
	1.00		$49.00

turning away customers due to lack of stock. Thus, it is important for the entrepreneur to realize that decision-making tools are just tools, and no more than that. In other words, while quantitative analysis minimizes risk by providing a rational approach to business problems, the entrepreneur's judgment is still the decisive factor.

Incident 13: Getting the Work Organized

When Pete restores a car, he takes it completely apart and reworks every piece. In effect, then, he has a disassembly line. When the pieces are all reworked and necessary new parts are obtained, the car is put back together. Sometimes parts are painted before assembly, sometimes after. It depends on both the type of car and the piece being handled.

At first, Pete had only one car to work on at a time. Now that his business has expanded, he has as many as six in various stages of work at once. Thus, he has increased his efficiency, since workers do not have to wait for parts to be fixed or for paint to dry to continue working. Instead they can move on to work on other cars.

Since each car is a different make and model, each one has to be considered as a special case. Thus, there is no possibility of ever getting any sort of serial production runs as a result.

Pete has read this chapter on production processes, and he rejects the entire thing. "Look," he said, "with the kind of business I've got, there's nothing in any book that can tell me what to do. Each job is unique, and each one has to be thought through as a special case. If we tried to go by the book, we'd be broke in a month. There's no book on our business, so we just have to play it by ear."

1. Reread the chapter. Take every major point covered, and indicate whether or not Pete is correct. Is it true that there is nothing here Pete can use? Is so, indicate why. If not, indicate how Pete might profitably use the material.
2. Are there many other types of small firms that might have problems similar to Pete's? If so, what 2 kinds of firms might they be?

Discussion Questions

1. Define the production process. What is the relationship between the production process and the design of a product?
2. Do you agree that a product "designer" should strive to design a product of the highest possible quality? Explain.
3. List and briefly discuss the functions of production planning and control.
4. Differentiate between an operation process chart and a flow process chart.

5. Distinguish between a product layout and a process layout. Give specific examples of small firms best suited for each layout.
6. What is the relationship between material handling costs and production layout?
7. Classify and evaluate the two types of plant maintenance. How does a small plant reach a proper balance between the two?
8. What is the objective of work improvement? How is this objective accomplished?
9. Explain the concept of work simplification.
10. List several important functions served by production standards. Give examples of each function.
11. How does the "time study" approach to establishing production standards differ from the "work sampling" approach?
12. Why is the setting of production standards not a one-time activity?
13. How does the proper control of inventories help save money?
14. Explain how the use of "economic order quantities" will affect inventory levels.
15. "Variation is the common denominator in quality control." Explain.
16. Distinguish between the two types of sampling-acceptance plans. Give examples of usage for each type.
17. What role does process stability play in the use of control charts?
18. Describe in some detail the control system(s) you would set up to control the production process in a small manufacturing plant.

Suggested Readings

Barnes, R. M., *Motion and Time Study: Design and Measurement of Work*, 6th ed. New York: John Wiley, 1968.

Begeman, M. L., *Manufacturing Processes*, 5th ed. New York: John Wiley, 1963.

Broom, H. N., and Longenecker, J., *Small Business Management*, 3rd ed. Cincinnati: South-Western Publishing, 1971. Ch. 24, 27.

Brown, Robert Goodell, *Management Decisions for Production Operations*. Hinsdale, Ill.: The Dryden Press, 1971.

Buffa, E. S., *Operations Management: Problems and Models*, 2nd ed. New York: John Wiley, 1968.

Buffa, E. S., *Basic Production Management*. New York: John Wiley, 1971.

Hobson, Leland S., and Schrader, George F., "Planning and Controlling Production for Efficiency," *Management Aids*, No. 177. Washington, D. C.: Small Business Administration, 1965.

Hoel, P. G., and Jessen, R. J., *Elementary Statistics for Business and Economics.* New York: John Wiley, 1971.

Kirkpatrick, E. G., *Quality Control for Managers and Engineers.* New York: John Wiley, 1970.

Klatt, Lawrence A., ed., *Managing the Dynamic Small Firm: Readings.* Belmont, Calif.: Wadsworth, 1971. Pp. 121–152.

Kline, John B., "Pointers on Scheduling Production," *Management Aids,* No. 207. Washington, D. C.: Small Business Administration, 1970.

Krentzman, Harvey C., *Managing for Profits.* Washington, D. C.: Small Business Administration, 1968.

Magee, J. F., and Boodman, D. M., *Production Planning and Inventory Control,* 2nd ed. New York: McGraw-Hill, 1967.

McCormick, E. J., *Human Factors Engineering,* 2nd ed. New York: McGraw-Hill, 1964.

Moore, F. G., and Jablanski, R., *Production Control,* 3rd ed. New York: McGraw-Hill, 1969.

Schneider, David, "Pointers on Raw Materials Inventory Control," *Management Aids,* No. 155. Washington, D. C.: Small Business Administration, 1963.

Stockton, R. Stansbury, *Introduction to Linear Programming.* Boston: Allyn and Bacon, 1963.

Starr, M. K., "Evolving Concepts in Production Management." In *Evolving Concepts in Management,* Academy of Management Proceedings, 24th Annual Meeting, December 1964.

The Truth About Wage Incentives and Work Measurement. Factory, April 1959.

Voris, W. *Production Control,* 3rd ed. Homewood, Ill.: Richard D. Irwin, 1966.

Part Five Resources for Managerial Decision Making

Chapter 14
Where to Go for Advice and Assistance

Large corporations typically have numerous specialized staffs with the training and experience to handle almost any problem, from planning a new location to settling labor disputes. In addition, large corporations frequently use law firms, management consultants, certified public accountants, and other outside sources to reduce the margin of error in managerial decision making.

The small businessman, on the other hand, does not generally have much specialized management assistance within his firm. In some cases, the entrepreneur is even his own board of directors, making all the important managerial decisions. At the same time, because of limited resources, he usually cannot afford more than a single costly error.

Fortunately for the entrepreneur, there are outside resources available to provide him with valuable advice and guidance, usually at a nominal cost. This chapter will familiarize the entrepreneur with those individuals and organizations who can provide him with such assistance.

The Professionals

Accounting. Accountants can help the small businessman in several areas of financial decision making. For example, they can set up a system of bookkeeping that is simple to follow on a day-to-day basis and valuable for auditing or determining taxes. They can also help set up systems for controlling cash and can suggest simple office and bookkeeping equipment, as well as procedures for effective flow of paper work.

Independent accountants and certified public accountants who are willing to work with small businesses can be located through bankers, attorneys, or the yellow pages. As with all professionals, the entrepreneur should confer with several accountants and check their references before selecting one.

Bankers. Bankers probably know more about business conditions in their area than any other professionals. They can suggest professionals and organizations that can assist with operating problems. Primarily, of course, they are sources of financial information about loans, lines of credit, and standard operating ratios. Since banks offer the small businessman the most complete financial service at the least cost, the importance of establishing a working relationship with a bank cannot be overemphasized. An earlier chapter on financial management has already discussed the different types of banks and the need to develop a relationship with a bank before applying for a loan. It is also a good practice for the entrepreneur to keep the bank informed about the progress of his business and any significant increases in growth or profits that may affect his line of credit with the bank.

Insurance agents. Insurance agents are more than willing to evaluate the insurance needs of small businesses and recommend a package to cover their specific needs. Since insurance is a highly technical field, the entrepreneur should seek out the services of a competent and reliable agent. He may be either an independent who deals with several insurance companies or a direct writer who is employed by and writing policies with one company. Again, the entrepreneur should discuss his needs with several agents, comparing coverage, costs, and convenience, before deciding on the program that best serves his overall business.

Lawyers. Every business needs legal advice from time to time. Theodore Voorhees has identified six areas of business activity in which an attorney is necessary or helpful:[1]

1. If a business is incorporated, the entrepreneur may need advice about directors' and stockholders' meetings, dividends, rights of stockholders, and so on.
2. Relationships with employees may require legal services in labor negotiations, proceedings before the National Labor Relations Board and boards of arbitration, and all other matters involving industrial relations.

---

[1] See Theodore Voorhees, "Selecting a Lawyer for Your Business," *Management Aids,* No. 8 (Washington, D. C.: Small Business Administration, 1962), pp. 66–73.

3. The entrepreneur may need advice about antitrust violations by his suppliers or about Robinson-Patman Act questions in sales to customers.
4. The company may encounter difficulties in its relations with the public—such as collection claims and claims for personal injury, property damage, and product liability. Somewhat less frequent are claims for libel, slander, defamation, false arrest, and malicious prosecution.
5. The legal problems of taxation—federal, state, and local—are faced almost daily by all business concerns.
6. There are other highly specialized fields of legal advice such as patent, copyright and trademark, Security and Exchange Commission financing, and practice before governmental agencies such as the Interstate Commerce Commission.

Legal counsel, of course, should be engaged only after a thorough, intelligent appraisal of the lawyer's or law firm's capability and potential usefulness to the business. Many small businessmen find it advantageous to arrange for a lawyer on a retainer basis. If legal questions come up with any degree of regularity, this arrangement will probably turn out to be less costly. It also assures that the lawyer will be more familiar with the business and therefore more understanding of legal problems. A competent attorney can be located through the entrepreneur's banker, accountant, consultant, other businessmen, or friends. In addition, the County Bar Association in most counties operates a lawyer-referral service.

Business consultants. Consultants are useful for analyzing and solving various management, operating, and technical problems that the entrepreneur, or his key people, are not able to do because of lack of time or specialized knowledge. An increasing number of owner–managers have recently realized the value of consultants, so more management consultants are tailoring their services to the needs of small businesses.

There are three managerial problems that especially lend themselves to outside consulting assistance:

1. A "one-shot" problem, such as solving a specific operating problem like setting up an advertising campaign or designing a plant layout.
2. A business appraisal, such as a periodic checkup of the business with recommendations for increasing overall effectiveness.
3. A feasibility study—for example, an objective evaluation of a nonrecurring problem such as where to locate a new store or which data-processing equipment to install.

The Small Business Administration has suggested several considerations in selecting a qualified consultant:[2]

1. Clarify in your own mind exactly what you want the consulting firm to accomplish.
2. Obtain information on the services offered and the general reputation of the consultant from your business friends, accountant, banker, or attorney. Ask the consultant for recent references on comparable assignments.
3. If it is a large consulting firm, talk to the men who will actually be assigned to work on your project. See if they are specialists in your problem area(s) and determine if they are the type of individuals with whom your company could work effectively.
4. Insist on a written proposal from each consulting firm interviewed that outlines what the work will cover, how the work will be performed, how long the study will take, whether a written report will be submitted, an estimate of the total cost, and how much time the principals of the consulting firm will spend on the assignment.
5. See if the consultant will put his recommendations into effect if your own people are not qualified to implement them. Get a written agreement about the cost of implementation. For example, will the consultant only instruct your people or will he install the recommendation?
6. Finally, do not be hesitant to discuss costs and beware of the high-pressure salesman offering a low-cost *packaged* survey.

Other sources. There are individuals in the community who the entrepreneur is likely to meet through business contacts and who may be able to provide valuable advice and assistance. For example, suppliers will want to help their customers sell so that they in turn will purchase more. Since suppliers have experience and knowledge of marketing practices in the entrepreneur's location, they are an excellent source for advice about general marketing practices and promotional strategies.

Customers are often overlooked as sources of advice and ideas, yet they are in a position to identify the entrepreneur's strong points or his competitive weaknesses. They can suggest new and unique uses for products or services, as well as ways to improve the business's public image.

Other valuable sources of advice and guidance are knowledgeable real-estate agents, members of local redevelopment councils, credit bureau managers, and other non-competing businessmen. All of these individuals are

---

[2] David R. Mayne, "Specialized Help for Small Business," *Small Marketers Aids,* No. 74 (Washington, D. C.: Small Business Administration, December 1961).

concerned with the growth of the local area and, therefore, are usually willing to provide counsel and/or assistance to the entrepreneur. The Small Business Administration also provides volunteers who counsel small businessmen and charge only their out-of-pocket expenses. More about this program will be discussed later in this chapter.

Small Business Administration[3]

This agency was created solely to "aid, counsel, assist, and protect, insofar as is possible, the interests of small business concerns in order to preserve free competitive enterprise." The SBA has four principal activities: financial assistance, procurement assistance, management assistance, and venture-capital assistance.

The first and last activities have been referred to in other chapters of this book. The procurement and management-assistance activities will be discussed in this section.

Procurement Assistance

In carrying out the responsibility of the Small Business Act, as amended, the SBA was directed by Congress:

1. To establish a program to set aside proposed procurements for competitive bidding and award to small business concerns, in order to insure that a fair proportion of the total purchases of supplies and services and property sold by the federal government will be awarded to small business.
2. To certify to government procurement officers, and offices, whether or not a small business concern has the capacity and credit to perform a specific government sales contract.
3. To counsel and assist small firms on government buying and selling methods.
4. To maintain an inventory of the productive facilities of small business concerns. The facilities inventory is used in assisting registered small concerns to obtain contracts to locate additional sources of supply for government agencies and to locate specialized skills and equipment.
5. To guide small business concerns in obtaining subcontract opportunities,

---

[3]Most of this section is based on information supplied by the SBA. For example, see "SBA, What It Is . . . What It Does" (Washington, D. C.: Small Business Administration, 1970).

also to develop subcontract opportunities with prime contractors and find small concerns to take advantage of such opportunities.
6. To assist small business concerns in obtaining government contracts for research and development and the benefits of research and development performed with government funds.

In order to accomplish these objectives, the SBA, through specialists in SBA field offices, counsels small businessmen on prime contracting and subcontracting. They direct them to government agencies that buy the products or services they supply, help them to get their names placed on bidders' lists, assist them in obtaining drawings and specifications for proposed purchases, and offer many other related services.

For example, the SBA develops subcontract opportunities for small firms by maintaining close contact with prime contractors and referring qualified small firms to them. The SBA also has authority to act as a prime contractor in government procurement contracts and may then subcontract with firms that will provide jobs for "difficult to employ" persons in depressed areas. In addition, if a small firm is low bidder on a federal contract and its ability to perform is questioned, the company may ask the SBA for a "Certificate of Competency" (COC). If the SBA, after an on-site study by one of its industrial specialists, concludes that the small firm has the necessary facilities and resources to perform successfully, it issues the COC attesting to the fact.

Management Assistance

The SBA offers a diversified program of training and management assistance to strengthen small firms and to improve their operations. Specialists in SBA field offices advise small businessmen on general managerial problems as well as offering assistance or information on specific types of business enterprises. (See the appendix to this chapter for a summary of SBA publications.)

Business management courses, cosponsored by SBA and public and private educational institutions and business associations, are offered to help increase small business management skills. These courses are generally held in the evening and are designed for owners, prospective owners, and managers of small firms. They deal with planning, organizing, directing, coordinating, and controlling a business, as distinguished from day-to-day operating activities.

In addition, the SBA cosponsors conferences, workshops, and clinics for small business firms. Conferences cover such subjects as working capital and business forecasting; workshops generally deal with problems relating to starting a new business; clinics consider specific problems within a particular industry. The cost to the small businessman for any of these is a nominal registration fee.

Finally, if the entrepreneur needs help to start or run a firm more profitably, he can obtain free counseling and guidance through two SBA programs: SCORE and ACE. Through SCORE (Service Corps of Retired Executives), more than 3,000 retired business executives throughout the nation assist prospective and existing small businessmen with their problems. The ACE (Active Corps of Executives) was organized to supplement SCORE by merging the expertise of active businessmen with that of SCORE volunteers.

Under these programs, a counselor visits the small businessman in his establishment. Through careful observation he makes a detailed analysis of the business and its problems. If it is a complex problem, he may call on other SCORE experts to assist. Finally, he will offer a plan to remedy the trouble and help the businessman through his critical period. This service is free, except for reimbursement of out-of-pocket expenses.

Trade Associations

Because of their close association and study of problems in a given line of business, trade associations are usually in a position to furnish practical advice to their members. For example, most trade associations hold regular meetings to encourage the exchange of ideas and information. They typically issue bulletins and journals with up-to-the-minute details on trends and practices in the industry. Some trade associations conduct studies and carry on other technical or commercial research, and almost all of them keep members posted on legal matters and pending legislation that affects them. Many associations sponsor training courses and seminars for owners and/or their employees and provide a clearinghouse for technical advice.

While dues vary according to the size of the association and the services rendered, typically the dues amount to a fraction of 1 percent of a member's annual volume. Considering the services rendered and the benefits received, the entrepreneur should consider this expense to be a wise investment in the future of his company.

Educational and Business Groups

Unless the entrepreneur is continuously aware of the need to update and increase his own knowledge through a self-improvement program and formal training, he will stagnate and place himself at a competitive disadvantage. Almost every city in the United States has a distributive education or adult education program offering technical and business courses. A growing number of universities with colleges of business are also offering courses in small business management. In addition, most colleges with bureaus of business research have consulting services available for the small business and also sponsor business seminars and business community studies.

For information on ratios, credit, and management practices, a branch office of Dun & Bradstreet can be consulted. Similarly, the National Cash Register Company has useful information in such areas as layout and design, window display, and selling techniques. Finally, the local chamber of commerce, which serves all businesses operating in a given geographic area, can assist a small businessman in locating desirable sites or in finding information about local matters.

Other Governmental Agencies

There are several other governmental groups that can provide useful information or assistance to the small businessman. The State Employment Service is a fruitful source of wage and labor market information as well as a source of employees (as discussed in an earlier chapter). The Department of Commerce publishes statistics on business in general and does studies on various types of businesses and industries. Similarly, the Internal Revenue Service publishes the "Tax Guide to Small Business" and advises on tax matters of small businessmen.

The Small Businessman Himself

We have seen in this chapter that there are numerous sources for advice and assistance. But in the last analysis, the difference between business success or failure is the entrepreneur himself. He can easily avail himself of a continuous flow of ideas and information covering almost every aspect of business administration and operation. His new ideas are great only if he follows them up and puts them to work. If he thinks about how his own business (or planned business) got started, he will recall the importance of his first ideas and instituting them. Once his business is moving, it is his job to keep up the flow of ideas.

In today's competitive economic climate, the small businessman can prosper only if he is growing. To remain small is to remain vulnerable to change—and in many cases, to perish. A business, like the businessman, can't stand still; it must seek out ways to grow or it will wither. But in seeking out ideas and growing, the entrepreneur may want to keep in mind the observation of Ben Jonson:

> No man is so wise that he may not easily err if he takes no other counsel than his own. He that is taught only by himself has a fool for a master.

In concluding, the following series of questions is intended to stimulate some thought about your use of sources of advice and assistance:

1. Do you subscribe to and read regularly at least one outstanding trade paper in your field? For nearly every type of business, a number of excellent periodicals—such as *Women's Wear Daily, Progressive Grocer,* and *Drug Topics*—keep their subscribers abreast of important developments. Many of these magazines conduct and report on store and consumer surveys that are valuable to management in selling strategy and control operations. As the business grows, the entrepreneur will probably want to subscribe to some of the more general business publications.

2. Do you subscribe to or have ready access to a sales promotion service, and do you use it in planning and executing your promotional events? Mat services carrying suggestions for headlines, copy, and illustrations can be of great value to the small businessman if he does not have an advertising staff. Other promotion services provide monthly sales planning guides that include a wealth of promotional material for every season of the year. Some trade associations publish such information as a part of their regular service to their members. And newspapers in many cities supply professional advertising assistance to their advertisers.

3. Have you considered joining a figure-exchange group that compares and analyzes the merchandising and expense data of its members? Many owners of small stores have found this analysis to be of great help in determining their own strengths and weaknesses and in discovering remedies for weakness. If membership in such a group is impractical, the entrepreneur can use figures published by his trade association to compare with data on his own operations.

4. Are you a member of your local credit bureau, and do you actively use the information it provides? If there is no credit bureau in the businessman's town or if membership is too costly for his operation, he can turn to his local banker for guidance in issuing credit to specific persons or businesses.

5. Do you retain a good lawyer to confer with on day-to-day problems that have legal implications? Long-term contracts, advertising practices, guarantees, price cutting below contract minimum or below cost, zoning regulations, landlord relationships, injury to customers or employees—all are matters on which the small businessman would do well to seek legal counsel.

6. To be sure you are not overpaying your tax obligation, do you retain a tax accountant to review your accounting records and prepare your more complicated tax returns? The entrepreneur, or an employee held responsible by him, can make routine preparations and file routine returns, but he should hire a tax accountant to go over his records and prepare the most elaborate returns.

7. Is your store insurance handled by a conscientious and knowledgeable agent? A small businessman usually has to rely almost entirely on outside professional guidance in insurance matters. Therefore, finding a reliable agent genuinely concerned with his insurance needs is essential.

8. Do you study industry data and compare the results of your operation with them? Published data on other businesses in the field give the entre-

preneur a basis of comparison for his determination of such elements as initial markup, cash discounts, gross margin, expenses, net operating profit, stock turnover, percent of old stock, average sales per customer, and sales per square foot.

9. Are you a member of the trade association or trade associations that serve your industry? Many large and small trade associations have stepped up the variety and quality of their services to members in recent years. Some groups do a great deal of research and educational work that may have practical application to small businesses. Virtually all have membership bulletins and special reports and furnish replies to individual questions.

10. Have you taken advantage of the educational facilities that are available to you? Schools, colleges, and universities are sources of both technical and management assistance. Members of the faculty in many of these schools are well qualified to provide small businessmen with management information. In addition, schools of business administration are giving more and more attention to adult training for owners and managers of going concerns. Administrative management courses, cosponsored by the Small Business Administration and business schools, are designed to broaden and strengthen small business management skills.

11. Have you given any thought to using a management consultant to solve a problem which up to now you considered beyond solution? Management consultants bring to unsolved problems a fresh viewpoint, an objective analysis, wide experience, a scientific approach, and an opportunity to devote the necessary time.

12. Are you grooming someone to succeed you as manager in the not too distant future? No matter how young the management of a business is, unforeseen disabilities can occur at any time. Someone should always be in training as a manager; otherwise, the business is no more secure than the health of its owner–manger. Furthermore, the small businessman should have a management reservoir in the event of business expansion.

Appendix: SBA Publications

SBA issues several series of management, technical, marketing, and research publications that have proved to be valuable aids to established or prospective managers of small firms. Copies of these series are available free from all SBA offices. These pamphlets are compiled into "annuals" periodically and are obtainable for a small fee from the Superintendent of Documents, U. S. Government Printing Office, Washington, D. C. 20402. Among the free publications are:

1. *Management Aids for Small Manufacturers.* Discussions of the various phases of managing a small manufacturing business including accounting, financial management, personnel management, purchasing, and market research.
2. *Technical Aids for Small Manufacturers.* Facts on significant developments in materials, processes, equipment, and maintenance.
3. *Small Business Bibliographies.* Reference sources for business owners and managers and prospective small businessmen.
4. *Small Marketers Aids.* Discussions of the various phases of managing a small retail service or wholesale business, including advertising, competitive strategy, controlling, and selling.

Among the publications for sale are:

1. *Aids Annuals.* Compilations of *Management Aids, Small Marketers Aids,* and *Technical Aids* that are no longer distributed individually.
2. *Small Business Management Series.* Booklets by recognized authorities in their fields on specific management subjects.
3. *Starting and Managing Series.* Booklets on general good practices in starting and managing a business, and other booklets on starting and managing specific kinds of businesses, such as restaurants, service stations, and so on.

In addition to these management aids, persons interested in SBA's services to small businessmen may receive without charge pamphlets describing programs of assistance.

For information on specific SBA publications in each of the above categories, the entrepreneur should contact his nearest SBA field office or write to the Small Business Administration, Washington, D. C. 20416.

Incident 14: The Manager

"Hey, Pete," Sam called, "how about sitting down for a cup of coffee."

Pete looked at his watch. "Well, OK, Sam. But I've got to run. Peterson—the fellow who imports parts—wants to see me. Seems there's a foul-up in production, and we may not get those Packard parts." He sat down on a box across from Sam and watched Sam pour him a cup of coffee.

"You know something, Pete?"

"What, Sam?"

"This is the first time we've had coffee together in maybe five months. It isn't like the old days, back in your kitchen, when we had all the time in the world."

"Yeah, and we kept griping about old man Martin," Pete said. "You know, Sam, in less than four years, I've got a bigger business than he had. Here we are, grossing over $100,000 per year, and even making a few bucks."

"And here I am," Sam mused, "still painting for six bucks an hour." He kicked at a piece of scrap metal. "Oh, I'm not griping, Pete—Lord knows, you're the best boss I ever had, and the work we do here makes me feel good. It's a long way from those quicky jobs I used to hate. Here a fellow can feel like his work will be appreciated. But, you know, you've changed a lot."

"How, Sam?"

"Oh, you're always running around in a hurry to go someplace. And you're more of a big businessman now than a body and fender man. When I hear you talking, it's about budgets and inventory and depreciation, and all sorts of things painters don't know anything about—or could care less about. But after those first few years, I see that you're the guy who's getting ahead. Martha's quit work now, and you have a new house. You wear a suit to work, and the banker calls you by your first name. And you go up to those customers' houses—you know, those hundred grand jobs, just like you were used to living there yourself."

"Yeah, Sam, I guess I am different." Pete smiled. "When I first started this business, all I knew was that we could paint and that maybe some guys would pay to get a really good job done. Then I found out that there's a lot more to business than that. All of a sudden, I had to do all sorts of things I didn't know anything about. I had to learn fast and work hard. Man, you know thinking is hard work? I never thought so, until I had to do some."

"So now you're the big businessman," Sam said. "And here I am, still painting. I'll be painting 'til the day I retire. If that crazy brother-in-law of mine hadn't gone broke with that pizza parlor, maybe I would have had the guts to try the game. But, it's too late now."

"It's never too late, Sam. But I hope you keep painting. You're the best—the very best, and I could never get another guy like you." Pete looked at his watch. "I have to run, Sam. Thanks for the coffee."

Sam waved and watched him walk briskly off, a neat, clean-cut young man in a hurry in his good suit and tie, ready to do some more business. He shook his head, put the thermos away, and began to think about the paint mix he had to work up for the job this afternoon. Six bucks an hour—it wasn't a bad life, and it ended every day at quitting time. At least he didn't have to take the job home with him.

As Pete walked away, he felt odd, because he had wanted to invite Sam to drop by that evening and have coffee, just like old times. But he somehow hadn't been able to give the invitation. Sam was a great guy, but he really didn't know the score. He just did the same old thing every day—he was a master craftsman, but he never learned new tricks. Somehow, in the past four years, Pete had been on a new kind of treadmill, experiencing a new kind of learning that *was* making him a different kind of man. It was hard work, but he wouldn't have traded it for the world.

1. Are owner–managers different from the craftsmen or employees they were before they went into business? Why or why not?
2. Do you see yourself as being more like Pete or Sam in 5 years? Why?

3. On the basis of this and the previous thirteen incidents, put together a self-improvement plan for Pete, the entrepreneur. Be sure to include the various sources he should consult for advice and assistance. Be specific and realistic.

Suggested Readings

Babson, Roger W., "Stimulating Small Business with Retired Executives," *Commercial and Financial Chronicle* CCI (January 14, 1965), 20.

Bauer, Robert J., "How Better Business Bureaus Help Small Business," *Small Marketers Aids Annual No. 4*. Washington, D. C.: Small Business Administration, 1962. Pp. 83–90.

Broom, H. N., and Longenecker, J. G., *Small Business Management*, 2nd ed. Cincinnati: South-Western-Publishing, 1966. Ch. 8, 29.

Cochrun, Irwin, and Olson, James R. G., "Marketing the Services of a C.P.A. to Small Business," *Journal of Small Business Management* I (October 1963), 3–7.

Crampon, L. J., *Communicating Information to Small Businessmen*, Small Business Management Research Report. Washington, D. C.: Small Business Administration, 1963.

Kelley, Pearce, Lawyer, C. K., and Baumback, C. M. *How to Organize and Operate a Small Business*, 4th ed. Englewood Cliffs, N. J.: Prentice-Hall, 1968. Ch. 9.

Klatt, Lawrence A., ed., *Managing the Dynamic Small Firm: Readings*. Belmont, Calif.: Wadsworth, 1971. See "External Services Available to the Small Business."

Krentzman, Harvey C., and Samaras, John N., "Can Small Businesses Use Consultants?" *Harvard Business Review* XXXVIII (May–June 1960), 126–136.

Mayne, David R., "Specialized Help for Small Business," *Small Marketers Aids Annual No. 7*. Washington, D. C.: Small Business Administration, 1965. Pp. 80–87.

Preston, Lee E., ed., *Managing the Independent Business*. Englewood Cliffs, N. J.: Prentice-Hall, 1962. Ch. 2.

"Sales Management Survey of Buying Power" Annual June 10th issue of *Sales Management*, 630 Third Avenue, New York, New York.

Small Business Administration, *Small Business Administration: What It Is, What It Does*. Washington: U. S. Government Printing Office (September 1964).

Sources of Assistance and Information, Administrative Management Course Program, Topic 15. Washington, D. C.: Small Business Administration, 1965.

Steinmetz, Lawrence L., Kline, J. B., and Stegall, D. P., *Managing the Small Business*. Homewood, Ill.: Richard D. Irwin, 1968. Ch. 27.

Survey of Current Business (Monthly), Office of Business Economics, U. S. Department of Commerce.

White, L. T., "Management Assistance for Small Business," *Harvard Business Review* XLIII (July–August 1965), 67–74.

Wingate, John W., *Management Audit*. Washington, D. C.: Small Business Administration, 1971.

Part Six　　Comprehensive Cases

The J & P Superette

Case Study 1   Corporate Organization

In 1962, Ed Jackson and Thomas Patrick formed a corporation for the purpose of buying and operating a supermarket. The corporation was called the J & P Superette, Incorporated, and had four stockholders. The stockholders were Ed Jackson and his wife and Thomas Patrick and his wife. Both Ed Jackson and Thomas Patrick had owned and operated supermarkets for more than twenty years. Each owned a store in his home community and at various times had owned and operated other supermarkets in nearby communities. Both men had owned and operated other types of retail establishments.

Mr. Jackson and Mr. Patrick had been personal friends many years and each had a high regard for the entrepreneurial ability of the other.

In 1962, the J & P Superette Corporation purchased a store in Williamsburg, Ohio. This store had been in operation for a number of years and was a successful operation. The store began to show a profit after a few months of operation and remained a good income producer.

The rationale behind the formation of the J & P Superette Corporation was to take advantage of an opportunity to purchase a going concern for a total personal capital investment of $10,000. The credit standing of the individuals enabled the balance of the operation to be financed. In addition to

---

This case was prepared by (Mrs.) Kathleen C. Brannen, under the supervision of Dr. William H. Brannen, Creighton University, as a basis for class discussion. Distributed by the Intercollegiate Case Clearing House, Soldiers Field, Boston, Mass. 02163. All rights reserved to the contributors. Reprinted with permission.

pooling their personal credit and entrepreneurial ability, there was another significant contribution that each made to the joint venture—time. Mr. Jackson would be responsible for personal visits to the store one month and Mr. Patrick would take over the following month. Under this arrangement each had sufficient time to manage his own supermarket operations. A store manager and an assistant store manager were hired to direct store operations. Mr. Jackson and Mr. Patrick directed the store at the policy level.

By 1965, the store in Williamsburg had generated enough excess cash to purchase another store in Mason City, Ohio. This store was not the immediate success which the store in Williamsburg had proved to be. After three years of unprofitable operation, the store in Mason City was sold for the original book value of the fixtures and current book value of the inventory.

The foregoing has been given as background material for the analysis of a chain of events in a third venture which began in 1965.

Mapleville, Indiana: Initial Investigation

Mapleville was first considered as a possible location for a third corporate store in April of 1965. Mapleville was a community of 8,000 people and the radius of the trading area was estimated to be twelve to fifteen miles. The nearest large city was fifty miles away. At that time there were four supermarkets in Mapleville which consisted of a national chain store, a regional chain store, and two independents. One of the independents, called Thrifty Food Store, had the unique feature of service meats.

The competitive environment looked favorable from the viewpoint of J & P because the two chain stores were locked in with high prices and trading stamps. The two independents were considered weak operations. J & P offered to buy one of the independents, but the offer was declined. The second independent had a live chicken, cream, and fertilizer operation in conjunction with the supermarket. J & P was not interested in acquiring this type of operation. The competitive strategy anticipated by the J & P Superette Corporation was to go into Mapleville with something different to appeal to the consumer; namely, low prices. The low-price operation would be possible because J & P would be in operation with low overhead, low-cost fixtures, and low depreciation. J & P expected to capture enough of the market through a policy of low prices to ensure a profitable operation.

Preopening Details

In January of 1966 a lease was signed on a building being vacated by the national chain store. The lease called for monthly payments of $625.00 and was for five years. The national chain store moved out of the building on February 15, 1966 and plans were made to open the J & P Superette on March 15, 1966.

A loan was negotiated with Thomas Credit Corporation of Cincinnati for $50,000. The interest rate on the note was 7% and payment was to be made in monthly installments of $500.00. In thirty-six months the balance was due and payable unless renewed by the holder. Thomas Credit Corporation was the financing subsidiary of a food supplier. It was understood that the Mapleville store would in turn give special promotional consideration to the products supplied by this company. J & P signed corporately and personally on the note. Actually, the loan was granted on the basis of the credit of other stores owned by Mr. Patrick and Mr. Jackson. The stated collateral was store fixtures using a cost replacement figure for valuation. The actual price paid for the store fixtures was $15,000. Note funds were used to purchase an inventory of $32,000. Prepaid insurance was $1,000. The store thus began operating with the balance sheet shown in Exhibit 1.

Exhibit 1. Balance Sheet, Beginning of Operations.

J & P Superette, Incorporated of Mapleville, Indiana

Assets	
Cash in bank	$ 2,000.00
Prepaid insurance	1,000.00
Inventory	32,000.00
Fixtures	15,000.00
	$50,000.00
Liabilities	
Thompson Credit Corporation note	$50,000.00
	$50,000.00
Owner's equity	−0−

The planned advertising policy was to spend 2% of sales on advertising. This money was to be spent on newspaper advertising except for 15% of the advertising budget to be spent on radio advertising the first few months of operation. When store profits had been established, it was planned to lower the advertising budget to $1\frac{1}{2}$% of sales.

The decision was made not to charge administrative expense until the store was profitable. In other words, Mr. Jackson and Mr. Patrick would receive no pay for their administrative contribution until profits were earned and the working capital ratio made withdrawal of capital feasible. Internal revenue regulations did not permit administrative expense to be charged against store operations unless the funds were paid out.

J & P Superette, Inc., was part of a group of independent retailers who had affiliated with and used the facilities of a voluntary group wholesaler. The wholesaler, in addition to being a supplier of merchandise, also provided services in the form of functional consultation and accounting statement preparation. Daily sales records were forwarded from stores to the wholesaler and balance sheet and income statements were prepared for each store by the wholesaler each time an inventory was taken. The voluntary group wholesaler sold merchandise to its affiliates for the wholesaler's cost plus a fee which averaged $2\frac{1}{2}\%$, plus freight. Freight charges to the Mapleville store averaged 2%. A cash discount of 2%, net 10 days was given. The service charge for conducting an inventory was $3.00 per $1,000 of retail inventory. The accounting fee was based on retail store sales volume. The average accounting fee charged the Mapleville store was estimated to be $80.00 per month.

Gary Schultz, the service meat manager for the Thrifty Food Store, was hired for the position of store manager at a salary of $160.00 per week and a bonus of 25% of the net profit.

Gary's brother, Terry Schultz, also a former employee at Thrifty, was hired to be the assistant store manager at a salary of $120 per week and a bonus of 4% of the net profit.

A meat manager, who previously had been an assistant meat manager for a chain store, was hired for $135.00 per week and 8% of the net profit of the meat department.

To train Gary Schultz for the job of store manager, he spent six weeks working under the direction of Mr. Jackson in one of the supermarkets personally owned and operated by Mr. Jackson. During this time he was shown the various store procedures involved in ordering merchandise, determining gross profit, banking, assuming credit, extending credit, etc. Mr. Schultz was made aware of all existing policies which he was expected to adopt in the Mapleville store. Mr. Jackson also tried to instill the importance of the management function of getting work done through others.

It was agreed that Mr. Patrick would visit Mason City more frequently than Mapleville, and Mr. Jackson would visit Mapleville more frequently than Mason City. This allocation was based on the proximity of the towns to the homes of Mr. Jackson and Mr. Patrick. Mr. Jackson visited the store in Mapleville twice weekly.

Between the time the lease for the building was signed and the store opened, a change in the competitive picture forced a change in general strategy. The national chain store dropped Gold trading stamps. The regional chain store dropped Red trading stamps and introduced the plan of Total Lower Cost. This move on the part of the chain stores was not the result of the entrance of the J & P Superette into Mapleville, but was the result of competitive pressure which existed in Cincinnati. The strategy change made in Cincinnati affected the entire area served by the metropolitan communications media. Consequently, J & P Superette acquired Gold trading stamps and opened with conventional prices. This strategy was believed necessary because the chain stores had better facilities.

Store Opening

The J & P Superette in Mapleville opened on March 15, 1966 with a grand opening splash which included a lot of give-aways including a color television set and merchandise loss leaders. Mr. Jackson and Mr. Patrick were apprehensive about the change in the makeup of the local competition and tried to compete in all areas where price comparisons would stand out the most. These areas were national brands and fast-moving merchandise such as coffee.

The store had several $15,000 weeks and then settled into a pattern of sales which ranged from $9,000 to $10,000 per week. Mr. Jackson and Mr. Patrick considered the $9,000 to $10,000 volume sufficient for a self-sustaining operation with proper supervision and management.

Eight weeks after opening the store, the first inventory was taken and statements were prepared. The income statement revealed that the store had purchased more meat than it had sold; i.e., the meat gross was negative. The meat manager departed. The situation was discussed with the store manager and Mr. Schultz said that he could eliminate the meat problem. Gary Schultz became the meat manager in addition to being store manager. Two men worked under Gary as meat cutters, but Mr. Schultz did all the ordering and pricing of meat. However, a subsequent income statement revealed a meat gross of 10%, still 11% below cost of operation. The produce department, however, did better than expected.

Mr. Jackson observed that the store manager, Gary Schultz, was delighted with his new role as store manager and seemed reluctant to participate in the affairs of the meat department. Mr. Schultz, however, spent too much time having coffee with salesmen and attending Rotary meetings.

The assistant store manager, Terry Schultz, was the worker on the management team. The physical appearance of the store was always excellent and Terry Schultz would come in each Sunday and scrub and wax the floors and clean the refrigerated cases.

Store Sale

By the fall of 1966 the J & P Superette in Mapleville had sustained a cumulative loss of $25,000. The operating loss appeared on the balance sheet as an increase in accounts payable. Mr. Jackson and Mr. Patrick offered to sell the store to the two key employees—Gary and Terry Schultz. Gary and Terry accepted the offer and contracts changed hands. The accounts representing the $25,000 operating loss were transferred to the books of the J & P Superette in Williamsburg. Gary and Terry put up $12,000 of their own money and contractually agreed to make the stipulated monthly payments on the Thompson Credit Corporation note. They took over the bank account, the accounts receivable, and the remaining accounts payable. The name of the store was changed to Gary and Terry's Superette.

Not long after the store was taken over by Gary and Terry Schultz, the regional chain store was destroyed by fire. For a couple of months Gary and Terry's Superette showed a profit. However, the regional chain rebuilt a larger store, installed new fixtures, and increased the size of their parking lot. When the regional chain store reopened, they quickly took the business back.

Competition became tougher and tougher as stores advertised more loss leaders at increasingly lower prices. The advertising policy of the two chain stores was determined in Cincinnati for the area served by metropolitan newspapers and television stations. Although advertising space in large city newspapers was greater than ads carried in small local newspapers, the number of items to be advertised and the prices were the same. Any exceptions to this general policy would be on a very few items.

The Corporate Split-Up

In June of 1967, Mr. Jackson and Mr. Patrick decided to split up the corporate partnership because the stores in Mason City and Mapleville were losing more than the store in Williamsburg was making. They agreed to use April 23, 1967 as the assessment date. The latest income statement was based on an inventory taken on April 23, 1967. The decision was made to put the Mason City store in one package and the Mapleville and Williamsburg stores in another package with an exchange of cash to equalize the transaction. Even though the J & P Corporation was not currently operating the Mapleville store, the corporation did have considerable assets and liabilities involved in that store in conjunction with their agreements with the Schultz brothers. Mr. Jackson and Mr. Patrick further agreed to draw straws with the understanding that if the loser did not like the choice available to him, the deal was off and an acceptable alternative deal would be sought. Thomas Patrick drew the winning straw and chose Mason City. Ed Jackson was pleased with the decision as he did not wish to give up the store in Williamsburg. Thomas Patrick received the store in Mason City and $10,000 in cash. Ed Jackson retained the corporation which then included the store in Williamsburg and all corporate interests and obligations of the store in Mapleville.

Mapleville Reacquired from the Schultz Brothers

By June of 1967 it appeared that Gary and Terry were going to lose the inventory, so Ed Jackson took the store off their hands. Although the store name was changed back to J & P Superette, Mr. Jackson's intention was to liquidate the operation as quickly as possible. Gary and Terry Schultz had sustained operating losses far in excess of their original investment of $12,000. Mr. and Mrs. Jackson, who now owned 100% of J & P Superette, Incorporated, were not aware of the total extent of these losses. The Schultz brothers were released of any financial obligations beyond their original investment. Ed Jackson was liable for the balance of the note held by Thompson Credit Corporation. When the store was reacquired it was determined that the inventory had suffered a shrinkage of $8,000 during the period since Gary and Terry Schultz had acquired the store. This $8,000 inventory shrinkage was a loss to the J & P Superette Corporation.

When Ed Jackson reacquired the store, he also found $4,000 of uncollectable accounts receivable. These uncollectable accounts were in the form of bad checks and forty customer credit accounts. In addition, the store had taken on an unprofitable restaurant business.

Between July and October, Mr. Jackson looked for a buyer for the Mapleville store. Only one good prospect appeared. A regional wholesaler agreed to back a buyer if Mr. Jackson would provide $20,000 of the financing. The offer was declined by Mr. Jackson.

To avoid operating the store through the winter, Mr. Jackson looked for someone to lease the building. On November 1, 1967 the building was leased to a national franchised discount store for $325.00 per month. Three months later the parking lot was leased to the Christian Church for $150.00 per month.

Final Finances

The store fixtures were sold for $5,300. Some of the nonrecoverable expenses included opening expense, operating supplies, small tools, signs, attorney and license fees. The uncollected accounts and bad checks were turned over to a collection agency and $1,100 was recovered. The inventory was transferred to other stores owned by Ed Jackson. The accounts payable representing the inventory on hand were transferred with the inventory. An outstanding bank note owed by the J & P Superette in Williamsburg was increased by $40,000 in order to retire the Thompson Credit Corporation note. Taxes and remaining accounts payable were paid with the existing cash. The store in Williamsburg, the only remaining supermarket of J & P Corporation, absorbed the $8,000 balance due on the note payable from the Mapleville store to the Williamsburg store and the lease obligation totaling $6,000. The statement in Exhibit 2 shows the balance sheet at the end of operations and after liquidation of assets. The total loss incurred in the Mapleville operation was $54,000. The details of this loss are shown in Exhibit 3.

In spite of the Mapleville losses, both men continued to show considerable profits in stores which they owned separately outside the J & P Corporation.

Exhibit 2. Balance Sheet, End of Operations and after Liquidation of Assets.

J & P Superette, Incorporated of Mapleville, Indiana

	End of Operations	After Liquidation
Assets		
Cash in bank	$ 2,000	$ 8,400
Inventory	23,000	
Accounts receivable	4,000	
Leasehold improvements	3,000	
Fixtures	12,000	
	$44,000	$ 8,400
Liabilities		
Taxes, payroll	$ 1,200	$ 1,200
Taxes, personal property	1,200	1,200
Accounts payable	24,700	2,000
Thompson credit note	41,000	41,000
Williamsburg store note	11,000	11,000
	$79,100	$56,400
Owner's equity	($35,100)	($48,000)

Also, the J & P Corporation had sufficient profits from the time the corporation was formed to absorb administrative expense in the form of a bonus paid to the owner (or owners) in the amount of $16,000 per year. By January 1, 1969 when the lease in Mapleville expired, the entire $54,000 loss of the J & P Superette in Mapleville had been used as a tax write-off against the profits of the store in Williamsburg.

Exhibit 3. Total Loss Incurred by the J & P Superette in Mapleville, Indiana.

Net loss during the time Mr. Jackson and Mr. Patrick were corporate partners	$25,000
Inventory shrinkage during the period when ownership was in the name of Gary and Terry Schultz	8,000
Operating loss last months	5,000
Loss on sale of fixtures (including leasehold improvements)	10,000
Lease shrinkage	6,000
	$54,000

Ed Jackson's Hindsight

In reviewing the unprofitable operation of the J & P Superette in Mapleville, Ed Jackson offered the following evaluation:

> Our attempt to make a store manager out of a meat manager was a judgmental mistake. It has been done, but probably has failed more frequently than it has succeeded.

Another fallacy is the idea that people will work harder for themselves than for someone else. They won't. Tom and I offered the store in Mapleville to Gary and Terry Schultz in the hope that a personal investment on their part would provide the motivation necessary to make the operation profitable. As a matter of fact, the policy changes which they made resulted in greater losses.

However, the situation in the meat department was the greatest single cause of failure. I should have followed up a weekly meat inventory. Poor buying practice was followed which largely was a matter of buying too much. Buying too much was partially the result of poor inventory control. The inventory is perishable. Pork, chicken, lunch meat, and ham spoil easily. To have a profitable meat operation it is essential to practice FIFO (first in-first out). A marking and storage system in the cooler must be in effect to ensure adherence to FIFO inventory movement.

The grocery department failed to produce a profit because of a lack of merchandising. Although the store was clean and orderly in appearance, these factors are only a part of merchandising. Strong competitive pressure dictated an advertising strategy of loss leaders which was not offset by increased turnover of other grocery items. Money can be lost a lot faster than it can be made. When a second grocery order comes in before payment on the first is due, cash flow can get out of hand very quickly.

Tom and I were taking care of our outside businesses. Nobody did any pushing and things just drifted which is a lousy way to run a business.

When asked if there was always agreement on policy changes between Thomas Patrick and himself, Mr. Jackson replied:

> There was too much agreement. One of the problems was that there were no disagreements. We were prone to give in on a point because of the high regard we have had for each other during our twenty-five years of personal friendship.

Areas for Discussion

1. How important is a profitable meat department to overall store profits?
2. If a supermarket has sales of $10,000 per week, what is the amount of

additional sales which must be generated to cover the 2% cost to the store for stamps? Is stamp cost the only expense which will be generated by increased sales?
3. What does the relationship between markup and turnover have to do with merchandising?
4. At various points in time, critical decisions were made by Mr. Jackson and Mr. Patrick which affected the strategy employed to obtain a profitable operation. Identify the critical decisions. State your agreement or disagreement with these decisions and the reasons for your choice. If you disagree with a decision, suggest feasible alternatives.

Air Comfort, Incorporated

Case Study 2

Joe Harris, President of Air Comfort, Incorporated, cast a rueful eye over the cost estimate that he would use as the basis for his bid on the Joy Building job tomorrow. It was already 7:00 P.M., the time he was due home each evening, and everyone else in the shop had gone. Stan, his right-hand man, had prepared the estimate and Joe had lots of confidence in it. Still, it was possible to leave something out on a job as big as this $40,000 to $50,000 and it would take twenty "average jobs" to reach this volume. As he wearily jammed the estimate in his briefcase to carry home, he triggered some basic reflections on Air Comfort, *his* company, and his position. He flipped the lights out, secured the front door and was soon in the scattered late traffic on his way home. His musings continued.

He had started Air Comfort three years ago when an "exclusive franchise" opportunity to be the Graff Company's representative in Metro had come his way. Graff is one of the big three in air conditioning and heating in the U.S. and with the trend for air conditioning in homes, stores, offices and public buildings such a franchise has considerable potential. This had seemed particularly true in Middle Atlantic Metro with an urban population approaching three million people. Well, it had worked out but what a sweat! Joe had always worked for large corporations after earning two degrees in mechanical engineering. His engineering training had made it easy for him

---

This case was prepared by Professor Presson S. Shane of the George Washington University, as a basis for class discussion. Distributed by the Intercollegiate Case Clearing House, Soldiers Field, Boston, Mass. 02163. All rights reserved to the contributors. Reprinted with permission.

to grasp the basics and a lot of the subtleties of air conditioning and heating. This same training had been a drawback in accepting some of the business situations that were now forced on him by trade practices, competition and less-than-scrupulous general contractors with whom he did business.

Air Comfort was occupying its second home, a splendid 6,000 sq. ft. plant leased for five years and providing plenty of space for office, shops, storage, and garaging for three of the seven trucks. The work force had settled back from the summer rush to twelve reliables:

> Joe, President and jack-of-all-trades
> Stan, Outside salesman and chief estimator
> Mary, Bookkeeper
> Helen, Clerk, typist, phone, etc.
> Refrigeration foreman plus three men
> Sheet metal foreman plus three men

Graff's equipment was good and they had proved to be a reliable business partner by guaranteeing some modest bank loans from time to time. Their sales promotion literature was good, but it was provided at cost beyond a certain free minimum so direct mail campaigns were costly to conduct.

Joe reflected on the overall aspects of his business. 1972 results had been:

	% of Sales	% Gross Margin*
Residential contracts for add-ons, conversions, replacements, etc.	45	25
Commercial contracts for general contractors on new buildings, houses, etc.	30	25
Service calls on both residential and commercial installations	25	40

*Gross margin is sales less all direct costs so consists of all overhead expenses plus income taxes and profit.

He had taken no vacation and had drawn a salary below what he had been making in the aerospace industry three years earlier. He valued, however, the psychic income and/or potential income of being an entrepreneur. But how much?

As he saw it, the problem is one of increasing business volume at a reasonable cost for getting the new volume. The new facilities will accommodate up to a 100% increase in volume. Employees could be added. The overhead expenses, which were $75,000 last year, need not increase very much with a larger volume so that the business could then move beyond the "critical size" and start to return the profits that seemed to be there.

Joe realized that his situation was critical. He had expanded his business and was faced with a declining economy. His cash flow position was deteriorating. He had to come up with a "second effort" sales plan to hold his position and avoid a savage retrenchment. He knew that an unsuccessful sales plan would push him back, dissipate his present team's capability, and destroy his business momentum. Where could the new volume be obtained, economically?

1. *Residential.* Direct mail, neatly painted trucks with phone numbers, word-of-mouth, etc. Junk mailings cost 12¢ each just for postage and material. A one-shot $2\frac{1}{2}" \times 5"$ advertisement in the local newspapers cost $200. The industry rule-of-thumb was that a line lead in season cost $40 of advertising money to get. These jobs were all Air Comfort's design and were of two types:
    a. Add-on: average job $1,200; capture rate 35%; 32% average gross margin. The market was highly seasonal and responded to advertising in season. Pay results good.
    b. New house: average job $1,800; capture rate 10%; 25% average gross margin. The market was not particularly susceptible to advertising but a busy builder who was "using you" was valuable. Pay results slow.
2. *Commercial.* Bidding jobs to general contractors had been low in productivity. Add-ons to Air Comfort's design had been ok but new construction to a general contractor's plans and specifications had been tricky. The two types:
    a. Add-on; average job $8,000; capture rate 25%; 33% average gross margin. The market was small stores, churches, restaurants, small office buildings, etc. This market was not particularly seasonal but it was hard to find it. There was high risk because of conflict of operating requirements with Air Comfort's schedules and hidden features in old buildings. Pay was ok.
    b. New jobs (to plans and specs by others): average job $50,000; capture rate 10%; 25% average gross margin. There was high risk in learning commercial procedures, interpreting specs, satisfying inspectors, etc., but the complex work offered a challenge for cost control, innovation, and management. The work was year-round but caused peaks and valleys for Air Comfort because jobs were so big. Pay results slow.
3. *Service and repair.* Highly seasonal and hard to get on a reasonable schedule. The first hot day in spring produced more than could be handled. The work was somewhat risky because of the low level of trouble-shooting skills in the available work force. Service clientele developed slowly but loyalty was showing up with good repeat business. The average job about $100 but the gross margin averaged 50%.

As Joe drove into the driveway, he had an inspiration. A friend of his was taking a course in small business management. He resolved to drop off some financial data to his friend and seek his advice. The financials are attached. You are the friend. Give Joe sound, concrete advice based on the information and data given in the case.

Exhibit 1. Air Comfort, Inc. Comparative Balance Sheet, March 31

	1972	1971
Cash	9,151	2,469
Trade accounts receivable	23,580	14,926
Note receivable	2,866	2,866
Materials and supplies	15,257	3,554
Work in process	23,702	22,440
Depreciable assets — Net of accumulated depreciation	8,545	6,665
Other assets	1,750	928
Assets	84,851	53,848
Trade accounts payable	33,566	7,480
Accrued taxes and payroll	7,705	3,495
Notes payable — Bank	10,000	10,000
Advance Billings	13,961	22,037
Liabilities	65,232	43,012
Common stock	12,000	12,000
Retained income (Deficit)	7,619	(1,164)
Stockholder's Equity	19,619	10,836
Liabilities and stockholder's equity	84,851	53,848

Exhibit 2. Air Comfort, Inc. Comparative Income Statement for the Year Ending March 31.

	1972	1971
Revenues	275,484	110,445
Cost of contracts completed schedules	188,707	71,820
Gross margin	86,777	38,625
Operating expenses (Schedule B)	75,458	36,339
Other income	(282)	(285)
Income (loss) before taxes on income and life insurance premium	11,601	2,571
Taxes on income	2,638	130
Insurance premium on officers' life	180	216
Income	8,783	2,225

Exhibit 3. Air Comfort, Inc. Schedules to Accompany Income Statement.

Schedule A

	1972	1971
Material and equipment	115,733	42,684
Labor	57,697	23,872
Subcontracts	13,813	4,401
Other direct costs	1,464	863
Cost of contracts completed	188,707	71,820

Schedule B

	1972	1971
Equipment maintenance	5,887	2,714
Payroll taxes	5,741	2,789
Unapplied labor	4,599	2,292
Employee benefits	3,545	1,559
Small tools and supplies	3,421	4,635
Office supplies and maintenance	2,556	1,450
Travel and entertainment	2,166	889
Losses on collection	1,381	
Total variable operating expenses	29,296	16,328
Salaries—Officer and office	31,698	15,664
Rent	3,930	3,600
Insurance	2,838	1,658
Professional services	2,300	825
Depreciation and amortization	2,023	1,668
Advertising	1,544	947
Miscellaneous other expenses	1,058	1,029
Interest	905	438
Total fixed operating expenses	46,296	25,829
Total operating expenses	75,458	42,157

Southern Mobile Homes, Inc.

Case Study 3

June 19, 1972

Mr. John Jones
Jones, Jones & Smith
Attorneys at Law
1101 High Towers
Fort Worth, Texas

Dear Mr. Jones:

As requested during our meeting on June 18, I am setting forth in this letter all the facts and information that I can remember concerning Southern Mobile Homes. And, as you stressed, I am including all the facts at my disposal, regardless as to how impertinent they may seem to me.

Perhaps the best place to start is to give you a brief outline of the recreational vehicle industry, which of course Southern Mobile is a part of. The recreational vehicle industry is composed of travel trailers, truck campers, camping trailers, and motor homes. And, as you have probably noticed while driving about, sales within this field have expanded at a rate which is almost unbelievable.

Recent statistics reveal that approximately 41% of the units sold were of the travel trailer variety. These trailers are offered in lengths of twelve to thirty-five feet with pricing from $900 to $10,000 or more for the more sophisticated models.

All names, dates, and places have been changed. This case was prepared by Kenneth Howard and Ben Tanksley under the direction of Professor Frank M. Rachel of North Texas State University, as a basis of class discussion. Distributed by the Intercollegiate Case Clearing House, Soldiers Field, Boston, Mass. 02163. All rights reserved to the contributors. Reprinted with permission.

Truck campers are designed for attachment to the truck bed of pick-up trucks either on a permanent or temporary basis. Prices for truck campers range from $1,200 to $4,800 and account for some 30 percent of all units sold within the industry.

Camping trailers are basically tent-like structures on two wheels which fold out to form sleeping quarters. Due to their costs, which range from $500 to $2,300 camping trailers appeal to the younger families.

Motor homes are the ultimate in recreational vehicles. Being constructed on the chassis of a truck or bus, motor homes are comfortable, self-contained, and self-propelled units. The costs usually start well over $5,500 and may even surpass $20,000 for some custom orders. However, average prices usually require an outlay of some $12,500. While accounting for only some 8% of the industry's total unit sales, the motor homes' popularity is increasing at a rapid rate.

Purchasers of the travel trailers and camping trailers have a propensity to "trade up," i.e., they initially purchase a small unit and then trade that unit back in for a larger, more expensive model. It is estimated that some 25% of dealer sales in travel trailers and camping trailers are derived from the sale of such used trade-ins.

Prior to becoming involved with Southern Mobile Homes, I had been an advertising account executive for Channel 14 Television for four years. In fact, this was the only job I had had since graduating from college. My success as an advertising salesman was apparently too successful since the management decided it was necessary to revise, downward of course, the sales incentive plan. Needless to say, I was frustrated and felt that to "get ahead," one must become an owner of his own business. I was in this disgruntled state of mind when I first met James Miller while on a sales call for the station.

Miller is one of those individuals which we term a natural in sales jargon. His delivery, which consists of ebullient optimism, sincerity, and warmth, completely disarmed any natural suspicions which I should have had, especially since I too was a salesman. At that time, he was a sales representative for Cruzar Motor Homes, but was also involved in a truck camper dealership which was about to discontinue operations. Miller convinced me that with just $1,500 capital, which I would provide, he could gain control of the truck camper dealership and pay me 25% of the profits from the operation. Payment of the 25% was to be made quarterly.

My first quarterly dividend amounted to $823, proving that my investment was sound. However, for a while I had my doubts since it was well into the fourth month and three of the checks were returned for insufficient funds before the fourth check cleared. Shortly thereafter, on or about November 15, Miller approached me with the idea of forming our own corporation to sell a full line of campers and Cruzar vehicles. I agreed immediately since my previous investment was doing so well and my desire to enter my own business was becoming even greater.

My initial investment, given to Miller on November 23rd, was for $10,000 cash. This was borrowed from my mother and stepfather against my inheritance. In return I was to receive 1,500 shares of stock—1,000 shares for the $10,000 cash investment and 500 shares for a release on the initial $1,500 investment. Miller began the necessary legal proceedings necessary for incorporation.

In January, Miller hired Mr. Charles Zudik as Sales Manager. Mr. Zudik lived at 921 Wedgewood Avenue and was about 55 years of age. According to Miller, Zudik was a real successful insurance salesman. I am convinced now that they had known each other for a long time; however, this is speculation on my part. Zudik was to have invested $5,000 in the firm in January.

On January 31, Miller called a meeting for the formal incorporation of Southern Mobile Homes. In attendance were Miller, myself, and Mr. Zudik. It was at this meeting that Miller informed me that Zudik would not be an officer as planned but would remain as an investor–employee. Miller also announced that a Paul Mason would become the Sales Manager and Secretary–Treasurer. Not to be slighted, I was to become the Executive Vice President. It was never made clear exactly what my duties as Executive Vice President were to consist of. Miller, of course, was the President of Southern Mobile Homes, with hire and fire authority.

Miller spoke very highly of Mason who was an experienced recreational vehicle salesman that he had known for many years. For Miller, it was fortunate for Southern Mobile Homes that Mason was available to go to work, having departed from his present employment in a dispute over commissions. Mason, like Zudik, was to also invest $5,000 in the corporation.

It was at this same meeting that Miller announced that Southern Mobile Homes had been granted a five-state distributorship for Util-Camp, Incorporated, a well respected and competitive manufacturer of truck campers. In addition, Miller informed us that papers which would name Southern Mobile Homes as an official distributor of Cruzar Motor Homes were being processed in Cruzar's home office. Until the processing was completed, Southern Mobile Homes would be permitted to sell Cruzar through a commission agreement with the Houston distributor.

As for financing, Miller stated that a line of credit for floor planning the inventory had been arranged at City National Bank. The line of credit, said Miller, was to enable us to handle only the top of the line.

It was agreed that I should give my present employer, Channel 14, six weeks notice so that I would join Southern Mobile Homes in March, well ahead of the peak season. And, at this point in time, things were looking great for our young organization.

Upon joining the organization on March 15, I was dismayed to learn that our shipments from Util-Camp, Incorporated, were being held up pending payment. Upon being pressed, Miller told me that he was not satisfied with the original floor plan stipulations at City National and was seeking better arrangements with other banks in the area. I discovered, however, that we have never even applied for a line of credit from City National. My first official act with Southern Mobile Homes was, out of necessity, to obtain financing.

Finally, with the help of Zudik, I was able to obtain a $100,000 line of credit from First State Bank. But, to do so, the bank required that Southern Mobile Homes apply $37,519.23 of the $100,000 to clear a previous debt of Miller's. This was consummated on March 28th.

On or about the 3rd of April, I opened the mail and was disturbed to see that the commission for the last three Cruzars sold had been applied to an outstanding account that Miller owed to the Houston dealer prior to the formation of Southern Mobile Homes. I immediately got on the phone and called the Houston dealer since Miller was out of town at this time. They informed me that not only had all previous commissions been applied to his account but that all furure commissions likewise would be applied until his account was cleared. There was nothing I could do since Miller had made the agreement with the Houston dealer in Southern Mobile Homes' name. In total, we had earned more than $6,100 dollars which was applied to Miller's debt.

I then called the home office for Cruzar to inquire about our dealership only to be told that Southern Mobile Homes had never applied for a Cruzar franchise. Within two weeks however, I had the franchise contract in my hands—after two quick trips to Cruzar's home office in Chicago. Miller seemed somewhat less than pleased over my efficiency in obtaining the dealership.

By May, we were still trying to build up an inventory and remain on good terms with our bank, which was becoming more and more difficult to do. Thus, on May 8, I invested another $11,000, taking a note payable in return; this amount was also borrowed from my mother and stepfather. The scope of my investment at this point was somewhat disconcerting, but my optimism for the future and the freedom of being my own boss with an unlimited expense account overshadowed any fears or doubts that I had.

It was also about this time that I had a serious altercation with Miller over the shop personnel. Back in February, he had hired a shop manager to take care of what few modifications and repairs our business required. Then, without any apparent need, two helpers were hired in April; and as if that was not enough, a fourth helper was hired in May. My protestations were unheeded since Miller said he had hire and fire authority and furthermore, he knew what was required to run our company. Current fixed expenses at this time looked something as follows:

Secretary	$ 900 per month
Shop foreman	960 per month
Mechanics (4)	2,400 per month
Rent	1,800 per month
Executives' salary (4)	4,800 per month
Interest (estimate)	2,100 per month

At this time, Miller informed me that the fourth helper was to be utilized as a coach driver to chauffeur couples to and from the World's Fair. It seems that he had formed a subsidiary known as Southern Mobile Motel by leasing back one of the Cruzars we had sold. Unfortunately, nothing ever came of this venture except some expensive repair bills for damage to the leased unit. The driver hired for this operation spent his time like the other helpers — playing dominoes.

On or about May 20th, Paul Mason performed what was to my knowledge his only act as Secretary–Treasurer. He discovered, by accident, that several checks were missing from the back of the checkbook; also, many of the check stubs were incomplete. It was then that we switched to the policy of requiring two signatures on all checks.

By the end of May, our need for cash became critical once again so I was able to pressure Mason into investing the $5,000 which he had agreed to contribute when he joined Southern Mobile Homes. However, I had little success with Zudik who continued to stall on investing his $5,000 of capital. Miller was to have deposited the $5,000 check from Mason on May 28.

On May 29, Miller left town on another of his frequent trips to establish sub-dealerships for Cruzar Mobile Homes, or so he said. But when the bank informed us that we were overdrawn on June 1, we began to understand what was happening. Miller had suddenly cashed the check at Mason's bank and left town. And, to make the situation even more frightening, he was travelling in our new deluxe model Cruzar which was worth more than $19,000. We agreed, then, that we would demand his resignation.

On June 11, Miller finally returned, looking somewhat hung over and with a damaged Cruzar. Our demands for resignation and replenishment of the funds were accepted lightly by Miller. To my knowledge, none of us ever saw Miller after that day. His last known address was the Del Rio Trailer Courts. Since his disappearance, I had a credit survey done on Miller and was surprised at his past occupations which included three suits in bankruptcy, a litigation over stock issues, and many, many sales positions with as many firms. Also, it appears that his fifth wife is suing for non-support.

After being informed of our overdrawn account on June 1, I got in touch with the C.P.A. Miller had retained on an hourly basis. At this point I was upset and demanded to know why we had never received a monthly statement or an opinion of our financial situation. To this, he replied that he was working only for Mr. Miller and had no obligation to any other person or persons. He did, however, turn over all his records to me when I informed him that Miller was not going to be utilizing his services any longer. These records were turned over to a Mr. Harvey Swift, C.P.A. who prepared, without audit, financial statements for our first five months of operations. Copies of these statements are enclosed.

Mason left Southern Mobile Homes this date to accept employment with a competitor here in the city. Zudik's untimely death last week leaves me as the sole surviving officer of Southern Mobile Homes. It also leaves me responsible for some 55,000 dollars of debt. I have not yet taken voluntary bankruptcy, but feel some significant move must be made soon else involuntary bankruptcy will occur.

This recaps, to the best of my knowledge, the short history of Southern Mobile Homes.

Your recommendations as to how to proceed with bankruptcy proceedings and whether legal action should be taken against Miller are anticipated in the very near future.

Respectfully,

Jim Baker, President
Southern Mobile Homes, Inc.

Exhibit 1

Harvey P. Swift
Certified Public Accountant
Walker Bldg. Suite 1001
Fort Worth, Texas 15986

June 9, 1972

Mr. Jim Baker, President
Southern Mobile Homes, Inc.
11051 Old Town Road
Fort Worth, Texas

Dear Mr. Baker:

I have prepared from your books of account a Statement of Financial Condition as of June 6, 1972, and a Statement of Results of Operations for the Four Month Period Then Ended. Since the financial statements were not audited by me, accordingly, I cannot express an opinion on them.

Rather than write a detailed analysis of the Statements, I would appreciate your reviewing them at your convenience in order that we might get together as soon as possible to discuss possible methods of controlling costs in several of your larger expense categories.

Respectfully submitted,

Harvey P. Swift

Exhibit 2. Southern Mobile Homes, Inc. Statement of Results of Operations as of June 6, 1972.

Assets		
Current Assets		
Cash in bank	$ 1,120.00	
Accounts receivable		
Trade	1,953.00	
Jim Miller	11,325.00	
Charles Zudik	3,850.00	
Paul Mason	3,499.00	
Inventory-finished goods — Notes 1 & 2	40,389.00	
Total current assets		$ 62,136.00
Fixed Assets		
Furniture & fixtures	$ 1,322.00	
Equipment	688.00	
Automotive	935.00	
Leasehold improvements	746.00	
Total	3,691.00	
Less, accumulated depreciation	440.00	
Total fixed assets		3,251.00
Other Assets		
Organizational expense (Net)	$ 475.00	
Deposits	830.00	
Total other assets		1,305.00
Total assets		$ 60,730.00
Liabilities & Net Worth		
Bank overdraft	$ 6,554.00	
Accounts payable — Trade	21,372.00	
Taxes payable	5,717.00	
Notes payable — First State Bank	54,723.00	
Total liabilities		$ 88,366.00
Net Worth		
Capital stock	$ 1,500.00	
Capital surplus	8,500.00	
Earned surplus — Exhibit B	(37,636.00)	
Total net worth		(27,636.00)
Total liabilities & net worth		$ 60,730.00

Prepared without audit.

Exhibit 3. Southern Mobile Homes, Inc. Statement of Results of Operations for the Four-Month Period Ending June 6, 1972.

Sales		$239,770.00
Cost of Goods Sold		
Inventory, February 12, 1972	$ 6,290.00	
Purchases—Note 1	229,994.00	
Parts & accessories—Note 2	16,135.00	
Total goods available for sale	$252,419.00	
Inventory, June 6, 1972	40,389.00	
Total cost of goods sold		212,030.00
Gross profit		$ 27,440.00
Expenses		
Advertising	12,879.00	
Amortization	210.00	
Auto & truck	832.00	
Commissions	1,077.00	
Depreciation	275.00	
Dues & subscriptions	55.00	
Entertainment and travel	4,940.00	
Freight	570.00	
Insurance	1,905.00	
Interest	838.00	
Maintenance and repairs	2,530.00	
Office supplies	1,950.00	
Professional fees	1,234.00	
Rent	2,791.00	
Salaries & wages	28,410.00	
Taxes	1,609.00	
Telephone	1,609.00	
Utilities	169.00	
Total expenses		65,076.00
Net loss		(37,636.00)

Prepared without audit.

Note 1. These figures do not include inventory purchased under floor plan, nor does the balance sheet reflect the liability.

Note 2. Included in "Parts & Accessories" are purchases of materials for the manufacture of pick-up covers, of which only the finished products were included in inventory.

Index

Accountants, for advice and assistance, 269
Accounting definitions, 194
Accounting equation, 195
Acid-test ratio, 199
Actuating:
  definition, 73
  as a management function, 73
Advertising, 166, 176
  basic appeals, 180
  budget, 185
  evaluating the ad, 186
  focus of, 179
  how to go about it, 178
  role of, 177
  selecting the media, 181
  sources for assistance, 186
  strengths and limitations, 177
Allen, Louis L., 20
Application forms, 223
Assets, 194
Assistance, for the entrepreneur, 269
Attorney, when to use, 276

Balance sheet, 196
Bankers, for advice and assistance, 270
Banks:
  dealing with, 135
  differences among, 129
Board of directors, 71
Break-even analysis, 200
Budgeting:
  capital, 203
  cash, 202
Bursk, Edward C., 11
Business consultants, 271
Business failures, 6
Buying a small business:
  advantages, 89
  determining the price, 92
  determining the profit, 94

Buying a small business (continued)
  disadvantages, 90
  factors to consider, 90
  final transaction, 96
Buying versus leasing, 211

Capital:
  budgeting, 203
  cost of, 204
  definition of, 125
  determining initial requirements, 126
  fixed, 125
  promotional, 125
  sources of initial funds, 128
  working, 125
Capitalizing future earnings, 93
Cash flow, 207
Channel strategy, 163
Collective bargaining (*see* Union-management relations)
Commercial finance companies, 131
Committee for Economic Development, 4
Committees, 71
Communication:
  principles, 77
  types of, 77
  understanding, 77
Comparative analysis (*see* Ratio analysis)
Compensating employees, 228
  factors to consider, 228
  job evaluation, 230
  wage supplements, 231
Competitors, 165, 172
Comprehensive cases, 285, 295, 301
Consultants (*see* Business consultants)
Consumer information, 161
Consumers, 160
Control charts, 254
Controlling:
  control systems, 80
  definition, 78
  problems, 80
  steps in, 79

Index

Control process, 79
Cost of goods sold, 95
Costs, pricing and, 171
Creativity:
  becoming more creative, 58
  brainstorming, 59
  definition, 57
  in planning, 57
  techniques, 59
Credit, 175
  establishing of, 134
  establishing a proper philosophy, 136
  as part of marketing, 175
  "truth in lending," 176
Credit cards, 208
Critical path method, 259
Current assets, 197
  financing, 208
  management, 207, 210
Current ratio, 199
Customers, 165

Decision making:
  process of, 55
  relationship to planning, 55
  role of creativity in, 57
  under uncertainty, 262
Depreciation, 95, 212
Dispatching, 243
Dun & Bradstreet, 6, 200

Economic-order-quantity formula, 251
Employee relations, 219
Entrepreneur:
  characteristics, 19
  introspection and self-selection, 20
  need for advice and assistance, 276
  rating scale for personal traits, 22
  self-analysis checklist, 21
"Entrepreneur" type, 18
Entrepreneurship:
  advantages, 16
  disadvantages, 16
Environmental factors, in marketing, 159
Expenses, 195

Financial management, 193
Financial planning, 200
Financial statement analysis, 198
Financial statements, 196
Financing current assets, 208
Fixed assets, 211
  financing, 212
  leasing, 211
Fixed costs, 200
Forms of organization:
  corporation, 117
  factors to consider, 118
  partnership, 116
  sole proprietorship, 115
Franchise:
  checklist for evaluating, 147
  factors to consider, 145
Franchising:
  advantages, 142
  description, 142
  disadvantages, 143
  feasibility of, 149
  finding opportunities, 143
  present scope, 141
Fringe benefits, 231
Future of small business, 10

Goals:
  establishing, 141
  getting the "big picture," 41
  implementing, 47
  methods, 48
  reaching, 65
  setting, 31
Government agencies, 276

Herzberg, Frederick, 76
Hiring new employees, 220
Human engineering, 246
Human relations in the small firm, 232
Human resources, management of, 219

Income statement, 196, 198
Industrial-development departments, for location assistance, 114
Informal communication, 77
Informal organization, 72
Initial funds (*see* Capital)
Inspection, in the production process, 256
Insurance agents, 270
International Franchise Association, 142

Index

Interviewing job applicants, 223
Introspection for the small businessman, 20
Inventory:
  costs, 250
  economic-order-quantity (EOQ), 251
  as part of pricing strategy, 170
  types of, 249
Inventory control, 249

Job description, 221
Job evaluation, 231

Labor laws, 235
Lawyers, when to use, 270
Layout, plant, 243–244
Leasing:
  assets, 211
  land, 112
Legal obligations, in employing workers, 229
Legal organization (*see* Forms of organization)
Legal structure of a business (*see* Forms of organization)
Liabilities, 194
Linear programming, 258
Loans:
  secured, 210
  short- and intermediate-term, 209
Location:
  comparing two different areas, 108
  factors influencing decision of, 105
  personal preferences, 106
  relationship to business failure, 107
  selecting the area within the town or city, 107
  selecting the proper site, 109
  selecting a town or city, 106
  sources for assistance, 113
  special consideration for different types of businesses, 109

Management:
  assistance, 269, 274
  as a cause of failure, 9
  definition, 219
  functions, 65
Manpower management, 219
Manufacturing (*see* Production)

Marketing:
  as a concept, 157
  decision making in, 158
  emergence of, 155
  environmental factors, 159
    in economic decisions, 159
    in legal decisions, 159
    in social decisions, 160
  functions, 163
  future of, 176
  information, 160
  stages of, 157
Marketing strategy, 160
Market segmentation, 162
Market study, 97
Markup, 171
Maslow, Abraham, 75
Mathematical models, 253
McGregor, Douglas, 74
Media, selecting, 181
Middlemen, in channel strategy, 163
Morale, 233
Motivation:
  basic concepts, 75
  Theory X and Y, 74
Mulvihill, Donald F., 167

National Federation of Independent Businessmen, 141
Net income, 198
Net present value, 203
Network analysis, 259

Objectives:
  formulating, 34
  relationship to planning, 37
  strategies, 40
Organization, informal, 72
Organizing:
  case example, 67
  guidelines, 66
  as a management function, 65
  principles, 66, 69
  proper structure, 66
Owner's equity, 194

Partnership, 116
Payback period, 203
Personal selling, 166

Personal traits, rating scale, 22
Personnel, 219
PERT method, 51
Pickle, H. B., 19
Planning:
   "commitment principle," 33
   file-folder method, 48
   function, 31
   long-range, 36
   need for creativity, 57
   and objectives, 37
   PERT method (Program Evaluation and Review Technique), 51
   "planning-forms" method, 49
   program, example of, 38
   short-range, 37
   steps in, 32
   time period, 33
Plant layout, 243
Plant maintenance, 245
Policies:
   establishing, 35
   guidelines, 35
Preferred stock, 205
Price, practices to help offset, 175
Pricing:
   relationship between markup and stock turnover, 171
   strategy, 169
   techniques, 169
Problem solving, 55
Product:
   design, 242
   life cycle, 163
   strategy, 162
Production:
   charts, 243
   process, 241
   standards, 248
Production planning and control, 242
Professionals, for advice, 269
Profitability of a business, determining, 91
Profits, 91, 94, 193
Pro forma statements, 193, 200
Promotional capital, 125
Promotional strategy, 166

Quality control, 252
   control charts, 257
   inspection, need for, 252
   methods, 253, 257

Quantitative analysis, 253
   techniques, 258

Ratio analysis, 198
Recruitment of employees, 220
Reference checks, 225
Resources for decision making, 267
Retailing:
   rate of failure, 7
   selecting a site for, 109
Retained earnings, 206
Revenue, 194
Routing, 242

Salaried employment:
   advantages, 17
   disadvantages, 18
Sales, 95
Sales promotion, 166
Sales volume, 171
Sampling, 252
SCORE, 275
Selecting a location (*see* Location)
Selecting new employees, 222
   application forms, 223
   interviewing, 223
   reference checks, 223
   testing, 223
Self-analysis for going into business, 21
Selling (*see* Personal selling)
Service business, location of, 109
Small business:
   defined, 3, 4
   and the economy, 3
   future outlook, 10
   problems, 10
   purchasing (*see* Buying a small business, 89)
   scope and trends of, 5
Small business failures:
   avoiding, 9
   factors in, 6
Small Business Administration:
   management assistance, 274
   procurement assistance, 273
   publications, 278
   types of loans available, 130
Small Business Investment Corporations (SBIC), 130
Sole proprietorship, 115
Sources of initial funds, 128
Standard time data, 249

Starting a new business:
  feasibility study, 97
    competition, 98
    income, 98
    population, 97
  reasons for, 96
  sources of information, 99
State Employment Service, 276
Statement of sources and application of funds, 198
Statistical quality control techniques, 253
Stock turnover, 171

Tax obligation, 212
Testing, 225
Theory X and Y, 74
Time study, 248
Trade association, 275
Trade credit, 209
  as a source of funds, 130
Training and developing employees, 226
  establishing needs, 226
  group, 227
  on-the-job, 227
  selecting the method, 226
  specialized, 228

Union contracts, 236
Union-management relations, 233
Unions, why workers join, 234

Valuation of a business, 90
Value analysis, 62
Variable expenses, 200
Vaughn, Charles L., 141
Venture capitalists, 131

Wages, 228, 237 (*see* Compensating employees)
Wage supplements, 231
White, L. T., 19
White, Wilford L., 147
Wholesaling, 110
Work improvement, 246
  principle of motion economy, 247
Work sampling, 249
Work simplification, 249
Working capital, 125
Workmen's Compensation, 230